THE BUZZ ON™

FASHION

Lori Newcomb
& Rusty Fischer

LF LEBHAR-FRIEDMAN BOOKS
NEW YORK · CHICAGO · LOS ANGELES · LONDON · PARIS · TOKYO

The Buzz On Fashion

Lebhar-Friedman Books
425 Park Avenue
New York, NY 10022

Published by Lebhar-Friedman Books
Lebhar-Friedman Books is a company of Lebhar-Friedman, Inc.

Printed in the United States of America

Library of Congress Cataloging-in-Publication Data

Fischer, Rusty.
The buzz on fashion / Rusty Fischer, Lori Newcomb.
p. cm
Includes index.
ISBN: 0-86730-816-8 (alk. paper)
1. Fashion--History--20th century. 2. Costume design--History--20th century. I. Newcomb, Lori. II. Title.

TT504 .F57 2000
746.9'2'0904--dc21   00-058363

Produced by Progressive Publishing
Editor: John Craddock; Creative Director: Nancy Lycan; Art Director: Peter Royland
Editorial Contributors: Julie Malpass, Justin Misik
Designers: Angela Connolly, Vivian Torres, William Setzer, Rena Bracey, Lee Gustainus, Gale Erwin, Suzanne Miller, Lanette Fitzpatrick

Visit our Web site at lfbooks.com

THE BUZZ ON™

FASHION

ACKNOWLEDGMENTS

The authors dutifully wish to thank the following for their contributions to this book:

Mari Davis, Webmaster and Fashion Diva, who has graciously allowed us to use the designer biographies found in this book, which also appear on her website, FashionWindows.com: http://www.fashionwindows.com.

Patrick Glynn, of Wireless Flash News, whose timely and topical news stories appear courtesy of WIRELESS FLASH, 827 Washington Street, San Diego, California 92103, and can also be found at http://www.flashnews.com.

Chris White, several of whose Top-5 lists appear in this book and who was a countless inspiration for those that don't! Chris is owner of TopFive.com, at http://www.topfive.com.

Thanks also to Marjory L. Walker at the National Cotton Council of America for her informative list of the uses for a bale of cotton.

Finally, a huge thank you to the friendly folks at The American Hair Loss Council for providing us with information on not only types of hair loss, but treatments for hair loss as well.

THE BUZZ ON FASHION

CONTENTS

intro
FASHION FANATICS

Fashion. What is it about this sensitive subject that causes flashbulbs to pop, wallets to fly open, and cash registers to sing like a chorus of crack-crazed canaries each shopping season? Aren't our closets full enough with last season's "hottest" trends? (Half of which we were too embarrassed to wear when they were popular!) But honestly. Why is fashion so interesting? And why do we spend so much time, effort, money, and hair-pulling over finding just the right tie to go with just the right shirt, or just the right shoes to go with just the right dress?

Is it because our parents didn't let us dress ourselves as little kids? (Or maybe even to this day.) Is it because we're that insecure about our own birthday suits? Is it because we're suckers for anything in black leather, mauve boa, or alligator skin? Is it because we just can't get enough of that lovable, kind-hearted Mr. Blackwell? Or maybe it's none of the above, after all. Maybe we're all just a bunch of fickle fashion fanatics!

TOP 5 REASONS TO READ THIS BOOK

It costs a lot less than that polyester leisure suit you've been admiring.

It's required reading at the Fashion Institute and Telemarketing Scam Academy.

Your girlfriend's giving you a quiz on it before your next date.

Finally, an answer to that age-old question: boxers vs. briefs.

Let's face it, it can't make you dress any worse!

Perhaps we just like the idea of clothes. New clothes, particularly. (Even if retro is all the rage right now.) More important, maybe we relish the idea of shopping for those new clothes: The whoosh of those automatic doors sliding open. (Just for us, of course.) The smell of "perfume alley" as we dodge past doctor's coat-clad sharpshooters with their spraying nozzles and far-flung cologne samples. The challenge of the inappropriately named "fitting room." The allure of those specially designed, three-in-a-row life-size mirrors.

(That let you see your bulging backside like you never have before!) The ka-ching of the cash register. The ring ring of the alarm as we try to dash out of the store with three brand new outfits. (Even though we only paid for two.)

Could it be that we're all just desperately trying to relive those blissfully peaceful moments with Mom and Dad at the end of every summer when we went to the big department store downtown and got our new clothes for school? Could it be that simple? That rudimentary? And if so, why don't we just give Mom or Dad a call each time we're feeling nostalgic, instead of running out to Macy's and doing irreparable damage to our otherwise flawless credit?

Whatever the reason, there is no denying that, whether we like to admit it or not, we are all fashion followers. From the closet clueless to the model wannabe, the idea of fashion holds an allure like none other. (Except maybe Hollywood and chocolate.) Fashion is a luxury enjoyed by all of us, despite our situation in life or our socio-economic status. From

TOP 5 SIGNS YOU MIGHT BE A FASHION FANATIC

5 Your Calvin Klein shrine.

4 Your shoe tree is an actual tree.

3 Your secret crush on Inspector #8.

2 Your three-bedroom walk-in closet.

1 Coffee? Nope. Tea? Nada. Coco? Yes, please!

those crisp new blue jeans at Kmart to that stunning silk Chanel scarf at Bergdorf's, the thrill is the same. (Although the price tag is quite different.)

Either way, one thing is for sure: this book is for fashion lovers. Big or small, rich or poor, size two or size twenty-two. What's in? What's out? Try both! After all, what's the fun in only seeing the fresh stuff? Sure, the latest styles are great to look at and even better to wear. And, yes, you have to know about them to shop for them.

But it's just as fun (if not more) to see what's gone out of style. (And how quickly that can happen.) Laugh your ascot off over those ridiculous bell bottom jeans of old. (Wait, aren't they back in style?) Guffaw over those hilarious tie-dye halter tops your mom used to wear, just after burning her bra down in Haight-Ashbury. (Nope, they're back in, too.) Okay, then, goof on those ridiculous Sonny & Cher sheepskin vests, Fruit Striped polyester pants, and thigh-high go-go boots. (You mean, they're back in vogue too?) Whatever, maybe some of the new stuff will make you laugh.

After all, if it's in fashion, then it's in *The Buzz On Fashion*. Read on.

CLOSET CLUELESS

FASHION FLASHBACK

Fashion as we know it really started around the turn of the 20th Century in a period the French call the Belle Époque (1900-14). It laid the foundation for today's nose rings, high-heeled sneakers, and the Gaspard Yurkievich gown you saw at the Oscars. It was a time when Coco Chanel took clothes out of men's closets and made them her own. It was a period when Paul Poiret created dramatic fashions with an anything-goes taste borrowed from the Oriental kimono, the peasants of the Ukraine, and the harems of the Middle East. He persuaded celebrities of his day to wear his creations on stage and out in public. He had his own displays in large Paris department stores, developed his own lines of fabric and furniture, and had his own brand of perfume ten years ahead of Chanel No. 5. He even held classes for people of modest means to learn to decorate their homes. He was the forerunner to every designer nook you see in today's department stores throughout the world, from Ralph Lauren to Donna Karan.

But what it took to make fashion an option for everyone was the growth in personal income and the rise of the world economies, especially in the United States. People could afford fashion (or anti-fashion) and fulfill their desire to make how they look a reflection of who they are—or want to be.

FASHION FLASHBACK, THE CENTURY IN REVIEW

During the past 100 years, fashion trends have come and gone and now a survey is showing which ones had staying power. According to a poll conducted by Dryel (a dry cleaning product) the No. 1 fashion innovation of the 20th century was wash and wear clothing, followed by online shopping, luggage on wheels, and the bikini. The rest of the Top 10 in descending order:

— Greta Garbo-style pants for women

— Denim

— Casual Friday garb

— Push-up bras

— The little black dress

— And the "Hippie Look" of the '60s

Freedom of movement, the trademark of the 20th century, profoundly affected what we wear today. Just over 100 years ago, women were still constrained by corsets, petticoats, and cumbersome skirts that swept the floor like walking curtains. These vestiges of the Victorian era were the first to be snipped. Women began campaigning for the right to vote and sought a professional domain (not realizing that all roads eventually led to cramped cubicles and glass ceilings). Corsets became a thing of the past, and so were all of the accompanying fainting spells caused by the lack of blood flow to the respiratory system and head. This changed the garment industry forever.

This mounting campaign of joining the work force and voting fit neatly with the concept of more freedom for female frocks. Can you imagine stuffing yourself, crinoline, corset, and petticoat into the driver's seat of your Jetta? Not to mention, where would you keep your cell phone?

No, it was time to loosen the laces. Dressing for success started with a little invention called "the shirtwaist" (which looked like a long men's shirt) and became the symbol of self-sufficient womanhood.

But what truly marked "freedom" was the creation of the revolutionary weapon in the female arsenal: *The Brassiere!*

With bras snugly on and new freedoms being battled for, what came next seemed inevitable: "modern" hair. A floppy bun piled atop your head was no fast and easy option for the working girl, so women began lopping off their long locks for the easy to wash 'n' wear "bob." Parents and husbands everywhere witnessed, in horror, women chopping off their pride-and-joy tresses of hair, for freedom of movement, ease, and comfort.

Another declaration of female fashion independence came about when women were finally "allowed" to wear what were once considered the sacred property of men: trousers. The trend began, albeit slowly,

COCO CHANEL

in the 1920s with Coco Chanel, advanced to the movie screen with Greta Garbo and Katharine Hepburn, and evolved continually, as designers like Yves Saint Laurent started making attractive, dressy pantsuits for women to wear not just at the workplace, but to restaurants and social engagements as well.

Parisian designer Chanel, with her simple, clean designs, was a pioneer in bringing women their overdue fashion freedom. She not only adapted trousers as part of her very own wardrobe, but helped to simplify fashion with the so-called "little black dress." And she had a short boyish haircut to match.

Mademoiselle Gabrielle Chanel began her career in Deauville, a seaside town in France. A *milliner* (hat maker) by trade, Coco was also an accomplished seamstress. Bored to

CHANEL

THE 1930s & ·40s

While the 1930s found the country mired in the depths of the Depression, Hollywood thrived as people sought escape from their dreary economic existence. Stars such as Hepburn and Marlene Dietrich in their male-tailored style made their mark, but so did actresses like Jean Harlow in their sexy, slinky gowns.

DIETRICH

HEPBURN

death by all of the bourgeois petticoats and corsets, she cut simple dresses out of knit jersey, which was previously only used for men's underwear. (Calvin Klein owes her big time.)

Wearing her own designs, which included a version of a man's cardigan sweater, Chanel drew attention. She was brilliant with marketing, and had a "stable" of wealthy admirers ready and willing to back her. She convinced women that what she was creating was "modern."

As the 1940s dawned and the country soon found itself at war, women found themselves called into the workplace and defense plants. Jumpsuits and coveralls suddenly became part of the whole "Swing Shift" fashion. And with the Paris fashion industry all but shut down, American designers were forced to pump up their own lines to reflect the no-nonsense styles of the period.

Claire McCardell was the Donna Karan of the '40s. Claire who? Oh well, she was the woman who decided that if it was good enough for Levi (Strauss, that is) than why not her?

A war was on, and American women were motivated to support the home team. "Sportswear" (casual clothing) began to take a strong root in the glamour industry. Style became less and less about formality and accessories. Claire McCardell led this trend.

She designed smart dresses, easy to pull over the head, in plain cotton fabrics like denim. She put flat shoes with her collections (something just not done until then), and the "ballet slipper" look was born. She

Like many talented, misunderstood artists, Claire did not truly gain her place among the fashion elite until after the war, in the 1950s. This is how she described her work: "It looks and feels like America, its freedom, its democracy, its casualness, its good health. Clothes can say all that." Where would Donna, Ralph, and Tommy be without the Mother of Casual?

In 1947, a different kind of H-bomb was dropped on women's fashion when Christian Dior premiered his "New Look," a style boasting longer, flared skirts and trim, belted waists.

sympathized with the limited resources of manufacturers and was aware of the importance of being free to move in one's clothing. *American Vogue* called it "personal futurama" (or as we call it today, "casual").

Not a big deal for those of us living in the new millennium, but back in the '40s it was an entirely new option. Claire worked wonders with denim, which was primarily used for work clothes. She even had the chutzpa to create designs out of mattress ticking (the blue and white stripe fabric). This was something no one, outside of hobos, had ever used before. It was all about what was available.

After years of women strutting around like tomboys, Dior's "New Look" marked the beginning of the return to the classic female hourglass form.

This "New Look" went in tandem with the Baby Boom. Marriage and motherhood had made a comeback. Women's careers were shelved, and crinolines, bras, and girdles were all put back in the top drawer, much to the delight of some manufacturers. The term "career-woman" meant, "a gal was a man-eating harpy, a miserable neurotic witch from whom man and child must flee for their very life," wrote Betty Friedan in the *Feminine Mystique*.

As for the fashion world, they salted, sugared, and devoured Dior's idea with a silver spoon. He was the darling of the fashion press, single-handedly changing women's closets all over the world. Dior brought back "pretty." Narrow pencil skirts, hats, gloves, little bags, tiny waists shown off in plumed suit coats, emphasized busts, and longer, crinolined hemlines soon followed. Emphasizing corsets and the bodices on evening gowns, and even accessorizing them with full arm-length gloves, it seemed as though women had suddenly been thrown into a nostalgic dream world of the 1900s. "Lady-like" was the way to look.

Even today, Dior's "New Look" resurfaces on runways. Femininity, constrained or loose, will always be stylish.

THE 1950s

This "New Look" was enough to bring Mme. Chanel out of exile. She was livid with the return of "absurdity" (corsets), as she called it. Coco began, once again, to perfect a woman's suit, using tweeds, returning to the cardigan shape, and embellishing them with chain necklaces. Her "new look" affected fashion forever. Even in the new millennium, a rite of passage among women is to buy their first Chanel suit.

Whatever. In 1957, Dior retired due to illness (some say Coco induced), and hired a young, docile man named Yves Saint Laurent. Yves quickly became the darling of Paris. He fell in, and out, of favor with the

MONROE

This was the beginning period of knock-off manufacturing, and even someone as savvy as Chanel was vulnerable to such exploits. Rather than fighting the imitators, she joined them. A Brit named Jeffrey Wallis was enjoying marvelous sales copying her trademark suits. Chanel recognized the numbers and the bottom line. She decided to send him twelve garments a season (twenty-four a year) to reproduce, thereby boosting the sales of her own line internationally.

It is reported that Coco said to Christian Dior, "I adore you, but you dress women like armchairs."

THE **1960s**

New inhabitants in the White House started the 1960s with Jackie Kennedy's tea suit and pillbox hat as the rage. Jacqueline Bouvier Kennedy became the First Lady and the most chic woman in America. She carefully selected her court of American designers.

JACKIE

French press for years to come, yet ultimately Yves evolved into the ultimate "monarch" of fashion butterflies. Yves was a smart choice by Dior for he understood the youth culture, and the style they would buy. He added zest to a stodgy couture house. He created the "puff-ball," trapeze dress, and designed jackets inspired by Marlon Brando out of crocodile and mink.

Also, along with milkshakes and drive-ins, the 1950s brought us shapely figures à la Marilyn Monroe, padded bras, and Lucille Ball-inspired poodle skirts.

In *The Seven Year Itch*, Monroe made a dress famous by buying it straight off the rack, i.e. not having it designed specifically *for* her. This was a big trend to come. She also boosted a celebrated fragrance to stardom with the quote, "All I wear to bed is Chanel No. 5."

Russian-born Oleg Cassini was her official style advisor, as well as Roy Halston, who was her milliner. Jackie dazzled us with her class, sophistication, and smile. She wore Givenchy, Chanel, and Balenciaga. The world continued to watch, photograph, and cover her wardrobe for the next three decades. Whatever Jackie wore was a guaranteed seller, and so was the knock-off.

In England, Mary Quant, her hubby Alexander Plunket-Greene (perfect name for a fashion mogul), and manager, Archie Mac Nair, opened a boutique called Baazar in London's King's Road—the Chelsea district. Her clothing was affordable, totally focused on

the youth, and thumbed in the face of the establishment. Explained Plunket-Greene, "Snobbery has gone out of fashion. We were rather socialist, partly because we had no money. We wanted to increase the availability of fun, which should be available to everyone. We felt that expensive things were almost immoral and the New Look was totally irrelevant to us."

In 1964, *Life* magazine ran a six page feature on Mary, and within months, The Beatles, the miniskirt, and all things British were embraced by America. London style fashion, aka the miniskirt, showed up in the JC Penney department store, but with a Puritan American twist: The hemline had been dropped eight inches. Still, it wasn't long before girls were being thrown out of school for indecent exposure.

The "baby doll" look was in, and who better to embody this than Twiggy? She was another woman who drew attention for a unique reason, her figure: Boyish, no-hip, underdeveloped bodies were to be

collections, feathers, beads, frills, and flowers were suddenly the thing to wear. Shawls, capes, and hooded jackets had resurged, and the romantic gypsy graced the fashionable avenues of many a city in the world.

Meanwhile, the couture houses were responding to the calls of working women who found peasant shirts and bell bottoms unwearable in the office.

Another Brit rose to fame and fortune: Jean Muir. Jean knew what the modern women of the time were looking for: freedom and comfort. She became famous for her comfortable matte jersey knit ensembles that hugged the curves of women's bodies. Following Muir's lead, other designers answered the demands for a return to the classics. Muir was labeled a "feminist

a preferred look of choice among Mod designers.

The musicians of the time also set a standard for how people should dress. Lots of velvet, Regency (i.e. Victorian-era) period coats, floppy hats, platform leather boots, and suddenly a new label for this presentation was coined: "Glam-Rock."

Also, hand crafts such as knitting, embroidery, hand-dyed fabrics (like tie-dye), and leathers of all kinds gained popularity for their back-to-basics appeal. Wholesome peasant looks flooded the runways, and there was a renewed interest in Asian spirituality, art, and mysticism. Native American–inspired

"Every generation laughs at the
old fashions, but follows religiously
the new."
                              -Henry David Thoreau

a longer length and dramatic split up to the thigh cut
in sheer fabrications, and was promptly rejected.

Next came the shortest short-shorts ever, "hot
pants," but let's be real: it flopped. Women were bored
with the unrealistic fashion antics and supported the
wearable styles of Saint Laurent, Muir, Sonia Rykiel,
Laura Biogitti, the Fendi sisters, and Missoni. Sonia Rykiel
devised her own system of sizing that was completely
unlike the "standard" sizes of the time. Laura Ashley
opened her first shop in London. The Victorian look
captivated Ashley and a young American designer
by the name of Ralph Lauren.

designer" but answered this by saying, "I design
feminine, not feminist, clothes."

Karl Lagerfeld was designing for an old Parisian
couture house called Chloe and became the current
favorite of the French fashion press. He was the
mastermind behind bringing back the lines, fabrics,
and neon colors of the glitzy Art Deco period.

A new skirt called the "midi" came to life, with

THE 1970s

No one disputes that the look of the sixties was at least entertaining, though it might have been unintentional. As times changed, the world's fashion brain seemed to lock up, then free fall into a "black hole" of taste, otherwise known as the '70s.

No other decade in history is subjected to more sneers, eye rolls, coughs, hissing, spitting, and general looks of horror than this time period. Discos flourished, men grew long side-burns and fluffy moustaches, pants stayed flared, polyester was cheap, and was produced at a pace that could wrap the world in giant stretch pants; platforms stayed and hats made a comeback. Leg warmers appeared, Nike began producing their running shoes, and designer jeans became a second skin. Punk broke out in the streets of London, T-shirts with logos made a debut, and the drug of choice was cocaine. The look was *Saturday Night Fever*, but with an occasional cool chic, like *American Gigolo*. Armani (Giorgio not gigolo) got his start in this decade.

By the seventies, American designers attracted real coverage by the fashion press, for their wearable, logical, sophisticated, modern, understated style. They put their focus on working women, who wanted wearable comfort from their clothing. Body-consciousness became an obsession, for to be able to wear the slinky designs of the Americans, a woman had to be narrow, literally.

What differentiated the American ready-to-wear houses from the French, was the design process.

The French were focused almost entirely on the "look" of an ensemble, aesthetics were first; comfort was not a priority. In the U.S., designers became totally client-oriented, and created clothing for a "modern life-style." Those modern life styles required comfort. The Americans did

A young New Yorker by the name of Calvin Klein got his start by creating coats. He took a dozen coat samples, on a rolling rack, from department store to boutique, until finally a visiting buyer discovered him in an elevator.

Klein was inspired by the paintings of Andrew Wyeth and Georgia O'Keeffe and based his colors around shades of stone and earth, taupes, warm, sun-tanned beiges, and buttery yellows. These were easy colors for women to wear, and to coordinate.

The line of his silhouette was quintessentially 1930s. No corsets, no boning, no restraint (cellulite alert!)— just fluid, soft, simple, easy-to-wear lines. Calvin was quite discouraged with the fabrics offered in the U.S and began a long-term battle with the American textile industry to offer better quality fabrics to designers. Thanks in part to him, today we have more diversity and choices.

The American designers were consistently promoted by *Women's Wear Daily* and *Vogue*, giving them the stage to acquire a broad retail and consumer following. France caught up, eventually. Besides Saint Laurent, Emanuel Ungaro gained popularity from his funky mix of prints with classic tweeds. Givenchy remained a standard of supreme elegance, and of course, Chanel offered her basics; "crème de la crème" suits accessorized with quilted bags and dripping in pearls.

the unheard of—they listened to the women they dressed. Bill Blass embarked on a tour with his new collections, like a diplomat on a mission, listening to the "ladies who lunch." East Coast vs. West also got his attention, and he learned that women on the Atlantic and Pacific needed different elements for their wardrobe. This simple, progressive observation soon drove his contemporaries to follow suit.

Other big names came to life: Valentino, Zandra Rhodes, Krizia, the Fendi sisters, Missoni, Thierry Mugler, Vivienne Westwood, and a handful of Japanese designers showing in Paris. They were all fairly gimmick oriented—they made for fabulous layouts, but were not the most approachable frocks in the world. The appeal of the Americans would last for decades to come.

Ralph Lauren became recognized as a designer with real staying power. He was discouraged with the fleeting whims of the European establishment and revitalized English classics. He introduced the Old West, and mixed it all up with Palm Beach chic. Ralph began his career as a tie designer, so tailoring was second nature to him. He continues to have a finger on the pulse of what Americans want from their clothing.

Anne Klein created the epitome of American sportswear, and Donna Karan was one of her assistants. Anne was the queen of career, before Liz Claiborne. She listened to career women, and understood what they needed from their clothing, because she was one of them. Anne strongly coordinated her ensembles to make them "no-brainers" for busy women. Donna listened too.

Designer jeans became all the rage. Sassoon, Sergio Valenti, Klein, and Fiorrucci's were sought, bought, and squeezed into. Who can ever forget laying down to put on your jeans?

Giorgio Armani, working at the Italian house of Fiorrucci, designed one of the first pair of these designer pants. Later Armani left Fiorrucci to open his own salon, and the world of fashion anointed its new Knight. Tan, fit, and gorgeous, Armani wore THE SUIT. No one, *repeat*, no one has ever created a suit like Armani. With superior taste, expert cutting, and the right amount of attention to detail, Armani saw his popularity skyrocket over the next decade, especially in Hollywood.

Hemlines went down, pants became narrow, and Japanese designers Kenzo and Issey Miyake presented a new idea—"the big look." Oversized (think long potato sack), unshapely tent dresses began to appear in the magazines. The unconventional designs offered by the Japanese tied in nicely to a continuing storm of individuality brewing in Europe. All these new looks were so unappealing that they just had to become cool. As the seventies closed, a new rebellion was about to begin, and London was its fortress.

OPULENCE AND ARROGANCE PERSONIFIED: THE 1980s

Anarchy blossomed in the UK in the late seventies, and took off by the early eighties. The "sensible" clothes designers hawked bored the youth. Individualism returned, androgyny created controversy—a key ingredient for press coverage—and "the look" of the moment was no look at all.

The street clothing of London influenced everyone, whether they admitted it or not. The look was bold, in-your-face tough, and dubbed "punk." And it was primarily homemade. Tartan kilts with ripped leggings, a Queen T-shirt, butt-kicking combat boots, and some variety of bizarre hair completed the ensemble. There was no uniform, no class system, and no particular boundaries to this way of dressing. It was very new, moody, and above all—primal.

There were several designers who stole some "starlight" of their own during this time of fashion malcontent. Designers who created costumes for pop-stars like Boy George, Adam Ant, the Sex Pistols, and

Annie Lennox caught the attention of the press. The antagonist androgyny found its way into mainstream fashion. The music video became a production medium by 1981, and youth all over

the world copied their favorite musicians.

In the U.S., the Reagans entered the White House, and opulence began. Seventh Avenue responded to their "California persona," meaning Hollywood, and produced collections Nancy would love. Oscar de la Renta, Bill Blass, Halston, and James Gallanos dressed the "Reaganites"—those ladies who lunch. As the economy went into a dizzying upswing, the focus shifted to luxury. *Dallas* and *Dynasty* became a prime example of the bourgeois exhibitionism in fashion—women wanted THAT LOOK. But there were also alternatives to wearing sequins to the supermarket.

A New York designer named Norma Kamali created the "sweat pant." Kamali was responsible for bringing exercise tights onto the street, hence the legging craze was started.

Ralph Lauren truly became the quintessential "style-maker" of the era, although he didn't consider himself a fashion designer. He approached his collections from an understanding that people appreciated familiarity. Sportswear and utility were a primary focus, so in the eighties he created a version of the popular Izod shirt, and embellished it with a polo player.

Donna Karan left the house of Anne Klein to start her own line of clothes that were "missing from her wardrobe." Her first collection was made primarily of black knit pieces (which could be rolled up into a suitcase) and was celebrated as a victory for the working woman. Her collection was hailed as genius by the fashion press—a DK cult following soon began.

In Paris it seemed to be all about sex, sex, and more sex. Body consciousness was the mantra. Karl Lagerfeld, in his dark shades and pony tail, left Chloe to take the helm at Chanel. He wanted to revolutionize 31 Rue de Cambon, and did just that with his own interpretation of Chanel, reviving it to a commercial titan.

In Milan, Gianni Versace became renowned. He created lightweight aluminum-mesh cloth and proved a master of leather, using lasers (which he learned in Japan) to bond the seams together, rather than sending the fabric through a sewing machine. Versace gained

tremendous popularity after rock stars such as Sting and Eric Clapton wore his designs. His clothes also appeared in the ever popular television series *Miami Vice*. He soon became a recognized, and respected, fashion force. Gianni knew the formula to sex appeal, and it was eaten up with a gilded spoon by all who could afford it.

Meanwhile on the street, short bi-level haircuts surfaced and layered clothes were reinterpreted. Those who were young in the early eighties can recall layering two Polo shirts at a time, and two pairs of socks, and two Swatch watches—excess was king.

Androgyny was pushed to the limit when French bad-boy, Jean Paul Gaultier, introduced skirts for men (What? Like the Scots never

existed). Other envelopes were pushed as well. Women cropped off their hair for "boy looks," Madonna's musical career was born, and being overtly sexy in ripped clothes took center stage. Bras came out of shirts, albeit beneath finely tailored suits. Makeup was strong, bold, and colorful.

Accessories had a banner decade with the philosophy that one could never wear "too many." Spandex blended with cotton became a revolutionary fabric, and body conscious looks were an alternative to the baggy potato sacking being shown by the Japanese. More was better, those with the most made headlines. But the materialistic gorge-a-thon was about to come to an end.

A JOURNEY: THE '90s

With grumpy George Bush and his frumpy wife, Barbara, in the White House, designers obviously had to look elsewhere for inspiration. The economy had a chronic migraine, and everyone was seeking a bargain. Wal-Mart's popularity soared, as did the popularity of thrift stores. Making due with what you had, and simplifying that wardrobe, became a rule of thumb.

In 1989, Mudhoney released a song called "Touch Me I'm Sick" and this opened a new trend called "grunge." This trend eventually found its way to the

Flannel shirts, long unwashed hair, camouflage, hiking boots, velvet coats, floppy hats, braids, tattoos, piercing, and all things remotely resembling the late sixties and early seventies were revived. Most of these accessories could be purchased from second hand clothing stores, or better yet, by raiding the attic in your parents' house. The freedom of wearing

whatever tickled your fancy became the trend. The fashion moguls noticed, regrouped, and sewed.

Pared down, simple, authentically individual looks (for the

runways of style quickly. Groups like Pearl Jam (Eddie Vedder = Jim Morrison resurrected), Stone Temple Pilots, and Nirvana set the stage, and the youth followed. Where the youth trends go, designers are never far behind.

A young designer named Marc Jacobs took the helm at the American house of Perry Ellis and chose grunge as a spring board of inspiration. The board of directors fired him and closed the women's division of the company. This didn't stop Marc; he started his own line and found success. Grunge was not popular with the establishment, but it was wearable, earthy, and required very little money to buy.

masses) were everywhere. Casual Friday became an institution, promoting a new realm in the rag business. Dockers Khakis, started in 1986, took a prominent role in menswear. People were encouraged to be comfortable and be themselves. The public became sensitive about price-points, so designers responded with second lines that cost less

money. Initials were used as an attempt to show modesty. Designers learned a tough lesson from the bold, in-your-face eighties. CK (Calvin Klein) and DKNY (Donna Karan New York) flourished. Other designers followed their lead. Tommy Hilfiger gained tremendous press with his "jock-prep-cool" look.

Exotic made a comeback with Indian, Chinese, and Arabic fabrics, prints, and silhouettes. Chinoserie (a popular oriental fabric), dragon tattoo printed T-shirts, straw bags, and chopstick hair ornaments spread like honey through Oolong tea.

A little known Belgium designer named Martin Margiela staged an unusual fashion show in Paris. He called it "Destroy Fashion" and featured ripped, unfinished clothes in an empty, rubble-strewn lot. A German named Helmut Newton presented militant, pared down punk looks in stark white, sparsely furnished studios. Dutch designer Dries Van Noten presented his unified global village collection in an empty warehouse in Paris, and was immediately labeled a new talent to watch. The minimalist movement soared through the fashion world. Accessories were discarded, vintage clothes were disassembled, improved, and knocked off in great numbers at the Italian house of Prada.

Bill and Hillary Clinton ascended into the White House, and gradually the financially war-torn landscape began to

heal. Employment surged, companies merged, and the fashion industry finally had people they *wanted* to dress. The Clinton White House was more laid back, into basics, partial to running shoes, sweatshirts, saxophones, McDonald's, and Elvis. Designers became inspired again.

Paris felt the earth move. The red, white, and blue of two continents besieged them as American and British designers did a major takeover of the couture establishment, with the assistance of a French financial wizard named Jean Arnault. Monsieur Arnault bought every Parisian couture house he could get his hands on, then hired young overseas talent to bring them back to prominence. Arnault, over the last decade, has financed major names such as Christian Lacroix, and boosted the careers of many a struggling genius.

When Hubert de Givenchy retired he hired a British punk designer named Alexander McQueen to take his throne. La Maison Givenchy, once the epitome of social elegance, became a war zone of controversy in the hands of this lad. Monsieur Givenchy's efforts to quiet the qualms of nervous socialites and the fashion press had little effect. McQueen had a thing for ripping into the classics, destroying any standard of elegance, and stomping over anyone who got in his way. He put a hard edge look into his collections for Givenchy, and his boldness took

unveiling of his creations. Galliano is "the" place to look for future trends. (Hint, hint.)

Karl Lagerfeld maintained his reign at Chanel. In the mid-nineties he began to work with young, uninhibited designers such as Jeremy Scott, who follow few fashion rules of days past. The house of Chloe got a face-lift as well. Stella McCartney was invited to renew its popularity among

several seasons to gain popularity.

Another Englishman, John Galliano, a true period costumer, breathed new life into the dusty halls of Dior (also owned by Arnault). Galliano is one of those designers the fashion nomads (editors) worship. He is a drama all his own. Inspired by the attics of wealthy socialites, he borrows old couture gowns and reinterprets them into headline-making frocks. The fashion nomads adore him, and fill their pages with glossy photographs of his creations. He has designed collections around eras like Belle Époque, artists such as Gustav Klimt, the style of Betty Boop, and music like the rumba. He weaves a tale behind his vision during backstage interviews, all setting the stage for the

the style-conscious youth. (Yes, that's right, Paul's little girl.) She was independently manufacturing her own label in London, to rave reviews, when she was approached. Chloe, in the able scissor-hands of Stella, has experienced a magical resurgence. Ms. McCartney attributes her success to her childhood memories of her mum Linda wearing Chloe in the seventies.

American-now-in-Paris, Marc Jacobs (the guy fired from Perry Ellis) became chief designer at camp Louis Vuitton. Marc, with his perfect understanding of what women need from their clothes, and American

Michael Kors, also a transplanted American fashion prince, has recently created pearls of beauty at the house of Celine. Together, Marc and Michael have revived the logo-mania, in a modern, understated way. American designers, even in Paris, seem to have a natural intuition for what professional women want.

Back in the USA, Calvin Klein's empire expanded. Model Kate Moss became his muse in the early nineties, and the battle of the "waif" was on.

Her naturally frail frame received gasps of horror from women—as if they'd never seen skinny before. It seemed unhealthy, unnatural, but most of all unattainable. All the controversy helped push sales to record numbers for Calvin, so naturally, he worked it. Along with Klein, Donna Karan perfected her design philosophy, and expanded her empire with DKNY, and a line of home furnishings, fragrance, and menswear. Her daughter, Gabby, assists mom in bringing forth a youth conscious, street-oriented clothing.

sportswear roots, has fueled the fire at Vuitton, and attracted quite a following. Marc is simply Marc, and creates what he feels is "the right thing to do." Simple in his own dress (a jeans and T-shirt kind of dude), he understands that fussiness just isn't a viable modern option.

Fashion designers gradually evolved into economic powerhouses. As the economy improved, Ralph Lauren, Donna Karan, and Tommy Hilfiger jumped on the prosperity bandwagon and went public, selling stock in

His approach to clothing was based solely on sex appeal. His dashing, delicious good looks didn't hurt the image of the house one bit. Everyone seemed to crave Gucci (and Tom). Stiletto heels, skinny pants, navel diving necklines, and dresses with keyhole cutouts were sought after, fought over, and sold out of retail stores everywhere. Tom has a typically American sportswear approach to style—it has to be comfortable, feel good on the body, and look incredibly sexy. Hollywood gorged themselves on Gucci, and Tom became the "golden boy" of the rag biz. Gucci ads were all about desire, seduction, and S-E-X! Hey, it sells.

their companies. Bill Blass retired and Versace was murdered in Miami. Versace's senseless assassination changed the house forever. His sister, and closest companion, Donatella, took the reins. Critics were skeptical that she could keep up with the instincts of Gianni, but she has and then some. Versace continues to be a glam-rock kind of clothing.

Near the end of the nineties, another American made headlines, but this time in Milan. The slumping house of Gucci desperately needed a revival, and Tom Ford was their man. Tom changed fashion more than anyone else in the late nineties.

GREATEST HITS

Now that you've experienced a brief fashion flashback, what exactly were the most important fashion developments of the 20th century? Here, in no particular order, are some of the key innovations of the past 100 years that any fashion fan would hate to live without (and why):

FASHION LANDMARKS OF THE 20TH CENTURY

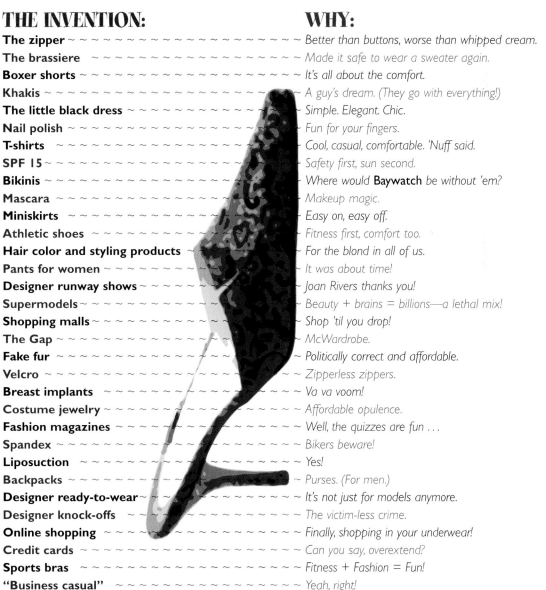

THE INVENTION:	WHY:
The zipper	Better than buttons, worse than whipped cream.
The brassiere	Made it safe to wear a sweater again.
Boxer shorts	It's all about the comfort.
Khakis	A guy's dream. (They go with everything!)
The little black dress	Simple. Elegant. Chic.
Nail polish	Fun for your fingers.
T-shirts	Cool, casual, comfortable. 'Nuff said.
SPF 15	Safety first, sun second.
Bikinis	Where would **Baywatch** be without 'em?
Mascara	Makeup magic.
Miniskirts	Easy on, easy off.
Athletic shoes	Fitness first, comfort too.
Hair color and styling products	For the blond in all of us.
Pants for women	It was about time!
Designer runway shows	Joan Rivers thanks you!
Supermodels	Beauty + brains = billions—a lethal mix!
Shopping malls	Shop 'til you drop!
The Gap	McWardrobe.
Fake fur	Politically correct and affordable.
Velcro	Zipperless zippers.
Breast implants	Va va voom!
Costume jewelry	Affordable opulence.
Fashion magazines	Well, the quizzes are fun . . .
Spandex	Bikers beware!
Liposuction	Yes!
Backpacks	Purses. (For men.)
Designer ready-to-wear	It's not just for models anymore.
Designer knock-offs	The victim-less crime.
Online shopping	Finally, shopping in your underwear!
Credit cards	Can you say, overextend?
Sports bras	Fitness + Fashion = Fun!
"Business casual"	Yeah, right!

HEMLINE TIMELINE

Explore a brief and factual history of fashion throughout the ages, from the Ice Age to Vanilla Ice, and learn the inevitable reason why no one can predict fashion's future and why most of us would like to forget fashion's past:

- **2620-2500 BC:** A polychrome stele of Princess Nefertiabet depicts her dining in a one-shoulder leopard-skin gown. It is now in The Louvre in Paris.

- **2000 BC:** The salty sand of the Taklimakan Desert in China helps preserve mummies wearing colorful robes, boots, stockings, and hats.

- **800 AD:** The inhabitants of the British Isles did not comb their hair until the Danes taught them how to do so at about this time.

- **1200:** Buttons were invented as a decoration to embellish hemlines, collars, and the sides of sleeves.

- **1470:** In Portugal, Princess Juana popularized the farthingale, a wide-hipped skirt stiffened by whalebone.

- **1499:** Anne of Brittany initiated the white wedding gown.

- **1772:** Shoelaces were invented in England.

- **1818:** People began wearing left and right shoes. Shoes were made identical for either foot prior to this.

- **1853:** Levi-Strauss and Co. got its start peddling tough pants to California gold miners. The first pairs sold for $13.50 a dozen.

- **1875:** The arrangement of three fruits—an apple, a pear, and a cluster of grapes—is adopted for the Fruit of the Loom underwear label.

- **1886:** The tuxedo dinner jacket made its American debut at the autumn ball in Tuxedo Park, N.Y.

- **1889:** The brassiere was invented in Paris.

- **1901:** King Camp Gillette, a former bottle-cap salesman, produced the first Gillette safety razor.

- **1904:** Guccio Gucci opened a small saddlery in Florence after quitting his doorman job at London's Savoy Hotel.

- **1908:** Helena Rubinstein, following her success in Australia, moved to London and opened a beauty salon.

- **1910:** In France, a hairdresser devised the permanent wave for hair.

- **1929:** French designer Coco Chanel introduces a collection of smart, practical clothing.

- **1930:** American men begin

wearing jockey-type underwear when the long john market "bottomed out" in the late 1920s.

• **1931:** Lawrence Gelb introduced Nestle's Clairol hair dye.

• **1933:** DuPont produces the first completely unnatural fiber, nylon. Suddenly, socks and underwear stay up of their own free will!

• **1934:** When Clark Gable stripped down in *It Happened One Night* to reveal nothing underneath his shirt but a bare chest, T-shirt sales plummeted by 75%.

• **1936:** Hart Schaffner introduced pants with the zip-up fly.

• **1939:** Women's nylon stockings sold for $1.15 a pair.

• **1940:** Max Factor invented Tru-Color lipstick, indelible lip rouge that did not smear or change color.

• **1942:** Humphrey Bogart's trademark trench coat in *Casablanca* created a look that still exists today.

• **1943:** The U.S. government passes the L-85 Restrictions, limiting the use of wool and silk in clothing manufacture.

• **1944:** *Seventeen* magazine begins publishing.

• **1945:** GIs return from overseas and begin wearing the leftover khaki pants from uniforms. Years later, khakis "swing" into The Gap's collection.

Stays Up!

• **1946:** The introduction of the bikini in Paris follows American atomic tests on the Bikini atoll in the South Pacific.

• **1946:** One of the first strapless dresses appeared on Rita Hayworth in *Gilda*.

• **1947:** Christian Dior's début collection is dubbed the "New Look" by the American fashion press.

• **1948:** As Dior tours the United States, American women protest the New Look's longer hemlines.

• **1950:** When Bette Davis tried on one of her dresses while filming *All About Eve*, the straps slipped down her arm, thereby starting the off-the-shoulder trend.

- **1952:** In an attempt to restrict unauthorized knock-offs, the French government rules that couture designs can be copyrighted for the duration of one fashion season.

- **1954:** What Clark Gable did to hurt the sale of T-shirts 20 years earlier, Marlon Brando reverses with the "rebellious" '50s look of jeans, T-shirt, and leather jacket when he appears in *The Wild One*.

- **1957:** Old Spice is introduced; over 40 years later, it remains one of the world's best-selling fragrances.

- **1960:** John Kennedy defeats Richard Nixon without wearing a hat. Hat sales plunge and never recover.

- **1960:** Mattel introduces Barbie, the first "fashion" doll.

- **1961:** Audrey Hepburn developed her legendary look in *Breakfast at Tiffany's*.

- **1962:** In London, Mary Quant introduces the first vinyl dresses and coats, and British *Vogue* endorses the thigh-high miniskirt.

- **1962:** Yves Saint Laurent opens his own couture house in Paris.

- **1963:** Diana Vreeland becomes editor-in-chief of *Vogue*, and soon coins the word "Youthquake" to describe the fashions of the times.

- **1966:** The sixteen-year-old Twiggy wins the "Face of the Year" contest, and her modeling career is subsequently launched.

- **1967:** *The Carol Burnett Show* premiered on CBS, with costumes by designer Bob Mackie.

- **1968:** September 24, *The Mod Squad* premiered on ABC. As ratings rose, so did hemlines across the country.

- **1969:** Levi's started to sell bell-bottomed jeans.

- **1970:** Ali MacGraw starts a major fashion trend after wearing an old crocheted hat in *Love Story*, which she reportedly just threw on during filming.

- **1971:** Southwest Airlines began operations; its stewardesses wore white boots and orange hot pants.

- **1972:** Nike Shoes began production.

- **1973:** Little-known talent Ralph Lauren designs the costumes for the movie *The Great Gatsby*.

- **1976:** Yves Saint Laurent revives the Paris couture with his opulent "Russian" collection.

- **1977:** In London, the Queen's Silver Jubilee coincides with an explosion of Punk rock music and anti-fashions, which appear in British *Vogue*.

- **1981:** August 1, the rock music video channel MTV made its debut, bringing "street fashion" into the homes of millions of young viewers.

- **1983:** What girl did not copy Jennifer Beals' off-the-shoulder sweatshirt in *Flashdance*, which turned into the look of the '80s?

- **1985:** In *Out of Africa*, Meryl Streep and Robert Redford appeared in safari outfits, thereby thrusting such outlets as Banana Republic to the forefront of fashion.

- **1986:** Dockers Khakis introduces its line of casual clothing.

Dockers Khakis

- **1991:** *Visionaire*, a fashion and art magazine, was founded.

- **1993:** High-tech fabric becomes popular, and Polartec fleece, Gore-Tex, sport sandals, hiking boots, and other sporty garments are worn everywhere.

- **1997:** In *I Know What You Did Last Summer*, Jennifer Love Hewitt continued the simple, yet undeniable trend in women's clothing: the tight, skimpy shirt.

- **1999:** ABC revives the quiz show format with its runaway hit, *Who Wants to Be a Millionaire?* Its host, Regis Philbin, popularizes the solid tie on matching solid shirt look.

TOP 5
SIGNS YOUR HEMLINE IS TOO HIGH

5 You suddenly find yourself leading a parade of construction workers.

4 George Michael keeps following you into public restrooms.

3 Your girlfriend keeps asking you where you got that "denim underwear."

2 People keep asking you where you got your linen bathing suit.

1 You can't seem to find that "full moon" everyone around you keeps giggling about.

2 TWO

FASHION BY DESIGN

Fashion designers are a special breed. (After all, who else could put up with all of those supermodels?) Their best friends are mannequins, needles and pins are their bread and butter, and they can't step foot out in public without being asked, "Does this belt go with these shoes?" They spend their days surrounded by bolts of fabric, ringing telephones, endless cups of tall lattes, frenzied personal assistants, stacks of 8 x 10 glossies, and ravenous fashion editors begging for the "latest scoop." And do you think they ever get to loaf around in ratty pink slippers, a sweat-stained ball cap, and pepperoni-stained boxer shorts? Forget about it.

So is it any wonder that these designing dictators take out their fashion frustrations on an eager public by making them suffer through ridiculous runway shows jam-packed with overblown styles, pointless accessories, and expensive fabrics no one in their right mind would wear out of doors? Let alone to a social function or, heaven forbid, work? Okay, that's the myth anyway. But read on to see how a select group of today's hottest designers have managed to create fashion lines that are not only wearable, but wearable in public!

GRUNGE GURU: MARC JACOBS

Although Marc Jacobs's current success is due to his clean-cut luxury sportwear, one thing is certain: he will go down in fashion history as the man who "invented" Grunge.

The 35-year-old New Yorker's infamous spring-summer 1993 collection for Perry Ellis displayed over-sized flannel shirts, slouchy sweaters, and chunky army boots paired with floral vintage-looking dresses. It became an overnight editorial sensation and an equally swift commercial disaster.

While the fashion elite raved that Jacobs's clothes broke new ground for women who wanted to dress more freely, consumers refused to pay $1,500 for a dress that looked like it came from a flea market. Perry Ellis sided with the customer, fired Jacobs, and discontinued the designer's line. But no matter how despised and ridiculed the grunge look was, no one can deny its impact: Once pierced waifs in rags had invaded the streets and magazines, fashion was never the same again, and Jacobs himself still looks on the fabled collection as his all-time favorite.

The young Jacobs had his mind set on design early. In 1981, he graduated from New York's High School of Art and Design and went on, like fellow star alumni Anna Sui, Steven Meisel, and Donna Karan, to the Parsons School of Design. He was quickly recognized as a fashion wunderkind: in 1984 he received the Perry Ellis Gold Thimble Award, the Chester Weinberg Gold Thimble Award, and Parsons's award for Best Student of the Year.

After a couple of years of designing for Reuben Thomas, Marc Jacobs and business partner Robert Duffy launched the first Marc Jacobs collection in 1986. In 1987, Jacobs was the youngest designer ever to win the prestigious CFDA Perry Ellis Award for New Fashion Talent. Two years later, Jacobs went to work for Perry Ellis. Though the grunge fiasco put an abrupt end to the collaboration, 1993 was not a complete write-off as Jacobs won the coveted CFDA Award for Best Womenswear Designer.

Jacobs took some time off, but returned to the fashion scene with a stellar fall '94 collection. The press raved about his sequined skirts, pants paired with red and apple-green leather tops, sheer fur-sleeved T-shirts, and hooded tweed jackets. In 1998 he won CFDA Best Womenswear Designer Award again. His luxury sportswear caught the attention of Bernard Arnault, head of the Louis Vuitton Moët Hennessy conglomerate, and eventually clinched him the position of artistic director of the prestigious leather goods manufacturer Louis Vuitton just as it was about to embark on its first-ever ready-to-wear collection.

After his debut show in Paris in April, 1999, Jacobs told British Vogue, "Vuitton is a luxury brand—it's functional, but it is also a status accessory. I decided status would be done my way, which is to say invisibly." A bit too invisibly for some: The pared-down collection was too understated for the French press, who found the flat-front trousers, long skirts, and cotton coats in white, gray, pale blue, and raspberry "boring."

The Anglo-Saxon press was more enthusiastic, and the British paper The Guardian called the collection "achingly hip." Since then, Jacobs has made himself at home at Vuitton and his designs continue to evolve in a more ironic, sexy, and colorful direction.

In an attempt to define his design philosophy, Jacobs told Harper's Bazaar, "Although it's tempting to deal with what I've learned from the past, I can only deal with the idea of the present. It could be that these rapidly changing, confusing times have in some strange way made the consistent aspect of classic clothing seem comforting. But I just like simple things in very luxurious fabrics."

DKNY-2K:
DONNA KARAN
IN THE NEW
MILLENNIUM

It is impossible to describe contemporary New York style without coming back to Donna Karan over and over again. "Donna Karan" is no longer a simple name; it is the label attached to a $600-million company that has combined comfort and style into a modern uniform for the American woman.

Born in New York in 1948, Donna Karan grew up with a tailor for a father and a model for a mother. Not surprisingly, she entered the Parsons School of Design to pursue a career in fashion. After her second year of study, an internship at Anne Klein turned into a permanent job, and she became associate designer in 1971. Karan's talent and loyalty paid off as she took over the company after Anne Klein's death in 1974. Along with Louis Dell'Olio, Karan designed for Anne Klein for the next ten years before branching off on her own in 1984.

Donna Karan's approach to fashion is very personal: She designs what she would like to wear herself, and in doing so, hit on a winning formula that emphasizes the universality of black, the versatility of basic, functional pieces, and the importance of comfort. Donna Karan does not try to entice her customers into buying a lot of different outfits; instead, she encourages them to combine a few key pieces in different ways.

When the Donna Karan New York line came out in the fall of 1985, it defined her philosophy of polished yet understated dressing. Built around seven easy pieces, the cornerstone of the collection was the black body suit, which could be worn with a wrap skirt, trousers, jeans, or under a suit. This sensible approach has not made Karan's fashion exciting or provocative; her clothes are meant to be wearable, not to push fashion boundaries.

Donna Karan has not stopped with high fashion; the name is well established in hosiery, beauty products, accessories, fragrance, eyewear, and home furnishings. There is also her extremely popular sportswear line, DKNY, and, inevitably, DKNY jeans. Karan takes pride in her empire and ensures an extremely high quality for her products. She has justified her expensive hosiery, for example, by insisting in *W* magazine, "With matte jersey, skinny knits, and layered sheers, with hemlines as variable as they are, no one can deny how important a pair of hose is. The legs support the whole body; they're the foundation and the stem to the soul."

One of fashion's great commercial successes, Donna Karan has also won critical awards. The fashion industry has bestowed numerous honors on her, such as the Coty American Fashion Award in 1977. Fashion Designers of America also named her Best Designer of the Year in 1985, 1990, 1992, and 1997.

However, the most obvious sign of her success is that her best friends, Barbra Streisand and Demi Moore, not to mention President Bill Clinton, all love being dressed by Donna.

TOP 5 SIGNS YOUR FASHION SHOW IS A FLOP

5 Madonna applauds.

4 The only ones left in the audience are the custodians, and even they don't like it!

3 Two words: mutinous models!

2 Those flashbulbs are the paparazzi taking pictures of themselves.

1 That's funny, you've never heard models heckled before.

"Just because a dress is red satin doesn't mean it will come off easily."

—Anonymous

Calvin Klein has always understood the greater ramifications of fashion; that it is not merely about clothing, but image, mood, and lifestyle. Over the last thirty years, Klein has managed to distill these same three elements—image, mood, and lifestyle—into a single image, usually in an ad campaign. Whether it's Brooke Shields purring that nothing gets between her and her Calvins or the unisex cool of his cK One gang, Klein is a master of manipulating the modern masses.

His celebrated name has spread far and wide on the waistbands of boxers and briefs, but Klein got his start in the less torrid business of women's coats. Born in the Bronx, New York, in 1942, Klein studied at the New York High School of Art and Design before enrolling in the Fashion Institute of Technology. Klein graduated from the Institute at the age of twenty and then worked five years for the Seventh Avenue manufacturer Dan Misstein. When he started his own business in 1968, he concentrated at first on coats, and by 1969 had already landed one cover of *Vogue*.

As of 1971 he had begun to experiment with sportswear, designing coatdresses, often in knits, hot-pants turnouts, jumpsuits, and classic blazer pantsuits that all shared certain constants of man-tailoring, notably in the way shirts, jackets, and pants were cut and in the use of topstitching. He did not neglect coats; these were available in a range from very casual, made in poplin lined with gingham, to dressier, in tweeds, to almost formal, in suede trimmed with fox.

In 1973, the year he won the first of three consecutive Coty awards, Calvin Klein emerged as a top designer who had his finger on the pulse of American women. Having learned, while touring the country, that women were becoming more name-conscious and that they wanted to be able to buy all their clothes from a single designer, he worked with the concept of a wardrobe of interrelated pieces.

One such grouping, all in the favorite 1970s beige, was composed of silk evening pants, tank top, shirt jacket, daytime trousers, cardigan sweater, polo shirt, and coat. With various combinations of these items a woman could be dressed for any occasion.

Although Klein designed dresses, like his 1973 strapless tube of black matte jersey, most of his evening looks remained fairly casual. Two-piece dresses were

"My mom says to me, 'If I see another picture of you with a Marlboro in your hand, I'm gonna kill you.'"
—Kate Moss, supermodel

made in silk charmeuse in lustrous pale tones of beige and burgundy or navy and brown. Often these dresses featured wrapped blouses, whose décolletage the wearer could adjust to suit her preference. The pieces that wrapped were held in place by a soft suede belt edged with brass beading or by wider cummerbunds of woven webbing.

By 1975 Calvin Klein had become a celebrity, and he changed his somewhat homespun earlier image (a 1973 advertisement quoted him saying this about his new collection, "I made a lot of things that go with things…") for a more glamorous one.

His advertisements began to feature photographs by Chris Von Wangenheim, Deborah Turbeville, and Guy Bourdin, who shot a 1976 ad that showed a Calvin Klein silk blouse on a wire hanger, with the label visible at the back of the neck, hanging next to a mirror in which a nude woman was reflected. More and more, Calvin Klein was trading on the idea that the appeal of his clothes, simple as they were, lay in the attitude of the wearer, who affected her look by how far she unbuttoned her shirt, or what she wore—or didn't wear—underneath her silk dress or her Calvin Klein jeans (his 1980 television ads starring Brooke Shields would become, in a word, notorious).

Klein quickly branched out into sportswear, and the rest, as they say, is history. Minimalist, practical and color neutral, Klein's clothing garbs a constellation of Hollywood stars, from Gwyneth Paltrow and Winona Ryder to Uma Thurman and Michelle Pfeiffer. He received the Council of Fashion Designers of America award for best womenswear and menswear designer in 1993, and has won the prestigious Coty Award for Design numerous times. His commercial empire has expanded as quickly as his list of awards, and now includes Calvin Klein for Men and Women, cK Calvin Klein for Men and Women, underwear, footwear, watches, fragrances, eyewear—the list goes on.

Klein has also culled useful notoriety from the publicity surrounding his outré advertisements. First, there was the pre-pubescent Brooke. Then, the erotic "Obsession" ads with Kate Moss and Marky Mark pressed against a wall. An advertising campaign launched in 1995 for cK Calvin Klein Jeans was quickly retracted after accusations of child pornography were filed. In February '99, there was a general uproar, led by New York City mayor Rudy Giuliani, over a Times Square billboard showing semi-naked tots gamboling in Calvin Klein's kids undies.

Though risqué publicity campaigns give the house edgy cachet and trend-setting status, wearable, mainstream clothing is what makes Calvin Klein the all-American designer—and with his name emblazoned on everything from bed sheets to dishware, truly a household name.

TOP

5 SIGNS YOU'RE AT A KIDDY CALVIN KLEIN PHOTO SHOOT

5 The shoot relocates every time you hear sirens.

4 The background music is the theme from *Sesame Street*.

3 Instead of snorting coke, all the models *drink* Coke.

2 The wrap party takes place at Chuck E. Cheese.

1 "Makeup" consists of baby powder and handy wipes.

DESIGNING WOMAN: ANNA SUI

Anna Sui (Get it right, people! It's pronounced "Swee," not "Sooey!" This is high fashion, after all. Not some Okie pig calling contest) draws inspiration from a hodgepodge of sources—Scandinavian furniture, the Bloomsbury group, and high-school preppies, just to name a few—but all of her collections have something in common: The decadent and whimsical touch of rock 'n' roll that makes Sui a favorite designer of models and musicians.

Just one look at the funky fashion diva tells you why Sui is the epitome of the cool New York lifestyle the rest of the world is just dying to emulate, even imitate. Always clad in head-to-toe black (which is even more emphasized with her black hair and shades), one might not realize that she is one of the most coveted designers among the young and funky. Yet her threads are frequently seen on the backs of young Hollywood. And after using rock stars like Dave Navarro of Jane's Addiction and the Red Hot Chili Peppers and James Iha of Smashing Pumpkins in her runway shows, even more of America has become aware of this talented designer.

Sui grew up in a Michigan suburb, the daughter of Chinese immigrants, with an older brother and a younger brother. Hers was the only Asian family in town, but she did not feel like an outsider.

"I was just special," says Sui. "I was a good student, belonged to all the social groups, and was on the best dressed list." She fell in love with fashion early on: She used to stage her own version of the Academy Awards and designed gala wear for toy dolls and soldiers. "I always wanted to be a fashion designer."

At the age of sixteen, Sui convinced her parents to send her to New York to study at Parsons School of Design. After leaving school two years later, Sui worked at different sportswear companies and freelanced as a stylist for famed fashion photographer Steven Meisel, whom she had met at Parsons.

Sui worked at a steady stream of different sportswear companies until 1981 when she designed some pieces of her own, which were bought by Macy's and featured in a full page *New York Times* ad. "My employer at the time gave me an ultimatum: Stop designing my own clothes or quit, so I quit," she says. Afterward, Sui decided to follow her dreams and devote herself full-time to designing her own collection. She set up a sewing machine in her apartment and started her own business.

But Sui's eccentric, vintage-inspired style never quite fit in with the slick, label-crazed '80s. She did not attain success until the beginning of the '90s, when her baby-doll dresses were suddenly in sync with the budding grunge movement and a "trashier" approach to fashion.

In 1991, Anna debuted her first

runway collection in New York. She initially became famous for the romantic pirate look she popularized in the early 1990s. Since then, she has become renowned for her eclectic style, mixing things like Chanel style suits with '70s glam. She has said that music is an extremely important influence on her and that there's nothing like going to a club and hearing live music. In her Spring '94 show, the grunge favorite baby-doll dress became her staple. She further showed her love of music in her Spring '97 collection, which featured handkerchief dresses that Stevie Nicks might have worn twenty years ago.

Not surprisingly, Anna credits both Nicks and Courtney Love as sources of inspiration. "I think everyone is influenced by their youth, by that time in your life when everything that happens seems critical, and certain songs become anthems for you."

Slowly but surely expanding her business, Anna Sui launched her bridge line SUI by Anna Sui in 1995. Unlike most designers, whose second collections are younger and more playful than their first line, Sui did it the other way around. The SUI clothes are more classic and modest versions of her funky signature designs. She opened two new shops in Japan in 1997 and, in that same year, premiered her Anna Sui shoe line. Staying true to the kooky Sui image, the shoes came in velvet, crocodile, and exotic skin. Future plans include a signature fragrance and a cosmetics line.

A fixture on the Manhattan club scene, along with pals Steven Meisel, Naomi Campbell, and Smashing Pumpkin's James Iha, Anna Sui keeps her finger on the pulse of pop-culture. The close connection to music is a vital part of her image. Her little Greene Street store is decorated with rock 'n' roll posters on velvet tapestry walls, and is stocked with all the accessories a groupie could want, from fluorescent nail polish and dazzling costume jewelry to S&M stiletto heels.

The designer says she's nearly obsessed by accessories. She does shoes from flats to platforms, decorates handbags, makes jewelry with features and beads, and puts hippie, flower-child wreaths in her models' hair.

"It's a touch of fantasy that you want," Sui says. "It adds just a touch of color, and you feel very feminine." Guess those mock Academy Awards finally paid off, after all.

TOP 5 SIGNS YOU WERE BORN TO BE A FASHION DESIGNER

5 Two words: monogrammed diapers.

4 No one could ever understand you growing up with all those pins in your mouth.

3 You kept calling that poor photographer from the yearbook "paparazzi."

2 None of the other guys in P. E. designed their own gym uniform.

1 Your best friends back in school were all mannequins.

"A woman's dress should be like a barbed-wire fence: serving its purpose without obstructing the view."

—Sophia Loren

Coco Chanel introduced a sophisticated, minimalized look for women who had become, as she had, "allergic" to frilly, corseted Belle Époque costumes. Her uncomplicated jersey dresses, riding jackets, sweaters, and—yes!—trousers became the dress uniform for women on their way to emancipation.

If you were to call up Coco Chanel's spirit at a seance and interrogate it, however, the grouchy, necklace-rattling gremlin would probably deny any such political agenda and disappear in a cloud of perfume. She designed only things *she* wanted to wear, and if a whole generation of women did too, well, that was just fine.

Gabrielle Chanel was born in Saumur in 1883. Orphaned at a young age, her grandmother put her in a convent where, somehow, the saucy girl got the idea to become a dancehall artist. On the café-concert circuit, her trademark song was something called, "Qui qu'a vu Coco," and the nickname stuck.

An elegant young man named Etienne Balsan rescued Coco from a tawdry diet of pancake makeup and burlesque, whisking her off to a mansion where she learned to ride horses and mix with the beau monde. With help from various moneyed lovers, Chanel opened boutiques on Paris' Rue Cambon and in the casino town of Deauville before World War I.

Chanel would be among the first to acknowledge that it was the war that made her such a success. Despite the phrase "guns or butter," women kept on buying clothes, but they no longer wanted to be encumbered by lavish dresses.

Propelled by her wartime popularity, Chanel refined her pared-down, androgynous look in the Roaring Twenties, earning the label, "soup-kitchen style." She chopped off her dark hair and started producing easy, dropped-hemline dresses, sleeveless evening gowns, and the famous Little Black Dress, paired with two-toned shoes. Chanel No. 5 came out in 1921, the perfume that Marilyn Monroe later famously said was the only thing she wore to bed.

The Second World War was not as fortuitous for Chanel as the First. She spent 1940-44 in Paris, arousing suspicions about her relations with the German occupation forces. When the war ended, Chanel left France for Switzerland.

This would have finished off most careers, but Chanel came out of retirement at

> "I don't mind living in a man's world as long as I can be a woman in it."
> —Marilyn Monroe

the age of 71 and reopened her shop in Paris. The collarless, braid-trimmed suits in jersey and tweed come from this period. Though she had eschewed all jewelry in her younger days, now she loaded down her suits with bracelets and strands of pearls, indiscriminately mixing real and fake gems. The quilted leather handbag with the interlinked, back-to-back "C" clasp came out in 1955.

Coco Chanel died, alone, in the Ritz hotel in Paris on January 10, 1971. The Chanel house was left to slide for the next twelve years until Karl Lagerfeld took over in 1983. Lagerfeld turned the house around, producing collections that pay tribute to, and occasionally poke fun at, the Chanel look: In the 1991 spring collection, he showed sequined Chanel jackets in fluorescent colors with Lycra leggings. He achieved enormous success in his fall/winter 1992-93 collection with his black leather biker style Chanel suit.

CHANEL

"SCORING" WITH
POLO:
RALPH LAUREN

As one our of our leading fashion designers, Ralph Lauren has a creative quest that drives his international business. His design philosophy is straightforward: "I believe in design that has integrity—design that lasts."

under the Polo label. In 1968, he became founder, designer, and chairman of Polo Fashions New York.

As a trendsetter, Ralph Lauren has been raising standards in the fashion industry for over thirty years. His insistence on classic form and function makes him an icon in this industry of more fickle and fleeting careers. His passion for detail and killer instinct has taken him from a startup company in 1967 to over $5 billion a year in sales today. He has the ability to envision beauty, and has the persistence to carry it through in every detail.

Lauren was born Ralph Lifshitz, on October 14, 1939, in the Bronx, New York, the youngest in a family of four in a middle-class Jewish family.

He studied at the City College of New York and served in the United States Army from 1962-1964. Lauren started his business in 1967 with an unusual line of ties called Polo. They were very classic and wide for their time. Lauren's fashion design is synonymous with natural elegance and enduring style. His designs go beyond the world of fashion into advertising, furniture, interior design, and even an assortment of household goods.

He created his famous English tweedy look

Ralph Lauren rose to world fame when he became the men's costume designer for *The Great Gatsby*, the film version of F. Scott Fitzgerald's novel starring Robert Redford. An astute businessman, he knew the power

TOP 5

IMITATION KNOCK-OFFS OF THE POLO BRANDNAME

5 OLEO

4 EBOLO

3 ROLO

2 CHOLO

1 SKOAL-O

sense. Yes, there are detractors of his designs, but for every detractor, there are ten who are just in love with his work. How do we prove that? Look around—Polo/Ralph Lauren for Men; Double RL; Ralph Lauren for Women; Ralph Lauren Home; even Ralph Lauren paint.

of Hollywood, just like a lot of his contemporaries (Giorgio Armani for *American Gigolo*; Gianni Versace for *Showgirls*). And it is not only Hollywood who loves him, Wall Street loves him too. The continued success of his companies is a good indication of that.

Lauren is known for combining innovation and tradition with inspirations that come from such varied influences as African safaris, English aristocracy, old Hollywood, Parisian café life, the Western frontier, Russian revolutionaries, Santa Fe adobes, Eastern prep schools, and even competitive sports!

Ralph Lauren's designs are classics in their own

The numerous Awards won by Ralph Lauren include:

- Coty Menswear Award, 1970
- Coty Fashion Award for Women's Wear, 1974
- Coty Hall of Fame, 1977
- Lifetime Achievement Award, Council of Fashion Designers of America, 1992

VIVA VERSACE!

"Oh, Versace."

"Oui, Versace."

"Si, Versace."

"Viva Versace!"

You know you're a fashion icon when you only need one name to be recognized:

"Oh, dear. Love the gown. Is that by Gianni—"

"What? Who? Never heard of him."

"You know? Gianni Versace?"

"Versace? *Versace?* Of course it's a Versace! Why didn't you say so in the first place…"

His grandiose clothes and opera-inspired lines may not have been for everybody, but for wealthy, thin, young-at-heart, wanna-be rock and rollers, no other designer could bring you farther backstage than Gianni Versace.

Born in 1946 in Reggio Calabria, Italy, Versace was literally raised on fashion: His mother was a *couturier*, or garment maker. Naturally, as a young boy, Versace unwittingly began his apprenticeship by helping his working mother find assorted accoutrements with which to embroider her dresses.

Versace studied architecture for a while, but when he was twenty-five he moved to Milan and worked as a freelance designer for such international apparel manufacturers as Genny, Complice, and Callaghan. In 1978, Versace showed his first women's collection, following it up the next year with his men's debut.

It is common knowledge that the worldly Versace had an unquenchable passion for the theater and the

opera. Fortunately, he also had a desire for translating the grandiose costumes and pageantry of his passion into wearable clothing. Versace's avant-garde approach, added with the sensuality of his clothes, caught the imagination of the rich and famous, launching Gianni Versace's career into fashion history.

Those who follow the fashion world know that there was nothing quite like a Versace catalog: Sumptuous clothes, the best fashion photographers (Herb Ritts, Richard Avedon, Helmut Newton, and Bruce Weber), and stunning models who somehow always managed to look even *more* stunning than they did anywhere else. Versace's bodacious catalogs were more luxuriously produced and larger than they had to be, but what else could you expect from a man whose vision, style, and grace was always larger than life?

And, despite detractors who often thought some of his stuff was a little (or a lot) "too-too," Versace remained faithful to that vision, creating flamboyant outfits that conformed to a totally glamorized vision of life. In fact, his first priority remained making people look beautiful. Yet he knew that fashion

was more than about the clothes: It's about creating a dream for people before they forget how to dream.

Perhaps more than any other designer, Gianni Versace knew how to seduce the press, using the most famous models for his shows and advertising campaigns. All of the big names in the modeling world showed for Versace. In fact, he was the one, with Karl Lagerfeld, who helped the supermodel phenomenon emerge. Being in Versace's cast was a breakthrough for a model. It meant access to a charmed circle, if not an outright guarantee of success. Assisted by top make-up artists and hairdressers, Versace reinvented his models each season to match the spirit of his collection.

Part of the game for Versace was to seat as many famous people as possible in the front row at his shows. (A practice that is *de rigueur* now.) He even convinced some of them to participate in his advertising campaigns. Jon Bon Jovi, Tina Turner, Elton John, and Madonna all pitched in. Their relationship was an intricate connection of mutual interest and friendship.

Versace's kinetic, kooky, kaleidoscope prints, biker leathers, and skinny silhouettes were designed for maximum attention. Remember Liz Hurley's safety-pin gown? Of course you do. And that was the point.

But Versace didn't just design for rock stars and beautiful women. His menswear line was just as popular.

TOP 5 REASONS TO GO TO WORK NAKED

5 To stop those dorks in IT from looking up your skirt.

4 Wasn't it your boss who said, "I wanna see your butt in here by 9:00!"

3 No one will want to steal your paper clips after they've seen where you keep them.

2 "I'd love to chip in, but I left my wallet in my pants."

1 No one will notice that you also came to work drunk.

However, the Versace man is not the guy-next-door.

He must be brave enough to go to work in a silk shirt emblazoned with a baroque pattern that would be more at home on a bathrobe. And if he's not? Well, he can at least allow himself a little private pleasure with Versace's Medusa underwear!

The victim of a gun-slaying on July 25, 1997, outside his villa in Miami, Florida, Gianni Versace was the king of fashion for the rock 'n' roll set, a throne he occupied alone for almost twenty years.

Today, the Versace sibling, Donatella heads a rapidly expanding empire that encompasses several fragrances, a line of home furnishings called "Home Signature," the "Versus" and "Istante" labels, and the "Vanitas" series of coffee-table books.

3
NOT READY TO WEAR

Sure, you've heard all about Calvin Klein, Coco Chanel, Marc Jacobs, and even Anna Sui, but what about more obscure designers like, say, Olay St. Enfant? (Okay, we haven't heard of him either.) Still, not every future fashion designer ends up watching supermodels strut their stuff down the glittering runways of New York and Paris. (Some have to work at The Dress Barn for a few years first.)

So forget what you've heard about the high-falutin', glamorous lush life of the overpaid fashion designer, and take a look behind the scenes. What happens when you don't get into the good fashion design school? (Or even the bad one?) Who really reviews all of those regal runway shows? And what does it take to be a super (or even not-so-super) model?

For a glimpse at those fashion folks who weren't born with a silver spoon in their mouths, sit back and read on to meet the people who are not quite ready to wear.

DESIGNER DILEMMA

Ever wondered who *really* decides what will hit the clothing stores next fashion season? As long as there have been fashions, there have been fashion designers. From the cretaceous creator of Fred Flinstone's saber tooth shirt to the genius who embroidered the ancient Romans' tasteful togas, there has always been that special breed of designing man or woman around. Of course, for centuries, they had little more than buffalo fur and seagull feathers to work with. But, nonetheless, they were always there to hand out such helpful advice as, "White and cream, never to be seen," or "You're not wearing those stripes with that ass, are you?"

Of course, nowadays fashion is big business. With a capital "B!"

From puffy sleeves to corseted waists, from thigh-high clogs to braided berets, an influx of money and a never-ending list of shameless backers allow today's fashion designers to do whatever they want with as much material as they want to do it with. (Regardless of the fact that few people will ever actually wear what they create.)

This is often known as the "stock-car racing syndrome." Chevrolet and Ford may gratefully create those supercharged, logo-covered, living matchbox machines we see whipping around the tracks each Saturday on ESPN 2. But neither company ever expects anyone to walk into its local showroom and plunk down several million dollars to special order one. In reality, what most often occurs is you run down to your local showroom and say something like, "I know you don't have Dale Earnhardt's #3 speed racer just lying around, but can you show me the next closest thing?"

At which point the delighted car salesman thinks to himself, "Jackpot," and gleefully shows you the latest race car rip-off.

TOP 5 WAYS TO TELL YOUR CLOTHES ARE DESIGNER KNOCK-OFFS

5 You have to cross a picket line consisting of Ralph Lauren and Calvin Klein to get in the store.

4 You get them out of a bubble-gum machine.

3 That telltale house arrest collar around the cashier's ankle.

2 *60 Minutes* asks you to wear a wire on your way to the cash register.

1 You hand the cashier twenty bucks for your entire winter wardrobe and still have enough change leftover for a biggie-size Happy Meal.

Well, fashion designers are not that different. (Although they probably dress a little better than car salesmen.)

Naturally, few people can afford to buy their latest creations. And, even if they could, few can get away with wearing a fifty-pound chain mail cocktail dress or see-through plastic overcoat with matching crotchless panties. Instead, their highbrow hijinx brings them name recognition, free publicity, and status, which in turn allows them to sell more sedate versions of their daring dresses at nonetheless exorbitant prices.

But don't be too worried. Knockoffs will always be available at your local department store. After all, us "little people" want to look good too.

Of course, if you want an "insider's" view of how it's done, why not consider the following fashion fable. Then stick around to read about life on the fashion fringes:

DESIGNER VS. DICTATOR

There's a certain young, up and coming fashion designer, we'll call him Olay St. Enfant. Olay's originally from Wisconsin, but we won't hold that against him. In junior high, Olay designed the costume for his school's "Buddy the Badger" mascot, and in high school he designed costumes for the senior drama production of *South Pacific*. (There was no *South Park*.) He stuck around long enough to get his degree at the nearby community college, where he wrote a short-lived fashion column for the local dairy trade paper until he finally got accepted into that "prestigious" fashion institute he'd found inside a matchbook cover a few weeks earlier.

After saying a sad farewell to his long-suffering family and a seemingly endless bus ride, Olay kissed the Dairy Belt good-bye and landed in a rough section of the Bronx. There he took classes at the Gotham Fashion Institute and Technical Trade School, which was really just a converted warehouse full of moldy mannequins and drab drape samples. He stayed at the YMCA just up the street and lucked into a part-time job patching balloons for the Macy's parades. (Naturally, he referred to this position on his resumé as "head assistant tailor.")

One of his 400-odd roommates at the Y had a distant relative who lived in Paris. So Olay took

a semester off to bum around the French countryside just long enough to pad his ever expanding resume with the names of enough fashion boutiques to look ambitious but not flighty. Of course, he didn't actually design for any of the boutiques, but who checks into those things anyway? When his Visa (card, that is) finally ran out, he returned to New York and the Gotham Fashion Institute (he wisely left off the "and Technical Trade School" part when speaking of his alma mater).

Just before graduation, which consisted of a flimsy certificate and a copper thimble, Olay landed a part-time job as a gofer for a trendy SoHo designer who just happened to be featured on the E! Channel's *Fashion Emergency* the very next week. Olay, conveniently enough, managed to worm one of his own designs into the broadcast. The design, a tube top woven out of tie-dyed six-pack rings, was a hit with the show's excitable host, who had even fewer credentials than Olay (but much more pull).

Ordering several of the design for herself and her crew, the news soon spread of her "SoHo 6-pack" discovery. Olay, brandishing pictures of himself and the show's host all over town, quickly parlayed the happy accident into an excellent opportunity by using the host's pseudo-impressive name to open previously locked doors to the well-guarded fashion kingdom.

He crashed cocktail parties, runway shows, and all of the receptionists' cubicles at the best fashion mags. In between, somehow he managed to design an entire line of recyclable clothing with retro images, merging two popular fads into one short-lived runway show of his own. Ill-conceived, ill-attended, and even ill-lit, Olay's catwalk catastrophe was just big enough of a draw to attract just enough fashion has-beens and wannabes with just enough name recognition to inspire just enough half-hearted rave reviews in most of the local fashion columns.

Taking advantage of a portfolio that currently runneth over, Olay somehow managed to talk up a few foreign investors at his post-show soiree, even securing a limited distribution deal to several of the nation's trendiest boutiques.

SIXPACK TUBETOPS?

Unfortunately, the investors backed out when they learned that Olay's six-pack tube tops had choked no less than seven house cats and three canaries shortly after his semi-successful show. However, enough pictures of the transparent tubes had appeared locally that knock-off artists were able to copy it in a more attractive (not to mention less dangerous) material that soon found legitimate backers with even wider distribution channels.

Which is why, just in time for the summer season, the affordable (and harmless) tube top rage has managed to appear in your local department store, starting at just under $40.

As for Olay, he used the limited proceeds from his limited success to shower the E! host with a new kitten to replace the one he and his one-hit wonderbra happened to strangle. The two excitable eccentrics wed shortly after signing a crafty prenuptial agreement that, when they divorced months later, nonetheless allowed Olay to keep his part-time job co-hosting the Sunday edition of the *Golden Hangers* show with Joan Rivers.

RUNWAY ROADKILL

When it comes to reviewing a top fashion designer's latest show, even the most seasoned runway reporter often finds herself shaking her well-coifed head. Take a catwalk down the fine line between a "runway runaway" and a "fashion flop" and find out why so few people can actually tell the difference:

"Maybe it's just me," you think to yourself as you flash your well worn "PRESS" pass and settle into your usual seat for the latest, hottest, and trendiest of the latest, hot, trendy fashion designer's latest, trendy, hot collection. "Maybe I'm just getting too old for this job."

You nod to the other old timers as they sit up straight, uncapping their pens and finding a clean page in their spiral notebook, while the cub reporters, newbies, and interns cuss, bend, and grope for a fresh dataport for their sleek, hi-tech laptops and Palm Pilots.

"Do I look as washed out and beat-up as they do?" you ask yourself, admiring the balding heads and bulging beehives of your pen-toting peers. "Can anyone as unfashionable as us actually be trusted to write *fashion* reviews?"

A young upstart barely clothed and smelling of B. O. eyes the vacant seat beside you and utters several obscenities when you inform him *politely* that you're saving it for your tardy couture co-worker.

The wide-eyed young reporter from another magazine sitting beside you gasps as the rude young man stomps away, revealing flip-flops on his feet and mustard stains on his backside. "Do you realize that you just dissed Hollywood's third highest moneymaker last year?" she asks you as you spot your partner in crime and wave her over to the seat you so successfully saved.

"You can thank me later," you explain. "Someone should tell that young man to invest a little of that money in a good bar of soap. He stank to high heavens

"I have lost friends, some by death, others through sheer inability to cross the street."
-Virginia Woolf

and if I'd let him sit here the two of us would have passed out long before the show began and then where would we be?"

"Sitting next to Hollywood's third highest moneymaker last year," your neighbor retorts, but by this time your co-worker is finally seated and the two of you are settling in for yet another of the season's funkiest fashion shows.

"What's that smell?" your partner asks, taking her seat and passing you the brand new box of Raisinets she'd promised in return for the fashion favor.

"Never you mind that," you dismiss her, knowing that, as the writer for your shared magazine's entertainment column, she would have gladly let that smelly young rascal sit on her lap for the entire duration of the show just for a measly exclusive interview. "Spell this designer's name for me, dear. I can never quite get it right."

She hands you a glossy brochure after underlining the designer's name and you scribble it onto your pad. You thank her around a mouthful of chocolate covered raisins and watch as the usual assortment of young, hip, artsy, and celebrity types fill the thriving room with their energy and enthusiasm.

"I hope they make the girls wear underwear for this show," your partner, Millie, opines in between jotting down the many names of the rich and famous in attendance for her chatty column. "I thought I had made a wrong turn and ended up in an adult bookstore at the last two shows we've attended."

"I agree," you snort. "And I hope they keep the music down this time. I had a screaming headache after that Galliano show last week."

Millie nods and hands you two foam earplugs, just in case.

Eventually the houselights dim, the inevitable fog machine begins pumping out its oozing, smoky moisture, multi-colored lasers shoot off in every direction, and, around a stifling yawn, you watch as two space creatures descend down the polished steel catwalk toward you.

STYLE TRENDS IN YOUR FASHION FUTURE!

- • **Smart fabrics that will control temperature and resist stains**
- • **Ribbon-trimmed crop pants**
- • **Cool white shirts**
- • **Bandanna prints**
- • **Metallic threads**
- • **Innocent, uncomplicated styles of the '50s**
- • **Wrap skirts**
- • **Animal prints**
- • **Contrast of the unexpected (i.e. silky smooth woolens with raw wool textured silks)**
- • **Metallic textures**
- • **Gauzy tunics**
- • **Monochromatic outfits for sophistication**
- • **Clothes that fit like a second skin (and even accommodate weight gain!)**
- • **Anything alligator!**

Shimmering metal collars fused to PVC-pipe vests adorn the rail-thin bodies of the runway models, who are finally exposed when they take off their space helmets to reveal gray eyeshadow and black blush on their cheekbone abundant faces.

Rolling your eyes at Millie, you nonetheless concentrate on your youngish neighbor, who is

SUPERMODEL

your neighbor and try and catch the tail end of her second glowing review: "Absolutely Amazon amazing," she coos, making you wish you'd worn those earplugs after all. "What a terrific concept, melding the modern love for athleticism with the ancient codpieces of yore…"

You like the "yore" part, switch "idea" for "concept" and wrap up yet another glowing review that you know will please your new editor, the one with the pierced eyebrow and platinum goatee who's young enough to be your grandchild.

Settling in while secretly scooting over, you suffer through several more hours of nauseatingly naïve writing and intolerably self-indulgent fashion designs. When the lasers, the fog, and the crowd have all magically dissipated mere minutes after the show's triumphant designer takes several unabashed (not to mention undeserved) bows, you glance at Millie and try and stifle a smile at the sight of your snoozing sidekick.

"Wake up, dear," you whisper, nudging her gently, as you well know that to wake her too abruptly after one of these affairs is to suffer a cranky cab ride back to the office. "Now tell me, what's the last ensemble you remember before nodding off?"

recording her rave review into a mini-cassette recorder, another piece of modern technology you just never got around to implementing.

"Masterful," she oozes into the handheld device as her eyes literally mist with emotion. "Completely captivating in its modern sense of rustic charm. I am overwhelmed by the sheer catharsis I felt when I unabashedly wept upon seeing this line for the first time…"

Dashing down the key phrases from your neighbor, as if cheating on the SATs, you change a few words around and add your own personal flair. Meanwhile, the houselights dim and the beating of drum music blares from speakers that are obviously located immediately in front of, behind, and to either side of you.

Two tan and limber young things eventually explode from the metallic curtain backstage and leap onto the catwalk, dancing amid the ever-thickening fog wearing nothing but see-through raincoats and camouflage combat gear. Clicking your tongue as they cavort mere inches away from you, you lean closer to

TOP 5

SIGNS YOU MIGHT NOT BE A SUCCESSFUL

RUNWAY MODEL

5 You show up at the airport and yell, "MAKEUP!"

4 The only flashbulbs going off are from the guys over at the *Guinness Book of World Records.*

3 You keep dropping pepperoni on the clothes during ten wardrobe changes.

2 It takes ten supermodels to tie your bikini strap.

1 That thunderous sound as you strut down the catwalk isn't applause.

"That dreadful hard-hat and macramé bikini combination," she groans, fixing her hair and retrieving her spiral notepad from the confetti and fog dust covering the floor.

"Lucky you," you sigh, helping her to her feet. "That means you missed the entire middle portion of the show, the one themed to combine the Renaissance with pro basketball—"

"Lucky me is right," she giggles as you amble over to the taxi stand outside. "Let me guess, you wrote another glowing review, though, didn't you?"

"Of course I did," you admit sheepishly. "What else am I to do? If I were to be honest, I would've hung up my Parker pen the day poor Audrey Hepburn passed away, God rest her soul."

"Ah, yes," remembers Millie. "Now there was a woman who knew how to wear a hat."

"Could you see Miss Hepburn," you ask,

"even a *young* Miss Hepburn, wearing a space helmet and a fig leaf, for Heaven's sakes?"

"Lord no," agrees Millie, frowning in reply. "But do you think our eyebrow-pierced editor would understand a review like that?"

"My dear," you predict, "he'll probably run out and buy the entire line once he hears *my* review."

LIFE AFTER FASHION SCHOOL, OR: WELCOME TO THE DRESS BARN

Like wanting to be a professional singer or a headlining magician, becoming a fashion designer is not something one finds an ad for in the Sunday classifieds each week. Designing fashion is a calling; something one is born with and learns to slowly integrate into one's professional life over years and years of trial and error.

In the beginning, this usually means picking out one's own clothes, not to mention the outfits of others, most likely at an early age.

Naturally, most kids don't have a whole lot of power at this point in their lives. For instance, it's a little difficult to take a child seriously when she's frowning at your choice of evening gown or spitting up on your favorite neon paisley tie from behind the bars of her crib.

Therefore, the "others" in this case usually end up in the form of dolls. And, whether it's Barbie or G. I. Joe, a burgeoning fashion designer's parents soon grow tired of dragging their Chanel and Dior wannabes into the toyshop for "…just one more outfit. Puh-leaze! I saw the cutest cheerleader uniform. If I can just drop the hemline and add some pizzazz, I'm sure Ken will ask her out this time—"

Over the years, a future fashion designer becomes more sophisticated in his or her artistic approach. Like a hardened criminal escalating from being a petty thief to a full-on cat burglar, the future fashioner naturally progresses from dolls to live victims. Pets are frequent experiments, donning birthday caps and miniature sweaters the designer has fashioned exclusively for them. Playmates come next, usually getting ambushed at a sleepover with subtle, helpful comments such as "You're not going to sleep in *that* are you? Flannel jumpers have been passé for quite some time now—"

Eventually school starts and opens up a whole new world to the neckline neophyte. There are those drab custodian uniforms to spruce up. Librarians to color coordinate. Teachers to de-school marm and principals to de-bow tie. And, of course, there is a veritable army of fellow students, pupils, and peers to work one's magic upon for nine glorious months out of every year.

Of course, most future fashion designers prefer to teach by example. After all, they've been telling others how to dress better for years, all to no avail.

TOP FASHION SCHOOLS

- **Paris Fashion Institute, Paris**
- **The Fashion Institute of Design & Merchandising, California**
- **Copenhagen Academy of Fashion Design, Denmark**
- **Fashion Design and Apparel Technology, California**
- **Fashion Institute of Technology, New York, NY**
- **International Academy of Design, Tampa, FL**
- **Instituto di Moda Burgo Milano, Italy**

What better way to lift the ignorant masses up from waistline wasteland to fashion's future than show them how it's done? Live…and in person?

So, naturally, the fashion designer begins her professional career by outfitting herself first. There is usually a hand-me-down sewing machine thrown into the mix, not to mention numerous, allowance-breaking trips to the fabric store for the latest, hottest materials.

(Or, at least, whatever's on the clearance racks that day.)

There are patterns to snip out of mom's *Woman's Day* and enough thread, buttons, and zippers to put any self-respecting sweatshop to shame. There are sketchpads and charcoal to pore over long after the rest of the world has drifted off to sleep, and needle and thread to work wonders with the next morning before school.

The bus stop is for finishing touches and the cafeteria is a no-trade zone since the future fashion designer spends every lunch break in the restroom nipping, tucking, and touching up in preparation for the second half of the dainty designer's day.

Of course, when one treats the halls of an elementary school or junior high as one gigantic cat-*walk*, there are bound to be a few cat-*fights* along the way. Not everyone, it seems, is as open-minded or as enlightened as you are about fashion's newest trends.

The new materials you try sometimes take a few weeks, months, or even years to catch on. Hemlines need to be adjusted, sleeves reattached, and those unpredictable growth spurts often turn bell-bottoms into clam diggers practically overnight.

But, eventually, high school rolls around and with it the chance to try one's haute couture hand at sprucing up band costumes, talent show gowns, and full-fledged dramatic productions of such classic period pieces as *Oklahoma!* and *Bye, Bye Birdie!*

Why, by the time senior year rolls around and your guidance counselor helps you put together your first real resume, it doesn't take a whole lot of fluffing to present you to the nearest Fashion Institute as their next Dior or Chanel.

And so, waiting for those letters of acceptance to start pouring in, you read through the glossy Fashion Institute brochures. Scouring over the pictures of bolts of fabric, industrial size spools of thread, and half-naked, anorexic models wearing futuristic clothing, you feel your pulse heat up and know that you've made the right career choice. Sleeping with the brochures under your pillow, you dream of blistering hot flash bulbs illuminating your face as you take your fifteenth bow amid the models who've just completed your very first fashion show. You bask in the audience's applause as they stand for what seems like hours—or at least, until you wake up anyway.

TOP 10

VIDEOS TO RENT BEFORE YOU ATTEND FASHION SCHOOL

10 Fashion Wars

9 Fashion Model

8 Fashion from New York

7 Fools of Fashion

6 Fashion Row

5 Madame Fashion

4 Parisian Fashion Frolic

3 Fashion Madness

2 Faithful in My Fashion

1 A Slave of Fashion

Eventually, after months of antsy anticipation, your third choice fashion institute accepts you and you head off, bound for dreams and glory. You share a nearby apartment with a likeminded individual such as yourself while the two of you hit the books and fly through semester after semester full of Fundamentals of Design, Color Theory, Fashion Illustration, Pattern Details, and Manufacturing Concepts.

Your portfolio bulges with junior and senior internships at Jessica McClintock and Gunnie Sax, where you swiftly fly from trim buyer to cutting assistant, assistant to designer to production assistant.

Your final project is to design your own graduation gown, and you spend weeks getting it just right, eventually using your own commencement picture as a coda to your perfectly plump portfolio. And so, a freshly laminated press shot of Anna Sui dangling from your rearview mirror for inspiration, you hit the bricks to find the hottest new designer to work for in order to soak up his or her infinite knowledge.

Only to find, of course, that the hottest, trendiest, hippest, freshest, best designers in town already have apprentices, gofers, errand boys, and do-girls, not to mention a waiting list a mile long should the holder of any of those four office positions suddenly and mysteriously drop dead. However, since such a "tragedy" is impossible, at least until you have enough money saved up to hire a good hit man, your only realistic option is to start, like so many other of your fashion forefathers, "from the ground up."

Which wouldn't be so bad, of course, if the "ground" in this case wasn't that waistline wasteland known as "fashion retail." And, since the rest of your graduating class saw the writing on the wall long before you and is already working at The Gap, you are forced to swim a little further down the fashion food chain. "Welcome to The Dress Barn," you find yourself announcing peppily one morning as a busload of gray-haired grannies from the local nursing home pulls up in front of your cash register for their monthly fashion field trip, at 10% off no less. "How can I help you?"

Oh, well, at least you'll be able to start saving up for that hit man now...

TOP 5
SIGNS YOU GRADUATED FROM A BAD FASHION SCHOOL

The theme for the reception dance is "Blue-Light Special!"

Your Class Valedictorian triumphantly announces her new job at The Dress Barn.

None of the graduation gowns fit right.

The only recruiters present are from Sears and Burger King.

Diploma signed by "Inspector #12."

LABEL UNCONSCIOUSNESS ??????????????

So you can't for the life of you figure out what in the world overtakes them each morning as they wake, bathe, and get ready to dress. Obviously, somewhere along the path to their college degree, someone, somewhere must have informed them that, among

There is a segment of today's young population that has decided *not* to look good—on purpose. They may bathe and accessorize and deodorize just like today's modern fashion plates—and, in fact, the mismatched and supposedly "generic" clothes they wear so proudly are often just as expensive as those bearing today's hottest designer labels—but the only way you'd know this by looking at them was if they pinned their cash register receipts to their over-wide, polyester retro lapels…

CLOTHING CLUELESS

They seem like perfectly reasonable people, at least to talk to anyway. They have cogent trains of thought, make good points, even hold good jobs, and apparently pull down normal incomes. They have families, roofs over their heads, food in their bellies, and plenty of lights on upstairs.

TOP-10 CDS
TO LISTEN TO WHILE GETTING DRESSED

10. **Alice Cooper**
    Flush The Fashion

9.) **Incredible Hangovers**
    At The Fashion Shop

8.) **Vince Gill**
    Emperor's New Clothes

7.) **Cake**
    Fashion Nugget

6.) **Fashionable Male**
    Fashionable Male

5.) **Laurie Macallister**
    These Old Clothes

4.) **Michael Stanley Band**
    You Can't Fight Fashion

3.) **Alien Fashion Show**
    Alien Fashion Show

2.) **Starflyer 59**
    Fashion Focus

1.) **Soozy Q**
    We Don't Have To Take Our Clothes Off

Color Trends
In Your Fashion
Future

- Anything brightly colored
- Colored plastic
- Metallic colors
- Oriental orange
- Clear/see-through

- Turquoise blue
- Liquid-like bluish tones
- White
  (i.e. new beginning, unspoiled year, new millennium, etc.)
- Anything alligator!

"Here we are!" their outfits scream. "Love us or leave us, just don't—ignore us. We are as needy, confused, and insecure as the rest of you, we just prefer to be a little more obvious about it!"

Yet who are we to judge such free spirits? Such nonconformists? Such—exhibitionists? Certainly, what they call "non-fashion" is, after all, a form of fashion in the strictest sense. Are they any less concerned about their appearance than many of us who, in the name of "fashion," suit up each day in our business suits of tweed and khaki, silk and rayon?

Are their paisleys, plaids, and polka dots any less inspiring than our navies, whites, and tans? What reaction do we get when standing in line for lunch or waiting for dinner, all of us alike and none of us different? Certainly no smiles, nods, points, giggles, or, in fact, any reaction of any kind, mar our way through most mind-numbing workdays.

So, in fact, we might even owe such Velcro victims and their fashion faux pas a passing nod of gratitude. At least they serve to brighten up our day just a bit. And, after all, isn't that what fashion's really all about?

other things, stripes clash with polka dots, not to mention many other assorted and various patterns.

They must have heard, if only through the grapevine or bad David Letterman jokes, that polyester, white dress shoes, reversible belts, beehive hairdos, cat-woman glasses, rainbow socks, and matching berets are most definitely "out." And have been for years. If not decades. Centuries even.

Yet still they persist in coming out of doors in such garish, hideous, tasteless apparel. Not, as we all have on one occasion or another, to do laundry, wash the car, or clean out our garages in. Such clothes, on such people suffering from such severe cases of "label unconsciousness" are in fact worn proudly to work, to dinner, to the theater, to restaurants any time of day or night, to clubs, to family's houses for Thanksgiving, to the grocery store, and, most definitely, on dates.

Like a badge of honor, such nasty dressers (as opposed to "natty," of course) proudly strut, vogue, and primp in their outdated, outmoded, and outclassed outfits, despite the fact that laughter, derision, and snide remarks constantly surround them like clouds of bad perfume.

TOP 5 SIGNS YOU'RE TOO LABEL CONSCIOUS

5 Your underwear costs more than your toaster.

4 You have enough miniature horses and riders in your closet to start your own polo team.

3 The police inform you that you were next on Andrew Cunanan's "Hit List."

2 You're prepared if Izod ever makes a comeback.

1 Calvin Klein writes you a personal letter thanking you for "last quarter earnings."

MODELS INC.

No chapter dealing with fashion fixations would be complete without the *ultimate* fashion fixation: becoming a model. Enjoy a behind-the-scenes look at fashion models and their marvelously mirrored world, which has become an entire industry unto itself. Learn the way even the most super supermodel got started and find out how to do so yourself. Unless, of course, you enjoy waiting around all of those coffee shops and soda jerks just waiting to be discovered…

MODEL CITIZEN(S)

So, you wanna be a model, huh? Well, get in line sister. Every teenybopper who's ever watched a Revlon ad or opened up a glossy issue of *Seventeen* magazine has dreamed of pouting for the photographer's flashbulbs or strutting down that never-ending catwalk to fashion fame and good cheekbone glory. But what does it take to make your dreams a reality?

Even the most novice model maniac has heard the old-line song and dance: "…an aspiring model should be at least 5'8" in height with clear skin, healthy hair, straight teeth, and a toned and well-proportioned body." Super. Great. You've got those covered.

Okay, well, most of those. All right, a *few* anyway. But what else will you need to be the next Christie, Tyra, or Niki?

Top New York Modeling Agencies

- **Boss Models**
- **Company Model Mgmt.**
- **Elite Model Mgmt.**
- **Ford Models**
- **IMG Models**
- **I D Model Mgmt.**
- **Metropolitan**
- **New York Models**
- **NEXT Model Mgmt.**
- **Q Model Mgmt.**
- **R & L Model Mgmt.**
- **Wilhelmina Models**

You can diet 'til you drop, place mounds of cucumbers over your eyes, bleach your teeth and spend hundreds of dollars on glamour shots if you want, but most industry experts agree that getting an agent is one surefire way to become a pretty player in the glamour game…

IN A NEW YORK MINUTE?

There are over 100 modeling agencies in New York City. And, as if that weren't overwhelming enough, supermodel sycophants must additionally decide who's a good guy and who's a grifter. Who's on the up and up and who's got mirrors on their Buster Browns to look up—as in, your skirt.

Where to start? People in the know are always a great source of information. However, if you're having trouble getting Christie Brinkley on the line, try the old tried and true method of pulling out a map and comparing addresses. Logic tells you, the closer a modeling agency is to Madison Avenue, the better it is. Likewise, the closer a modeling agency is to, say, Hell's Kitchen, well, you do the math.

Even the briefest glance through New York's listing of active modeling agencies should reveal how varied today's modeling agencies have become. For example, there are no-nonsense agencies that don't mince words, such as Model Scout USA, Model Search America, Models Mart Ltd., and Mega Model Management.

Then again, there are agencies that sound like they might just be fronts for something else, like the good people down at Screen Test Inc., Jewel Escort & Modeling, Click Shows, and Hollywood Image Photo Studio.

There are agencies whose names don't exactly inspire much confidence, such as The Stoned Modeling Agency, Real People Management, not to mention Trouble in New York. And there are agencies that do, like Spotlight Models Inc., Star Makers Inc., and Image & Esteem Team Inc.

Then there's the agency that is the generic equivalent of the fashion blue-light special: Barbizon Model & Talent Mgmt., established way back in 1939 and specializing in modeling schools that recruit directly from their "talent agency" arm. As in, "Well, your portfolio full of Garanimals ads and local CrimeWatch clippings looks promising, but a few years at our local Barbizon Modeling School should really polish you off."

There are modeling agencies whose names are obviously designed to appeal to a model's inherent sense of exhibitionism, as witnessed in companies like Flaunt, Desire, Fame Talent Agency, Beautiful People Unlimited, Pretty People Model Management, and even Better Bodies Inc.

MODELS INC.

BODY PARTS

There are young, fresh, hip agencies formed in the last ten years, for example, Like Metropolitan, established in 1990 and DNA Model Mgmt., established in 1995. And there are even agencies nodding to the new millennium, like the folks at Online Model Mgmt.

Many agencies have chosen to specialize in a certain segment of the modeling community. Parts Models, for instance, is one of the few modeling agencies specializing in "body parts," such as hands for watch ads and feet for—sock ads? But body parts aren't the only specialty-modeling agency around these days. There are agencies that specialize in men only, such as Nitro Inc. and Maxx Men. There are agencies specializing in athletic types, like The Lyons Group.

There are even agencies that get a jump-start on finding the next decade's supermodels just a little bit early, such as New York Kids Models & Talent and Rachel's Totz 'N Teenz Model.

And you'll be inspired to know that of the numerous modeling agencies surrounding Madison Avenue, that bastion of all things advertising, at least one agency specializes in larger models: Plus Model Mgmt.

There are agencies that sound more like they're representing porn stars, such as the We Do It Models agency, and there are agencies that sound more like law firms, like Schiffman, Ekman, Morrison & Marx.

Finally, there are the "big dogs," with their instant name recognition, haughty receptionists, and Hollywood set-like office suites. These damsel divas, such as Wilhelmina Models and Ford Models, not only have their own Web addresses, but their own AOL Keywords. Hook up with one of these bad boys (or girls) and you can pretty much write your own ticket to fame, fortune, and a lifelong battle with a legitimate eating disorder.

However, the world of fashion models is only slightly less fickle than the world of fashion itself. Therefore, even if you *do* look like Tyra, Cindy or Niki, chances are by the time you make it past the wily receptionists inside one of these ivory towers, whatever "look" you had going for you will already be over and done with.

"What exactly do agencies do?" you might be asking yourself. Well, for one thing, they find "new" faces to replace last month's "old" ones. (Naturally, "old" here is a relative term, since models are often

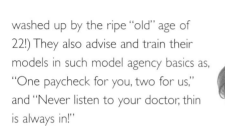
washed up by the ripe "old" age of 22!) They also advise and train their models in such model agency basics as, "One paycheck for you, two for us," and "Never listen to your doctor, thin is always in!"

Of course, they promote their models as well as scheduling and booking them on photo shoots, TV commercials, and publicity stills. Lastly, of course, they bill clients who have benefited from their models' beauty and collect fees for such a privilege. Big fees, if they're good ones. Big with a capital "B"! All in all, not a bad gig!

SPOTLIGHT
ON SCAMS

Of course, just because some creep hangs out his shingle and calls himself a "modeling agency" doesn't mean he really is one. The harsh reality surrounding the lucrative modeling industry is that for every fashion icon, millionaire supermodel, there are literally thousands of attractive, eager, and naïve girls who get ripped off before they ever get started. Whether they lose just their money, or worse, their innocence, no one wants you to get hurt just because you want to be a model. Therefore, a few scam warnings are obviously in effect.

It may sound cruel, but modeling is a dog-eat-dog business. Therefore, it's always a good idea to bring along a short, generally non-glamorous friend (i.e. "dog") whom you are sure has no modeling

potential whatsoever to any open call with you. Next, persuade her ever-so-gently to go in first. Obviously, if your friend comes out with stars in her eyes and brags that the agency just told her she's going to be the next Christy Turlington if she signs with them, then you'll know to beware of that particular agency's scam potential. (Once you get your friend to calm down, that is.)

Another fashion agency faux pas is known as the "school scam." Most industry insiders feel that it is never necessary to take a modeling course to become a model. After all, reputable agencies will train you themselves—for free. However, if you have extra money just falling out of your purse and are tired of tripping over it on your way to the shopping mall, Dempsey dumpster, or casino, by all means go ahead and sign up for modeling classes. Otherwise, makeup counters like Lancome and Esteé Lauder will often give free makeup lessons, sometimes up to twice in one day, if you wait for the shift change!

If an agency tells you that you'll be working immediately or that you'll be a star, be wary. Such promises are unrealistic and reputable agencies and schools do not say such things. Unless, of course, they feel that you *will* be working immediately or *will* be a star. In which case, ignore this advice and go for it!

Also, like those proverbial come-ons offering "natural bust size enhancement" or "wrinkle-free

TOP 5 WAYS TO TELL YOU MAY BE TOO THIN

5 That girl from Ally McBeal keeps asking you to be in the picture with her.

4 You count on your ribs instead of your fingers.

3 The only time you use a belt anymore is to beat off the vultures.

2 Stretch pants don't.

1 You need suspenders for your thong underwear.

immediately. Instead you will be expected to take their course.

Furthermore, reputable agencies will not insist that you use "their" photographer because "he is the best." A good agency will recommend a few photographers and let you meet with them to look at their portfolios before you decide on one, not the other way around.

BREAK A LEG?

Now that you've learned what an agency does and which ones you'd like to have do those things for you, it's time to go about getting one. How? Well, if it were that easy, you probably wouldn't be reading this book because you'd be so busy shielding your eyes from the harsh glare of the paparazzi at your latest runway triumph, Hollywood premiere, or courtroom appearance.

However, the only sure way to start is by getting your picture taken. And we're not talking by Aunt Sally's disposable camera or the friendly schmoe down at your local department store. Quality "head shots," as they're known in the industry, will often cost you a few hundred dollars (or more) if you want them done right.

These first photos are the beginning of what will eventually become, if you hang in there long enough anyway, your portfolio. Like a thin, classy photo album, only without those embarrassing shots of you naked on a bear skin rug (unless you're vying for an entirely different type of modeling career, that is) a portfolio is basically your resume told in pretty pictures.

forever creams," pay no attention to the agency ads in the back of magazines. (Especially if they appear in the back of magazines you had to stand in line behind Pee Wee Herman to purchase.)

Reputable agencies do not normally advertise in the classifieds. Ads that say, "Models needed immediately. No experience necessary," typically will not have you working

TOP

5 BEST MOVIES ABOUT MODELS

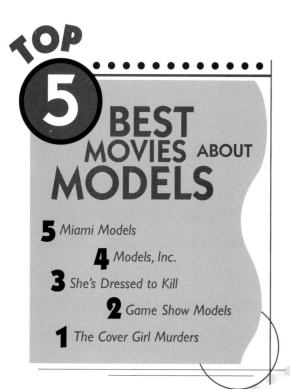

5 *Miami Models*

4 *Models, Inc.*

3 *She's Dressed to Kill*

2 *Game Show Models*

1 *The Cover Girl Murders*

office lamps and turn away most of this week's hopefuls lined up in the hall.

Naturally, the hopeful model is forced to go the way of the hopeful actor, the hopeful screenwriter, the hopeful artist, and the hopeful singer—to the local bar or restaurant to apply for a "real" job. It's a tough choice, but at least you'll be gainfully employed.

Take your pick ladies. What's it to be? Bartender at the local dive? Or waitress at the Burger Barn? Either way, after all of this expert advice, you're sure to look just stunning in your uniform.

And, while many of the modeling agencies named above require a mailed head shot to get your foot in the door, they most definitely will be looking at your portfolio if you actually make it that far.

Naturally, that doesn't mean you should show up at the modeling agency office looking like you just stepped out of an episode of *Cops*. Hair rollers, flip-flops, moustache creams, and tube tops, not to mention Spandex, polyester, or plaid are most definitely *not* to your advantage in such a situation.

Some agencies, however, actually have open calls, where aspiring models can show up, portfolio in hand, and try and pitch themselves like human advertising campaigns. While this prospect sounds promising on the surface, in reality such "open calls" are usually only afforded once a week, and most of them only last about thirty minutes!

Furthermore, they often occur right around lunchtime, when the bigwigs step out for a three martini lunch down at the Russian Tea Room. Thus the administrative assistants, gofers, and Fed Ex guys (who always "just happen" to be in the office at such times) are left with the run of the store until they eventually bar the doors with the art deco

GLOSSY GLAMOUR:
ADS VS. ARTICLES

Fashion magazines. You gotta love 'em. For one thing, they smell really good. (Thanks to all those useless perfume samples.) For another, they make great paper weights. (Wait a minute, they *are* paper.) They're perfect for killing spiders. (Wham!) And they're quite useful in the bedroom. (If you're having trouble sleeping, just try reading one of the articles!) Either way, they look great on the coffee table. ("Have you seen the latest issue of *Vogue*, darling? It *smells* divine!")

Despite their presence in every grocery store, bodega, bookseller, and beauty parlor in the country, fashion magazines to be profitable require Herculean skills akin to climbing Mt. Everest. Only, you have to do it every single month!

For one thing, editors at magazines like *Vogue*, *Elle*, *Cosmopolitan*, and *GQ* are often forced to wear just as many hats as they feature in their fall, "Hail to Hats" layouts. From keeping up with the latest trends (polka dot pashminas—really?) to attending those never ending runway shows (poor things), from interviewing supermodels (fascinating) to color coordinating their file cabinets (purple for Paris, red for New York), a fashion editor's job is rarely ever done.

What will be the next big thing? What's my deadline? Where will it come from? Man, it's almost my deadline again. Who will design it? Is it my deadline already? Who will buy it? Can I "buy" a few more hours to meet my deadline? Who will knock it off first?

Whoops, missed another deadline! Fortunately, a bumper crop of new subscribers is constantly graduating (or dropping out) from high schools, fashion institutes, private colleges,

buy them to look trendy, both by wearing what they see on the models inside, and by boastfully carrying them everywhere they go! Fashion devotees, from buyers for the local Gap outlet to cashiers at The Dress Barn, subscribe faithfully and use them as bibles

BETTER SEX TODAY

state universities, and beauty schools around the globe every day. From high school girls wanting to look older, to mid-level managers wanting to look younger, the reading demographic for many of today's hottest fashion magazines are ever-changing.

Housewives read them for a quick flight of fancy or a few practical tips on what to wear if their hubby ever gets that big raise, promotion, or leveraged buyout. College co-eds

for their very own fashion religion.

Single girls use them to get guys, attached girls use them to stay trendy in case the guys they have go south, and married women use them for the

TOP Fashion/ Lifestyle Magazines

Vogue

Elle

Mademoiselle

W

Bikini

Maxim

GQ

Essence

Allure

Marie Claire

Glamour

Self

Jane

classified ads in the back advertising "Better Sex Today!"

But those glossy, glamorous fashion mags aren't just for the ladies anymore. Guys, you're buying them too. Maybe it's only to see what's "hot" just in time for your girlfriend's birthday. Maybe you just can't get enough of those wacky diets. Or perhaps you dig the half-naked models in those racy depilatory ads. Either way, don't believe the guy

standing in line next to you in the grocery store flipping through the latest issue of *Cosmo* who says, "Oh, this? It's for my girlfriend." Otherwise, why would he be mentally calculating his score from that "Is he really good in bed?" quiz?

And so, from co-eds to concubines, model wannabes to male models, the vibrant, topsy-turvy world of fashion magazines is in no danger of crashing anytime soon. But just what exactly is it like working at one of these top-notch glamour rags, er, mags?

Let's check in with our fashion newbie to find out:

NEWBIE NIGHTMARE

It's your first day on the job at *PHAT! SHEN!*, the newest, hippest, hottest, glossiest, slickest fashion magazine on the market. Your editor, who looks like she just stepped off the cover of an old Cher album, complete with Egyptian wig and blaring belly button, invites you into her office for a little first-day pep talk just before lunch.

"Don't forget the coffee, hon," she says on your way in. "Two sugars for me, light on the cream. You take it however you want it."

Bringing in her coffee, you sit at a funky, new wave chair loaded with fabric swatches and try not to mentally de-lint her belly button across her clear acrylic desk.

"I hear you've already had a run-in with marketing, hon," she announces casually, before grimacing at her first taste of coffee. "Something about our projected ad to article ratio."

"I wouldn't really call it a run-in," you explain diplomatically. "I simply mentioned to somebody at the water cooler, who I'll never speak to again, by the way, that I was hoping this magazine would be a little different than all of the others."

"How so, dear?" asks your boss, barely feigning interest at your peon-esque comments as she picks at—something—inside her coffee mug.

"I just noticed," you admit sheepishly, " after glancing through our premiere issue that there were just as many slick, artsy ads in *PHAT! SHEN!* as there are in say, *Vogue* or *Elle*. That's all. I just thought a magazine as hip as ours would be concentrating more on the articles. You know, enriching people's lives instead of just selling them what 'haute couture' considers the latest thing."

"I see," she murmurs, glancing at the caller I.D. box on her futuristic phone and deciding to ignore the obviously non-important caller. "Let me put it this way. Instead of giving you the long story on why we decided to run with as many ads as the competition, I'm going to give you a little assignment that should be, even to someone as new to the industry as yourself, quite illuminating.

"I'd like you to go downstairs," she explains, looking out her 30th floor window as if for emphasis, "and ask a few passersby a simple question: What does fashion mean—to *you?*

"Can you do that for me?" she sums up, sliding over a box of neon pink T-shirts with the funky *PHAT! SHEN!* logo emblazoned across the chest in lime green. "Hand out these T-shirts to every brave soul who answers you honestly, and by the time this box is empty I dare say you'll never argue with our advertising policy again."

Barely refraining yourself from saying, "Yes, ma'am,"

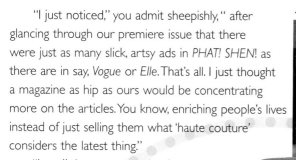

you lug the box and a legal pad into the elevator and descend to the lobby, grumbling the entire way.

"Does she have *that* low an opinion of her readers?" you wonder as you set up shop next to a wilting potted palm in the dimly lit lobby. "Who in their right mind would prefer *ads* to *my* crisp, clear writing style?"

You find out, of course, much sooner than expected. Your first customer, a harried UPS man who nonetheless notices your hastily scrawled *"FREE T-shirts"* sign on the side of your box, stands at attention in front of you while you "interview" him.

"That's easy," he says, wiping perspiration off of his furrowed brow. "Fashion is this," he says, pointing to his

Hershey brown uniform. "It's simple, easy."

"Yeah, but," you argue, holding onto the shirt in your hand until you get what you came for. "What about when you're *not* working. What does fashion mean to you then?"

"Same thing," he brags. "I wear a certain kind of uniform then, too. We all do. You know. Jeans. A T-shirt. Some shoes. That's about it. I'm all about comfort, lady, now—can I have my shirt, I've got a lot more stops to make before Miller time. Hey, does that shirt come in brown?"

Your next pollster is even more illuminating. A glib teenager who's just handed off an application to be a secretary in one of the many offices upstairs slinks over in bell bottoms and a paisley tank top, a hoop earring in her left nostril, three topaz studs in her right cheek.

"Fashion is my life," she insists. "See this outfit? It took me seventy-three minutes to pick it out this morning. I wanted to make a definite statement when I went to apply for that job just now."

"And what statement is that?" you ask, dumbfounded, before handing over her free T-shirt.

"What do you think?" she practically shouts. "That I'm the right person for the job. Duh! Now gimme that shirt, lady."

After you've recovered from the un-called for "lady" jab, you confront a long string of clothing clueless clones who answer your probing question with a series of tired tirades that makes you hand out two T-shirts for every one answer just to get rid of them in half the time:

"Fashion is all about trust. Personally, I trust my personal god Xena: the Wardrobe Warrior to guide my hand into the closet each morning and wear the first thing I pick."

"Fashion smashion. As long as my socks match, I'm good to go."

"For me, fashion is a passion. Take this outfit I'm wearing now. The yellow symbolizes my zest for life. Lemons. Zest. Get it? Red expresses my anger at a male dominated world. Purple is all about power. The aqua symbolizes my equilibrium with all things dolphin. And wearing two different shoes is just a clear cut case of bootleg brilliance."

"Fashion? Isn't that the TV show where the kids

FASHION IS PASSION

pour into the streets and dance on top of the taxi to that funky beat?"

"Don't tell me. I'm on *Candid Camera*, right? That T-shirt's see through or something, isn't it? Am I right?"

"Fashion is against my religious beliefs."

"Don't tell anyone, but I'm not wearing any underwear right now. Do I still get a shirt?"

After a mere twenty minutes you finally understood what your boss was getting at all along: For most people, fashion, like snowflakes, was never meant to mean the same exact thing to two different people.

You could have stood in that lobby and given a brilliant dissertation on fashion and its true meaning, and everyone would've walked away scratching their heads. It was easier to say it with pictures. Big, glossy, artsy pictures like the ones your magazine's ritzy clients provided for free and then *paid* you to publish.

And with the prices your magazine was charging those ritzy designers, a picture was worth a lot more than a thousand words.

Let alone bucks.

FRESH FASHION FETISHES, OR: YOU HAVE STYLE?

You may not believe it, but chances are you have a style all your own. Now don't get so excited. There's a big difference between stylish and just plain, old style. Cameron Diaz is stylish. You and your Star Wars boxer shorts are what's considered a style, sort of. But take heart. Today, possibly more so than ever before, individual style is slowly becoming more appreciated than simply being "stylish." After all, anyone can follow the whims and fancy of every fashion trend highlighted in the same old fashion magazines on the same old newsstands each and every month. But it takes real style to combine a polka dot tube top, crested blazer, poodle skirt, and combat boots over those little smiley face socks. (Especially if you're a guy. Now that's style!)

AMY, QUEEN OF DARKNESS

Much seriousness has been attributed to the Goth movement, assuming, incorrectly, that all Goth guys and gals are suicidal maniacs just waiting to graduate from fashion victim to serial killer. A more innocent notion, however, not to mention a more accurate one, is that while some people dress each day as if they were attending prom or going on a job interview, others enjoy "holiday dressing."

In this case, the holiday of choice is merely Halloween.

HAIR

If hair can make or break you, black hair makes for the best hair. While some Goth opt for streaks of blond or orange (or even green or red), make sure there's just enough black left to keep your current Goth status intact.

GOTH ACCESSORIES

You'll need a watch (after all, how else will you be able to tell when the sun is coming up?), but others include crucifixes, dog collars, fishnet stockings, corsets, canes, and, of course, don't forget your plastic fangs.

CAPES

… aren't a Goth accessory, they're a Goth necessity. While not all of them have to be this long, one cape is a must-have for any Goth girl or guy.

BLACK IS BACK!

Black is your friend. Not just because it's slimming, but because it's so darn cool. Black lipstick, black nail polish, (double) black eyeliner, and definitely black panties are all not only acceptable, but advisable.

SHOES

Despite their physical location, shoes are at the center of Goth culture. Whether it's combat boots or square toed mules, shoes are at the heart of the matter. (Can you guess what color we suggest?)

GUYS 'N GOTHS

Although you're getting just a little too long in the tooth for such sophomoric shenanigans, you'd read about the club in the local paper and felt an instant kinship with the troubled, ill-dressed loners lurking quietly in the background of the review's accompanying series of photographs.

Of course, you've heard of Goth before. (Didn't everybody see the *E! True Hollywood Story* about Brandon Lee?) But, as a retiring corporate clone caught up in your meager 401(k) plan and the daily grind of your capitalist cubicle, you've had little time to dwell on the fashion subculture that was slowly but surely sweeping the nation.

Still, it's been months since you've actually entered a club at all, much less one constructed to look entirely like the inside of a huge bat cave. So, on a boring Wednesday evening in between girlfriends, you slip into your old pair of black jeans (a little snug), your favorite black turtleneck (a little mature), and your black Gucci loafers (a little too "too") and head to the recently reviewed nightclub. Sure. Why not?

The Labyrinth, as it's known, looks just like what you would have expected it to. Dim lighting, lots of damp ooze on the blood red walls, candelabras instead of track lighting, and plenty of dry ice bubbling from the wall sconces. There are a few hanging bats thrown in just for the tourists, and the obligatory Marilyn Manson and Nine-Inch Nails tracks blaring from the dismal DJ booth.

You sidle up to the coffin-shaped bar, order a Budweiser, receiving your 100th glare of the evening from the anorexic, goateed bartender in the flowing cape and dangling cross, and sip it cheerily from your velvet-covered barstool.

Peering out across the sea of bobbing, dancing, vogueing vampire wannabes, you are unimpressed by the pancake makeup, army boots, raccoon eyes, and hairspray-by-the-gallon inspired 'dos. The Labyrinth looks just like any club you'd gone to in your younger days, just with a little less skin and a lot more tattooed tears.

Sexes blend and merge, it must be hard to look either too feminine or too masculine in the same uniform of capes, cloaks, and black boots, until eventually a perky vampira slinks over wearing a black tank top with a spiked dog collar and not much else.

GOTH GOTTA-HAVES

- Choke collar
- Eye shadow
- Pancake makeup
- Black jeans, T-shirts, leggings, and skirts
- Fishnet stockings
- Parasol
- A lace-up pirate shirt
- Long black skirt (for boys and girls)
- Boots (preferably black)

- Black coat
- Sunglasses
- Gloves
- Net shirts
- Circle cloak
- Bondage pants
- Long black veil
- Bat wing, skull, or cross jewelry
- Long vest
- Tattered tank dress
- Coffin (optional)

"Hi," she says as you order her a drink, glad that the rules of barstool etiquette still apply. "What's a suit like you doing in a dump like this?" she asks.

"How do you know I'm a 'suit'?" you ask, clinking bottles with her good-naturedly.

"Let's see," she leans back cockily, sizing you up. "No tattoos, no makeup, no suicide attempt scars marring your hairy wrists, no boots, no crosses, no fangs, no swollen, baggy eyes from lack of sleep spent lamenting the fate of the universe. Should I keep going?"

"So, what" you say, laughing. "Look at you. I don't see any fangs or capes slowing you down."

"It's Wednesday," she points out. Seeing the uncomprehending look on your face, however, she adds condescendingly: "casual night."

A few hours later, driving her home from the club, police lights magically appear in your rearview mirror and, despite the momentary flutter of your heart, you're infinitely grateful that the gloom and doom of the Labyrinth has killed your buzz a long time ago.

"License and registration, please," the cop says, peering quizzically at your gothic guest with a foot-long flashlight. "You too, miss."

"It's okay," your pallid passenger explains. "I get harassed like this all the time."

After a brief warning to "slow it down" and another furtive glance at your lifeless lady friend, the mistress of the dark, the officer lets you off the hook and hands back both of your I.D.s. Glancing quickly at hers before returning it, you notice an unfamiliar face beaming back at you from the positively perky photograph: a smiling co-ed with flowing blond locks and bright eyes stares back at you from above a blindingly white Hanson T-shirt. Quickly, you check the stranger's name: Amy Logan.

"Amy?" you cry, finally handing her back the license. "Your name is—Amy?"

"That's just my street name," she explains sheepishly, quickly cringing at her former self on the front of the license. "But my coven name is Pandora, Perpetrator of Pandemonium."

"Uh huh," you mutter, pulling up in front of her place shortly after. "Sure it is."

"Aren't you coming in?" she asks, hurt and standing stubbornly in the driveway.

TOP 5 SIGNS YOU MIGHT BE GOTH

5 People keep saying, "Hey, how come I can't see your reflection?"

4 You can go out in sunlight, you just don't.

3 Your biggest pet peeve is the squeaky hinges on your coffin.

2 You keep your Halloween decorations up all year.

1 Marilyn Manson calls you up for fashion tips.

"No thanks, Pandora, er, Amy," you say. "But I'll watch 'til you get in safely."

"Whatever," she sneers. "I knew you were a suit, inside and out."

Not even waving, she slams the front door of a decidedly normal looking townhouse on the better side of town.

"Amy," you sigh on the way home.

If you'd wanted some girl named Amy to bite you on the neck, you could have just gone to a sports bar.

"I often think that the night is more alive and more richly colored than the day."
-Vincent Van Gogh

CYBER
COOL?

The rise of the Internet and the decline in expense of personal computers and laptops have given the once former geeks who work in the technology field an entirely new and unexpected status: cool. But can newfound power and prestige turn a semiconductor's ear into a software purse?

CYBER COOL?

Like the rest of technology, cyber cool is still so new that (almost) anything goes. Colors can (and should) clash and, since (fashion) seasons are very *out*, your old G. I. Joe lunchbox is back *in* (vogue)!

CYBER COOL is

... actually a heady blend of retro cool and cyber chic, so drag out your older brother's ratty Devo concert shirts, *Incredible Hulk* Underoos, and *Planet of the Apes* backpacks.

PANTS

Any pair of pants will do. New or old, khaki or plaid, drawstring or button fly. Just make sure that there are plenty of pockets to hold all of your floppy discs, tic tacs, and *X-Files* action figures.

SUNGLASSES

...are optional, as most cyber studs are near- or far-sighted anyway. If you do go for shades, make sure they're prescription, to avoid accidents.

CYBER ACCESSORIES?

These are up for grabs as well. Naturally, any and all techno-toys will do, from cell phones to laptops, from beepers to Discmen. However, since "geeks just wanna have fun," any other gadgets or doo-dads are just peachy as well. From plastic phasers to *Star Wars* watches, the world is your oyster, cyber studs and studettes, so start taking chances.(And start looking cool.)

DIGITAL DARLING

So you're finally home after a long day of writing code and hacking glitches in your rapidly rising software company's game programs. You pour yourself a glass of chocolate milk and settle down with your cat, cleverly named "Unix," and flip on the TV. In between the game shows and vapid entertainment news, you are naturally forced to watch several commercials.

They are for cars. They are for cellular phones. They are for shoes and ties and toothpaste and soap. The stars are not painfully pretty models or hipsters or oldsters or even mega-rich hip-hop stars. They are, in fact, just like you. Thinnish, pasty-ish, bookish, geekish folk in expensive but mismatched clothes and butchered hair complete with Cat Woman glasses and their old man's shoes.

They all look like they just stepped out of a Microsoft convention and even the buzz words in the commercials are things you hear all day: "code," "Cobol," "Internet," "interface," "software," "network," "hardware," etc. You drain the last of your chocolate drink as you

"If you have any trouble sounding condescending, find a Unix user to show you how it's done."
—Scott Adams

suddenly realize, for the first time in your life—you are *cool!* You *are* it. *You* are the latest thing.

The whole evening goes like that. Market reports on CNN tout Internet stocks left and right. Web sites are alluded to on the nightly news, true crime dramas, national exposés, and even sitcoms! Everywhere you flip, TV characters, hosts, or interviewers are logging on and hitchhiking down the information superhighway.

You are suddenly the movie star, the rap artist, and the runway model all rolled into one. You check your look in the mirror and realize you could be a poster boy for the nerd revolution, yet you suddenly don't mind the appellation. Miraculously, the word *nerd* doesn't sound so bad anymore. *Geek* is not so offensive either. Neither are *brainiac, egghead, bookworm,* or *professor.* If only your friends from school could see you now! (Although, you secretly admit, they'd still probably beat you up.)

"It's about time!" you think, sorting through your closet and finding that, despite your aversion to anything even resembling the word "fashion," by no fault of your own, you are most definitely "in."

The polyesters and plaids. The off-grays and the dull-whites. The bowling shoes and Archie Bunker socks and even pocket protectors are suddenly all the rage. Those hokey Apple logo or Yahoo! T-shirts you've been hiding for years are actually priceless and even the *Star Trek* ties are suddenly in vogue.

It must have happened while you were bent over your laptop at work, buried under stacks of e-mail and straining your young eyes at the glowing computer screen, but it happened nonetheless. You are definitely hot. Hip. With-it.

Dare you say, even—cool?

But there is just one thing that troubles you as you drift off to sleep in your single bed covered with those soft, cuddly *Star Wars* sheets: "What now?"

TOP 5 SIGNS YOU'RE NOT READY FOR A LAPTOP

5 You keep asking where the mouse is.

4 You keep saying, "These things will never get off the ground."

3 You wonder out loud, "Why can't they just call it a 'briefcase' like they used to?"

2 You keep asking if it doubles as a TV tray.

1 The salesman threatens to eject you from the store if you keep saying, "Oh look at that one, it's so cute!"

IF THE SUIT FITS...

So, you've decided to take the big plunge and actually invest in that first step up the long ladder of manhood: a suit. Whether you're fresh out of school, starting a new career, or going to your first ballet, buying a suit is an integral part of accepting your role as a man. In fact, history has proven that men who wear suits demand a certain level of respect superior to that of men who wear, say, Lycra or Spandex. So accept your fate and enjoy the entire experience of shopping for a suit. And just remember, no matter how busy your tailor is, be sure to insist that he remove your pants before making any alterations. Unless, of course, you like your new suit so much you never want to take it off.

ACCESSORIES

Certain accessories are a must with the power suit: a good briefcase, a pair of tortoise shell glasses, or a classy watch all help to round out the picture. As for gadgets? Skip the cufflinks. Cell phones and Palm Pilots are today's answer to handkerchiefs.

TIE

If you're wearing a suit, then a good tie is an absolute must. Fortunately, society is much more tolerant of goofy ties than they were back in, say, the, '50s. Dancing Christmas trees? Great. Snoopy? Super. Hula dancers? Fab. Daffy Duck? Grand. Anything goes, as long as it doesn't require a nine-volt battery or an extension chord.

SHIRTS

Although you don't see much of it, your suit's not complete without the right shirt underneath. Solid colors are hot, especially if they match the color of your jacket and tie (à la Regis Philbin or the cast from *Casino*). If not, stick with white. It matches everything and hides wrinkles better than many other colors.

JACKET

In a proper jacket, the right fit is as important as the right material. Loose is good, baggy is bad. (Tight is worse!) And whatever you do, don't borrow your Dad's jacket, especially if he's 6'2" and you're only 5'2".

PANTS

Pants should fit well, too. As with the jacket: loose is good, baggy is "Bad." With a capital "B." Crisp, classy creases are always in style, and whatever you do, make sure the bottoms are hemmed. The cuff should just hit the back of your dress shoe, not the back of your calf!

SUITS ME JUST FINE

This is where a girlfriend, wife, or mistress comes in handy. Someone belonging to a member of a sex that was actually born with that "fashion" gene, which men are so sadly lacking. Someone who can at least tell when colors, patterns, socks, or lapels clash, often horribly. Someone who actually knows the difference between blended and worsted. Someone who's not afraid to say things like, "You want my honest opinion, right? Well, your beer belly honestly looks *huge* in that. *Honestly.*"

More important, someone who's not working on commission.

However, despite the fact that girls enjoy shopping more than say, breathing, they also know the inherent "break up" potential that is part of the whole "shopping for a suit" package. As in, "Honey, if you tell me to suck in my gut one more time I'll never speak to you again." Therefore, they usually find some pleasant excuse to avoid going with you. As in, "Oh, shoot, it's my turn to check the freshness dates on all of our dairy products. Maybe next time, sweetie."

So, when it comes to buying a suit, it's usually left to you and your own good, bad, or indifferent taste. However, don't let this fact dissuade you from your ultimate goal. Buying a suit is one of the most important clothing decisions you'll make—ever. Consider it an investment in your fashion future.

Now, for the uninformed, there are several types of suit buyers out there.

The first type of suit buyer only intends to wear a suit about once a year. Chances are, the last real matching-coat-and-pants suit this type of fellow had was the classy green denim and brass ensemble his mother dressed him up in for his kindergarten graduation back in 1976.

Generally, this man has been forced into finally investing in a suit of his own by some upcoming gala or event, i.e. a wedding or a funeral. Most likely, the first thing out of this suit shopper's mouth upon entering

The Stuff That Suits Are Made Of

- **Wool:** A natural animal fiber.
- **Gabardine:** A type of fabric that can be made from either wool or cotton.
- **Oxford:** A type of fabric usually made of cotton.
- **Hopsacking:** A fabric typically made of wool or cotton.
- **Serge:** A fabric often made of wool.
- **Tweed:** Usually made of wool, this fabric has a rough appearance.
- **Bedford Cord:** A ribbed weave.
- **Flannel:** A soft-filled cotton twill brushed on one side.
- **Herringbone Twill:** A broken twill weave composed of vertical sections that are alternately right hand and left hand in direction.
- **Hi-Twist:** A term used to describe a cloth made from a worsted yarn that has been twisted by 40 to 60%.
- **Houndstooth:** Popular wool pattern made with a variation of the twill weave to form jagged, broken checks.
- **Poplin:** A fine quality fabric produced by using very fine warp yarns with slightly thicker filling yarns.
- **Rayon:** A fiber created by the mixing of plant cellulose and chemicals.
- **Polyester:** A man-made fiber. It resists wrinkling because it is resilient.
- **Acrylic:** A man-made fiber produced from a form of plastic.

the men's store will be something similar to, "I'm here to buy a suit. Yes sirree Bob, an honest-to-goodness wool blend, three-button-coat-and-pleated-trousers kind of a suit. Can anyone help me?" In which case every available salesman on the floor will fight to the death for the chance to sell this sucker the most expensive suit, or entire *rack* of suits, in the store.

In order to avoid such a clothing catastrophe, just in case the above description sounds like something you might possibly do, decide on a plan before stepping foot into the suit store. In fact, a good idea is to think about the following questions first:

"What shade of color is light enough to hide my dandruff and dark enough to pass muster when my boss kicks the bucket?"

"How many pockets can I get away with before looking like a Boy Scout?"

"When are those hilarious black and white tuxedo T-shirts going to come back in style?"

Finally, when you do enter the store to pick out your one and only suit, try to choose something neutral enough to get yourself through fifty years of weddings, funerals, and trips to the ballet, yet sturdy enough to last until your own funeral.

Another type of suit buyer is the man that plans to wear a suit more than twice a year, but not *much* more. Generally, this is a man who plans on switching jobs

often and doesn't want to be bothered by the task of remembering which suit he wore to which interview on which day.

Occasional suit users need only invest in two suits, one light and one dark. This, of course, is in order to accommodate for different social occasions, seasons, side dishes, hot dog toppings, etc. Gray and navy are the standards in this case, and one rule of thumb when straying from solid colors is, "horizontal stripes exaggerate, vertical pinstripes elevate." (Hint, hint.)

The most notorious and discriminating suit buyer is, naturally, the man who must wear a suit to work every day. Obviously, if this is the case, you'll need more than one suit. In fact, it's a good idea to have at least one suit for every day of the week, especially if you're a sloppy eater or profuse sweater. It's a good idea to choose suits that are different from each other, as well, so that everybody at work doesn't just think you're wearing the same navy suit each day, when you've actually gone ahead and shelled out the bucks for five identical suits. If you *are* partial to one color, go with different shades and subtle patterns of that color, so that at least the women at work will know the difference anyway. (After all, who cares about the guys?)

And then, of course, there is that very special breed of suit shopper who never actually intends on buying a suit at all. Ever. This is the troubled man in search of cheap therapy, à la that ever present source of wondrous wisdom from the superior suit salesman.

After all, buying a suit is a real ego-building experience that everyone should try, even if they don't need a suit in the first place. Walking into the men's store, you will often be able to tell by the salesman's brown nose and complimentary demeanor that he is working on commission. But no matter. You don't owe him anything, after all. You're simply there for the Freudian fringe benefits.

In fact, a good salesman in action is a sheer thing of beauty. Often a sharp dresser himself, he usually looks like a pro. Strong hands, eagle eyes, and a gentle touch are the other tools of his trade. But his words, his fabulous, flowing, flattering words, are the true key to a salesman's ultimate success.

"That suit really looks sharp on you, sir. It's a good look for you. A *very* good look. That fabric really hangs nicely on your shoulders. It goes great with your complexion, too."

By the time an expert salesman is done with a normal suit shopper, of course, the poor sod is likely to buy up half the store. But for this special breed of suit-less soul searcher, the salesman's glowing words of praise are satisfaction enough. He leaves the store unfettered by doubt, worries, insecurity, or fear, not to mention anything as weighty and cumbersome as a brand new suit.

Now that you've figured out what kind of suit shopper you are, there are a few easy rules to remember when actually picking out your suit:

- Make sure the shoulders fit. If it doesn't sit right around your neck, it won't sit right anywhere else.

- To alter or falter? You should be able to hug yourself wearing a coat and not feel like you're wearing a straight jacket. Fitted doesn't necessarily mean tight. Unless, of course, you're going for the John Travolta circa *Saturday Night Fever* look.

- Sleeves are a touchy subject. You don't want it to look as if you're wearing your father's jacket, with your fingers barely visible. On the other hand, you don't want to look as if you outgrew a coat you bought in junior high.

- Length: Too long, and your jacket will look like an outerwear coat. Too short, and you'll look like a bullfighter. As a rule of thumb: You should be able to run your fingers along the bottom of the coat with your arms dangling naturally. Remember that Frankenstein was *not* a fashion plate.

- As with coats, trousers should emphasize a more body-conscious fit that should never be tight. Trousers should drape slightly, have a break before the hem, and fit comfortably—that means you shouldn't show off the pockets' lining if you've gained weight.

- Every man should have at least one pair of pants with safe, standard one-and-a-quarter-inch cuffs. However, watch trousers that are too short. Otherwise, people will want to know where the flood is.

And there it is, suit shopping in a nutshell. Remember that buying a suit is not a duty, it's an honor. After all, you *want* to look like Donald Trump, right?

Right?

TOP 5

SIGNS YOUR OFFICE DRESS CODE IS TOO STRICT

5 "Casual Day" means you "get" to wear bow ties.

4 "Jeans" are something in your DNA.

3 Every third cubicle is a shoeshine stand.

2 Company picnic + tuxedo = fun, fun, fun!

1 Mr. Blackwell posts his "10 Worst Dressed Employees" list in the break room daily.

STILL PREPPY AFTER ALL THESE YEARS

Although their Ivy-league degrees may have become yellowed and frayed, much like their tattered copies of *The Preppy Handbook*, don't think for a minute that the country club set has banished their Izod sweaters and Bass Weejuns to the back of the closet.

In fact, it's doubtful that they've changed their way of dressing one iota over the years. After all, if the rest of us can't even get a guest membership into the club, how are we to know *what* they wear?

HAIR

… is a preppy no-brainer. The shorter the better, although stop just "short" of skinhead. Business cuts are standard, and facial hair is grounds for being taken out of the will.

VESTS

… are another natty necessity. However, since most prepsters wear their powder blue Oxfords a little baggy, make sure to get yours a few sizes too big. (The tie is optional.)

ACCESSORIES

Aside from a nice, thick stack of books, of course, a golf club is still *the* preppy fashion accessory. (Aside from a thick stack of money, that is.) However, any snooty sports staff will do, including polo or croquet mallets or even a lacrosse stick. (These are also helpful to fend off much cooler attackers when they chase you in the mall.)

KHAKI

… is a must-have color for any peppy preppy. Whether it's slacks or shorts, purse coverings or canvas sneakers, the blandness of khaki makes a wonderful contrast for all of that blinding pink, green, and madras.

PASTEL SHIRTS

… are the rule of the day, but pastel shirts with some brash designer label on the chest is even better. It used to be lizards, but now it's little tiny men riding little tiny horses while trying to hit little tiny balls. (Coincidence?)

I (STILL) ZOD

It is quite possible, you've suddenly come to realize, to be fashionable without even knowing it. Of course, it's much more likely, as in your case, to be *out* of fashion and only realize it when it's suddenly called to your attention, out of the blue, by an overheard conversation.

Which, of course, is exactly what happened to you at work the other day. Standing in the supply room, looking for the jumbo paper clips and finding only the miniature version, you were surprised to hear your name mentioned by a co-worker at the water cooler around the corner.

"You know," the speaker replied when the speak-ee failed to recognize your name. "The preppy guy in human resources."

"Preppy?" you whispered to yourself as you leaned against the supply room wall, if only to keep from fainting. "Who? Me?"

Later, after the offending party had moved on and your legs had returned to the consistency of firm Jell-O, you stood in the men's room splashing water on our face to try and regain some sense of composure. Glancing in the mirror as you dried yourself off, you tried to see how someone, anyone, anywhere, anyhow could ever consider you, of all people, a preppy.

Yet the reflection was the same as it had always been: Clean shaven face. Short, business cut hair. The yellow designer tie, the powder blue Oxford shirt, carefully buttoned down at the collar and bearing the respectable equestrian logo, the leather belt, Duckhead khakis, argyle socks and, gulp, penny loafers. (Complete with the pennies, of course.)

Could they be—right? Could you be, gulp, a preppy? Still? After all these years?

But, you'd been to a state university! You'd even

skipped a class or two. (Well, okay, gym.) And experimented with drugs (your first roommate was a pot head and, though you'd never actually toked, you sure smelled it on his clothes often enough) and alcohol (what was a good frat party without a couple of beers?). Why, you'd even had casual sex. More than once!

So how could anyone still call you a preppy? Yet, the mirror didn't lie. The person staring back at you over the men's room sink was, indeed, looking suspiciously prepster-ish.

And so, after work, no longer able to deny the ugly truth, you swing by the mall for a fashion transfusion. The problem is, you've been cloistered in cotton and khaki for so long that you're finding it a little hard to branch out. The baggy jeans and ski cap look is definitely not you. Neither is the surf dog, vampire, rock star, pen-protector, athletic, hip-hop, or burnout look.

You're not suave or debonair enough to go for the silk slacks and ribbed crew neck approach. Neither are you a pimp, mobster, or FBI agent, leaving you lost and confused in the suit racks.

Invariably, shying away from rayon and glitter, razzle and dazzle, you find yourself drawn to the golf ties and dress socks. Like a madras magnet, any color but tan, wheat, harvest, or sand actually *hurts* your eyes. You even find yourself eager to wrap sweaters around the shoulder of every scantily clad male mannequin you see.

And so, like a crack head to his pipe, you succumb to the guilty pleasure of yet another reversible duck decoy belt and matching bow tie.

"Some battles," you think to yourself as you slide into your Volvo for the short drive home to your townhouse on the 18th hole, "are simply too hard to fight."

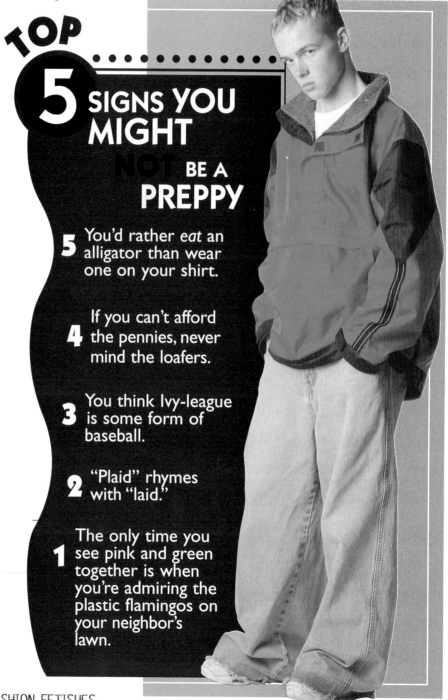

TOP 5 SIGNS YOU MIGHT NOT BE A PREPPY

5 You'd rather *eat* an alligator than wear one on your shirt.

4 If you can't afford the pennies, never mind the loafers.

3 You think Ivy-league is some form of baseball.

2 "Plaid" rhymes with "laid."

1 The only time you see pink and green together is when you're admiring the plastic flamingos on your neighbor's lawn.

WANNA BEATNIKS

You can blame it on all of the new coffeehouses that have sprung up, as if Juan Valdez had planted each one himself, over the last couple of years. Never mind the fact that Jack Kerouac would have surely been tossed out on his ear from these hopelessly retro establishments with their "two cup minimums" and blandly stale "open mikes" held at microphone stands right next to signs reading, "No Profanity, Please!" A whole new bumper crop of sensitive, goateed souls have discovered snapping fingers and gone *On the Road* to find a poetic, not to mention fashion, style all their own.

BERETS

... yes. Baseball caps, no. Berets are great for hiding tiny scraps of paper (i.e. poetry).

PIPES

... yes. Chewing tobacco, no. Other accessories include patchouli and Kerouac's *On the Road*. (Natch!)

SHIRTS

Whatever the weather, a nice black sweater is always flattering on the wanna beatnik. Turtlenecks are great, crew necks are fine, but avoid V-necks and anything with a golden bear, smiling alligator, or miniature polo player on the chest.

PANTS

As long as your pants are black and baggy, anything really goes. Black denim, black cotton, black silk, whatever. Just make sure there are plenty of pockets to hold your brilliant scribblings on all of those café cocktail napkins.

BLACK

... is always in fashion, the blacker the better. If you can't muster all black, then a nice combination of white and black is fine. In general, avoid bright colors. (In fact, the only red you use should be in your poems about flowers.)

POETIC (IN) JUSTICE

The poetry contest was just a joke. Sort of. True, you'd gone back to school even though you'd vowed not to the minute you threw your graduation cap in the air nearly seven years earlier. And, it *was* also true that your Creative Writing 101 instructor, the cute one in the tweed and horn rimmed glasses, had suggested the contest as a way of "broadening your horizons," as he put it.

But you'd actually done it just to meet guys. Plain and simple. Well, what else were you supposed to do? The bars, clubs, and hot spots downtown were getting old. It was nothing but girls working at your office building in the Research Park. And the last three blind dates you'd had ended up in tears, leers, and jeers, respectively.

And so, you'd sat down one night and written your great opus, "Ode to the Food Lion up the Street." It was a joke, anyone could see that. Lots of references to ketchup and Pringles. The lazy symbolism between cash registers and organized religion. It was every bad free verse cliché known to man all rolled into one and you were quite sure the local Arts Alliance, proud sponsors of the event, would laugh it right off of the judge's table and into the circular file.

Still, it was a class requirement and you were just glad it was over with. That is, until you got the call that Sunday evening a couple of weeks later in between parts one and two of the Betty Broderick story on the Lifetime Channel.

"Congratulations," said the ephemeral voice from the answering machine, since you certainly weren't picking up the phone on your Grandmother's only 5 cents a minute night. "Your poem, 'Ode to the Food Lion up the Street' has been selected as this year's 2nd prize winner. Please join us at the Barnes & Noble on Jones Street next Saturday evening at 6 to read your poem out loud along with the other talented winners."

And so, for an entire week, you sweated bullets while reading your stupid poem over and over again to your tired reflection in the bathroom mirror. Come Saturday night, you'd already been at the mega-bookstore for two hours just so you wouldn't chicken out. Accordingly, you'd had no less than three of those ultra-fattening Frozen Mocha

Wanna Beatnik Must-Haves

Beret (Preferably black)	**Black pants**
Turtleneck (Preferably black)	**Socks (black)**
Goatee	**Shoes (black)**
Pipe (Beige will do)	**Patchouli (Duh!)**
Swashbuckling silk shirt	**Tattered copy of *On the Road* tucked under your arm**

Java Jigglers from the built-in Café, where the biggest freaks in the world had been setting up a makeshift poetry stage ever since you'd arrived.

Slowly, as the sun set and evening dawned and poetry lovers of all shapes and sizes began to stream in, you noticed a definite new trend in the fashion annals of literary history. Jack Kerouac, Allen Ginsberg, and their ilk had suddenly been resurrected in the form of a horde of pale, pasty, twenty-something man-boys smelling of patchouli, tic-tacs, and those cloying clove cigarettes.

With their already-thinning hair either spiked or finger combed straight down onto their wide, intelligent foreheads, to a man they each had the nearly identical goatee or fu-Manchu beard perfectly trimmed to match.

They eagerly lined the café in their black vests and leather pants. Though the stereotypical berets were in absence this night, you were quite sure each "wanna beatnik" had left theirs at home on the off chance that it might be windy on the way to the Café.

Sipping from the cups of coffee in their skinny, big-knuckled fingers, the wanna beatniks eagerly awaited the poetry reading. Although you noticed pointedly that none of them wore the special "reader ribbons" like the one that was currently ruining the brand new dramatic, blood red blouse you'd bought especially for the occasion.

And so, just like clockwork, your best-laid plans had come to pass. You'd taken the night-class, stayed away from the bars, won the damn poetry contest and now, like a booby prize in some celestial clothing comedy, you'd certainly have your pick of identical hipsters once they heard your dreadful drivel read aloud.

What to do? What to do?

Oh, well, you'd never dated a guy with a goatee before. Or leather pants, for that matter. Maybe they'd be a turn on. Besides, you'd had too much caffeine to sleep tonight anyway. Quite possibly, you could get one of the wanna beatniks to "Howl" before the night was done. What the heck, it might even be worth extra credit.

REASONS POETRY'S NOT MORE POPULAR

5 Ranting and raving about tubers is just not the turn-on it used to be.

4 After "Roses are red," what's the big deal?

3 Wasn't high school bad enough?

2 "Poetry schmoetry, where's the hunks?"

1 So few words rhyme with "penis."

IT'S NO DRAG

Gay or straight, rich or poor, tall or short, big or little, cross-dressers come in all shapes and sizes. While they may not proudly strut across the catwalks and glossy magazine pages of mainstream American fashion (unless you're talking about RuPaul) this ever-growing, confident contingent has no intention of backing into the closet anytime soon. Unless, that is, it's to pick out that darling little sequined number dangling at the back…

FALSE BREASTS

Fake breasts are key. Too big, and they ruin that tiny little sequined number you spent all day sewing. Too small, and you might as well not even wear any at all. Shoot for somewhere in the middle and spend the extra few bucks for the good ones. (Otherwise you might as well just stuff tissue in there, à la Laverne & Shirley.)

SHOES

Shoes may make the woman, but they do even better for the man who dresses like a woman. While flats may be more comfortable, on your size 12 feet they'll probably just look like loafers. And heels? Forget 'em unless you opt for the extra week it will take you to learn how to walk in them. A simple pair of pumps are fine. Whatever you do, avoid sandals. (Unless you enjoy shaving your feet, that is.)

HAIR

Beside breast forms, wigs are possibly the most important cross-dressing accessory. While many guys go for blond, blond doesn't go for that many guys. Take some time to pick out a color that flatters your face. (Or, at least, your facial hair.)

MAKEUP

Makeup is another key factor to cross-dressing, and while any guy can do it, not every guy can do it well. Buy a book or get the Malibu Barbie makeup CD-ROM and spend an evening checking it out instead of cruising all of those cyberporn sites like usual. Once you get ready for your first makeover, just keep repeating to yourself, "Less is more, less is more." Then practice what you preach!

CLOTHES

While your (fake) breasts may get a second look, you can believe that your dress will be all that matters. Just because you're not a girl doesn't mean you should use excuses. Find a dress that fits, with plenty of room to sit down in. Other than that, let your conscience (and your credit card) be your guide.

WALK-OUT
(OF THE) CLOSET

There is no greater lover of all things "fashion" than the fresh-out-of-the closet cross-dresser, i.e. "female impersonator." You personally discovered this "transsexual truism" one normal weekday afternoon when your boss let your small advertising company off early from work. Innocently, you thought you'd surprise your boyfriend with a little imported beer and take-out Chinese for lunch. Little did you know he was having his own, unique brand of "afternoon delight" all by himself!

Since your soul mate worked nights at the local Home Depot as manager of the wallpaper department, you thought it would be nice to spend more than five minutes waving at each other on your way in and his way out the door.

Like evidence from a crime scene, however, you picked up clues from the minute that you'd arrived home. While the Weather Girl's disco hit, "It's Raining Men," blared from your CD player, you noticed a glass of wine on the kitchen counter, spotted with rather large lipstick stains smeared indelicately on the rim.

Depositing your forgotten lunch on the counter next to it, you entered the bedroom more than fully prepared to see your new housemate and an illicit lover tumbling ungracefully beneath your brand new sheets.

Instead, you heard the shower running in the bathroom and saw your clothes, your best clothes, scattered across the bed. Your finest silks, richest scarves, most glamorous evening gowns and crispest blazers were laid out as if amidst a grand shopping spree.

For a brief moment the wild notion that you were possibly being robbed by the local "closet cat burglar" signaled your feet to flee.

Curiosity, however, forced you into the wicker rocker by the bed in the hopes of

CROSS-DRESSING ESSENTIALS

Silicone or Latex breast forms

A gaff (to conceal or hide the male genitalia)

High-heels

Wigs

A waist cincher or corset

A pair of coverage hose in nude

Proper lingerie and panties

A beard shadow cover

Hormones (consult your physician)

Foundation or blush

A cosmetic box with eyeshadow, eyeliner, mascara, lipstick, etc.

The odd French maid (or naughty schoolgirl) uniform

catching your live-in and *his* lover exiting from a passionate, steamy shower together. Shortly the water turned off and the sound of high-heels clattered across the bathroom tile.

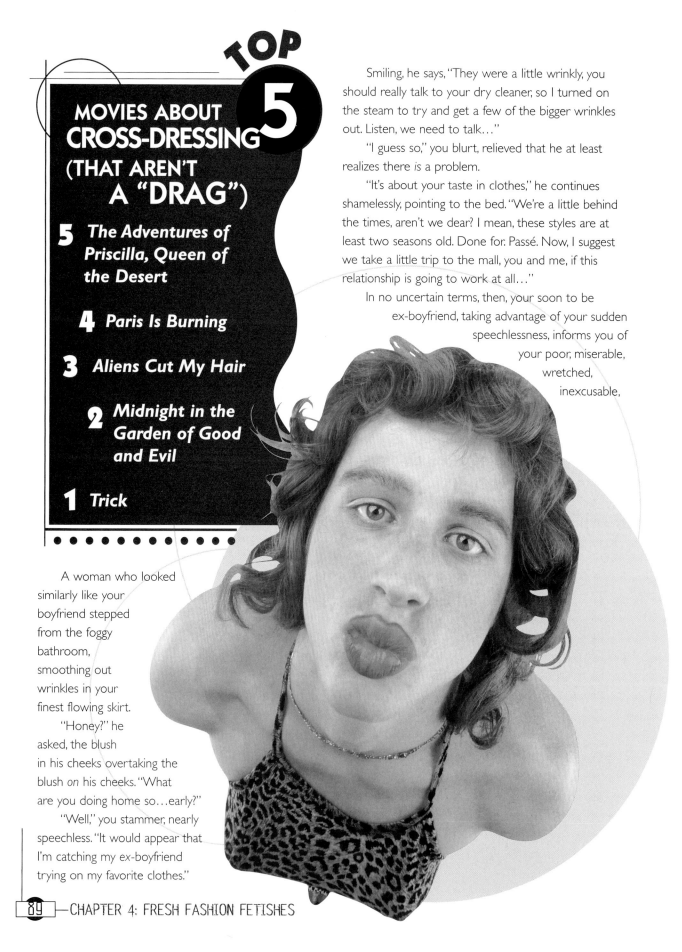

MOVIES ABOUT CROSS-DRESSING (THAT AREN'T A "DRAG")

5 The Adventures of Priscilla, Queen of the Desert

4 Paris Is Burning

3 Aliens Cut My Hair

2 Midnight in the Garden of Good and Evil

1 Trick

Smiling, he says, "They were a little wrinkly, you should really talk to your dry cleaner, so I turned on the steam to try and get a few of the bigger wrinkles out. Listen, we need to talk…"

"I guess so," you blurt, relieved that he at least realizes there *is* a problem.

"It's about your taste in clothes," he continues shamelessly, pointing to the bed. "We're a little behind the times, aren't we dear? I mean, these styles are at least two seasons old. Done for. Passé. Now, I suggest we take a little trip to the mall, you and me, if this relationship is going to work at all…"

In no uncertain terms, then, your soon to be ex-boyfriend, taking advantage of your sudden speechlessness, informs you of your poor, miserable, wretched, inexcusable,

A woman who looked similarly like your boyfriend stepped from the foggy bathroom, smoothing out wrinkles in your finest flowing skirt.

"Honey?" he asked, the blush in his cheeks overtaking the blush *on* his cheeks. "What are you doing home so…early?"

"Well," you stammer, nearly speechless. "It would appear that I'm catching my *ex*-boyfriend trying on my favorite clothes."

downright *bad* taste. From your generic panty hose to your knock-off purses, he lists your fashion faults from Angora to Zebra skin, all the while strutting to and fro in your favorite heels and those generic panty hose he's so offended by.

You guess you should have realized the clues from the very beginning. His hairless body (he told you he'd just joined the "Y" and wanted to "shave" a few seconds off his backstroke). His manicured fingers ("It really helps in my line of work," he'd explained). His nightly Oil of Olay, Noxzema, and Seabreeze ritual (the doctor had told him it was good for his pores).

But, like the trusting soul you'd always been, you wound up duped yet again.

"I'm not into guys," he explained insincerely. "I just … like … fashion."

"*Ladies'* fashion," you correct.

"Honey," he says, rolling his eyes in the direction of your closet. "I wouldn't exactly call what you've got in there 'ladies' fashion'!"

Which, of course, is the final straw. You might have been able to go to couple's therapy to work out the issues, baggage, and inner child at play in his sexually confused sandbox. You might have been able to overlook the stretched-out stockings. And, quite possibly, you could have even shared your favorite bottle of expensive perfume.

But no *man* was going to tell you that you had bad taste. Not in this lifetime anyway . . .

TOP 5

SIGNS YOUR BOYFRIEND MAY BE A CROSS-DRESSER

5 That lipstick on his collar is his own.

4 Keeps telling you how lucky you are to be able to wear panty hose.

3 He actually leaves the toilet seat down.

2 He has better taste in clothes than you do.

1 Wants the two of you to go as Cagney & Lacey for Halloween.

JOCKS

Perhaps it's because everything always came so easily to them back in school. Perhaps it's because the anabolic steroids have made them color blind. Perhaps all that Gatorade had a negative effect on their fashion sense. Or maybe they just plain like the feel of those pumpkin orange polyester coaching shorts against their skin. Either way, there's no sense teaching an old jock new tricks…

HATS

… are a must for all jocks. For one, they cover up that nasty bald spot from all of those grungy football helmets. For another, they're a great place to hide your steroids.

TANK TOPS

… are a jock gotta-have. The color doesn't matter, as long as there are no sleeves. This allows for optimum armpit exposure while at the same time avoiding those unsightly sweat stains after lunch hour arm-wrestling competitions.

STOPWATCHES

… are another athletic accessory. Not only can you see how fast you still run the forty yard dash, but it comes in handy when you and your jock buddies hold an impromptu "longest burp" contest.

SHORTS

No matter the weather, shorts are in. Not just one pair, either. That's for sissies. Two pairs provide plenty of protection in case you should spontaneously decide to join the local triathlon on your way to the grocery store.

SHOES

… whether tennis, hi-top, or running, are always in. Whether you're wearing jeans or sweats, a tuxedo or pajamas, your shoes/sneakers define your jock status.

SOCKS

… are a necessity and, like shorts, are often layered. Whatever you do and no matter how many pairs you wear, just make sure to roll them down. Unless, that is, you're going for the "jocks in *The Revenge of the Nerds*" look.

JUST JOCK!

Dear Editor,

In response to last week's inflammatory letter to the editor, sarcastically entitled "Jocks and Fashion: Oil and Water," I would just like to say that I have been a confirmed "jock" for years and always thought I was doing everything fashionably possible.

After all, it never occurred to me that XXXL was not an acceptable size. I never once considered wearing anything but sneakers out to dinner. (Unless I was eating at the golf course, where I always kept an extra pair of soft spikes.) Underwear? That's what jock straps are for. And the last time I took off my ball cap was on my wedding night. 'Nuff said.

Of course I realize that fashion has four seasons: football, baseball, basketball, and hockey. Likewise, my closet boasts a wide variety of colors. Red and black for my hockey team. Blue and silver for when I'm watching my team play hoops. Pinstripes are always appropriate for baseball. And garnet and gold are rather classy come the weekly "pigskin preview." What other colors are there?

As for formal wear? What about those snazzy black slacks they let me keep for refereeing all of those softball games that one summer a few years back. Of course, my beer gut's grown considerably since then, but my reversible jersey should cover it quite nicely.

And besides, what about my vast tie collection? I'd like to have a word with the man who doesn't spell "classy" with tiny baseballs, yo-yos, or hockey pucks.

Furthermore, I pride myself on several other very fashionable aspects of my sportsman's personality:

I make sure my coaching shorts always have back pockets to fit my chewing tobacco.

I never wear my whistle out in public.

I never show a gal my trick knee until the third date.

Friends are always welcome to borrow from my vast baseball cap collection.

And my Dan Marino watch is 14-karat gold.

Now, I ask you, what's not fashionable about all that?

Your readers might want to try a new equation after reading *this* letter to the editor: jocks + fashion = home runs and hot dogs!

After all, what other form of fashion allows you to hide mustard stains and wrinkles so gosh darn well?

TOP 5 REASONS TO DATE A JOCK

5 If you melt down all his old trophies you'll have enough gold for most of an earring.

4 Orgasms are overrated.

3 Shiny whistles have always been a turn-on.

2 You sort of like it when he snaps your butt with a towel.

1 You love a man in uniform. (Even a softball referee's uniform.)

WORKPLACE
WOES

Congratulations! You finally got that job you've been after for the last few weeks. (Okay, months.) So, let's see. You've called your Mom. (Twice!) You've celebrated with your friends. (Sort of, they already *had* jobs and had to go home early.) And you've studied the handy employee handbook the recruiter gave you after signing on the dotted line. (Sort of, your "cat" spilled sparkling grape juice on it during your half-hearted celebration.)

In fact, the only section of the handbook to escape "death by grape juice" was a little addendum there at the end discussing the dreaded "d" word: dress code. Unfortunately, you'd been so worried about actually getting the job, you'd forgotten to check out what the other employees (especially the females) were wearing to work!

Well, you're in luck. Your cat may have been subconsciously trying to sabotage your leaving the house five days out of seven a week, but we've prepared a quick primer on dress code dos and don'ts just in time for your first day of work:

SHOES

When it comes to shoes in the workplace, comfort is key. If you must have heels, make sure there are plenty of cubicles to lean on for support on your way to the water cooler.

YOUR HAIR?

When it comes to follicle fashion in the workplace, think Demi Moore in *Disclosure*, not Joan Cusack in *Working Girl*.

MAKEUP

At work, as it does everywhere else, makeup matters. Wear too much and don't be surprised when people start calling you "Mimi" behind your back. Wear too little, and your handle might be *Creepshow!*

THE ATTIRE

Even corporate casual doesn't mean "sensibly sloppy." Those three-piece power suits you saw in *Wall Street* may be out, but a nice jacket and slacks combo will always be in style.

ACCESSORIES

Occupational accessories are different for every job (i.e. White House vs. crack house) but a good pen or pencil is a must. Not only do they make good weapons in the parking lot after hours, but they always look great tucked in your hair, tied back in a bun, or resting just so against your cheek or teeth in a business meeting.

PLAY IT SAFE

For the first few days, anyway. You've already got the "power" interview suit, the "school marm" dress, and the "backup beige" sweater and skirt ensemble. Why not alternate them for those first few tentative days until you've gotten a feel for what the rest of the staff is into?

After all, even if you *had* read the employee handbook, who's to say it wasn't written in 1938? ("Hey, you're a *girl*. You can't wear pants!") And even if it was written in the past decade, many office branches would rather sell their stock-options than adhere to unfair edicts straight from the home office.

So running out and tracking down the latest and greatest outfits in "corporate casual" could all have been for naught if you had showed up on Monday to find a sea of blue jean-clad, coffee sucking hipsters in various shades of Hanes T-shirts, tank tops, and dashikis. (Come on, you know what those dot.com crews are like!)

There's no danger in dressing "up" your first few days. After all, when you scream for help after your twelfth paper jam of the morning, it's not going to matter what you wore. You're still a greenhorn, so why not act like one? Your boss will thank you for going the extra mile, and your coworkers aren't going to eat lunch with you until Thursday anyway!

In the end, your collection of skirts and blouses, slacks and blazers, and the odd power suit or two thrown in for good measure, should see you through just about any job in today's professional marketplace.

DRESS FOR (CASUAL) SUCCESS
(Follow these guidelines to avoid "dress-code demerits")

- Casual doesn't mean "sloppy." Use an iron!
- Leave your printed T-shirts at home.
- Save sweats for the gym and beachwear for the beach.
- Keep shoes shined and scuff-free.
- Combine items from your business wardrobe with casual attire.
- Wear a vest instead of a blazer.
- Is it okay to be colorful? Yes. Is it okay to clash? No.
- Match your belt to your shoes for a polished coordinated look.

DRESS CODE DEFINITIONS

Now that you've got the job, you'll want to fit in. No, this doesn't mean eating lunch with the office ass-kiss or leading the "I love my job" cheer from your office cubicle each morning at 9:01. However, it does mean eyeballing your coworkers and dressing down, or up, accordingly. To assist you, here are some down-and-dirty dress code definitions:

- **Business casual:** What you'd see if you ever made it past the secretary in one of those high-rise buildings downtown. Lots of pleated slacks, Oxford shirts, and loafers on the guys, plenty of power suits, beige skirts, and short-sleeved silk blouses on the ladies. The only thing casual about it is the fact that you don't have to wear your hair in a bun or shine your shoes each morning.

• **Tie-optional:** Um, not really. The inventors of this tight-ass dress code were obviously tired of the bitching and whining of their sad-sack employees and decided to give them one small, weak sign of bowing by letting them not wear a tie with their three-piece suits and dress shoes. In short, even though the handbook says "tie optional," they'd prefer you wear one. Especially come your anniversary date!

• **Wacky Wednesday:** Or Tacky Tuesday, whatever. This is another one of those "appease the peons" days where some flunky in Human Resources suggests everyone in the office wears pink socks one week, Hawaiian shirts the next. Fun for a month or so, until you get tired of running out every Tuesday night to buy pink socks or Hawaiian shirts!

• **Corporate casual:** Probably the most popular of today's dress codes, corporate casual is a relatively new concept brought about by those funky Kia commercials and the proliferation of twenty-something, dot.com millionaires who used to hate their dorky dress code from way back in the days when they still worked for Kinko's. (Instead of owning 51 percent of the shares, that is.)

Heavy on the funky kind of trendy stuff you see in Old Navy commercials and in *Yahoo! Life* magazine, this is a comfortable mix of stylish clothes with individual flair mixed in. (E.g. your favorite Lucky Charms T-shirt and a pair of cargo pants.)

• **Dress-down days:** These often fall on days when most of the office is in Vegas for that big "convention," and the rest of you losers are left to meet that big deadline the boss conveniently called from the airport to remind you about. Tennis shoes, capri pants, khakis, even jeans proliferate. (Sort of like what you'd wear to the office on a Saturday if it was just you and that creep from Accounting working. Minus the Mace, that is.)

TOP 5

MOVIES GUARANTEED TO MAKE YOUR OFFICE SEEM BETTER

5 *The Temp*

4 *9 to 5*

3 *Office Space*

2 *Die Hard*

1 *Office Killer*

full of prints your granddad favored, hairstyles even your mom wouldn't admit to wearing (even though you have proof), and plenty of techno gadgets sticking out of any and all pockets. (Think Bill Gates. In high school.)

"Dew knot trussed yore spell chequer two fined awl yore mistakes."
—Brendan Hills

• **Casual Friday:** The one day of the week your tight-ass boss allows you to come in wearing pants without pleats, shoes without tassels, and shirts that aren't starched. (Also known as "Appease the Peons One Day a Week Day.")

• **Urban hip:** A grown-up term for what your parents, and possibly some of your older friends, call, "...that crap they wear on MTV." Heavy on only the hottest name brands of the moment, bigger-than-your-pocket logos, fresh colors, fly fabrics, droopy drawstrings, bold buttons, happening hoods, plenty of pockets, zowie zippers, and anything else your girlfriend (unless you're having an office romance) would be ashamed to go out with you in. (Think L. L. Cool J meets *Dilbert*.)

• **Silicon Valley chic:** This is a "dressed up" term for "geek chic." Heavy on clothes that used to be cool and are now cool again, i.e. "retro," geek chic is

• **Jeans-only:** This is another "statement" dress code. Naturally, jeans are similar to khakis or capri pants, but the fact that you're being "forced," for lack of a better term, to wear jeans is just as corporate crazy as insisting you wear a tie to work. (Just a little more comfortable.)

OCCUPATIONAL HAZARDS

Naturally, some jobs carry their own dress codes, i.e. uniforms. Those frisky bike messengers, for instance, would be out of luck without their spandex and backpacks. Those folks at UPS need their daily dose of mocha brown. The post office salutes red, white, and blue. Strippers don't do well without a daily dose of leopard skin and faux fur boas. And if you work at Burger King, well, you have our sympathies.

Of course, many such "corporate clone converters" leave your hair, face, and hands relatively unscathed. (Except for Burger King, that is.) So if you don't have to wear a hair net or chicken hat, try some of those funky barrettes or chop sticks to add a personal touch to your uniform blues. Rings are nice. (One per finger, please.) An ankle bracelet or two never hurt anybody. And, even if nobody can see them, you'll know they're there. (Hey, any distraction helps when it's only 1:30 and you've already started your "happy hour after work" countdown!)

TRUST YOUR INSTINCTS

Regardless of what your dress code actually is, or isn't, common sense is always in style. So go with your gut. If your boss tosses off words like "corporate casual" and "urban hip" in your interview, yet everyone is wearing khakis and sweaters, ignore the lingo and head to the Gap.

On the other hand, if everyone seems to be wearing something different regardless of age, sex, race, or day of the week, try slipping into what you'd wear out to the movies or dinner and see what happens. If nobody drops their coffee mug in the lobby come Monday morning, you know you're okay.

Speaking of common sense, very few dress codes address the matter of personal hygiene. This is probably because they assume if you got the job, you passed the first test. Therefore, it's a given that no matter what your style of corporate, shabby, or urban dress, cleanliness counts.

Clothes should be clean, wrinkle-free, appropriate for mixed company, and above all, fit well. (Did we mention clean?)

TOP 5

SYNONYMS FOR YOUR CUBICLE

5 Paperclip Purgatory

4 Cyberporn Central

3 The Alley of the Damned

2 Fortress o' Flatulence

1 Silicon Valley Sweatshop

FLANNEL
FALLOUT

It must have surprised the close-knit group of Seattle slackers when not only did other residents of Seattle start dressing like them, but the whole country did as well. One can hear the inevitable refrain from coffeehouses and Rave clubs across the perpetually rainy city, "How are we supposed to look grungy now, when everyone else is copying us? To stand out at all, we'll have to start dressing up."

FLANNEL

… is a must, whether it's a shirt, a bandana, or the three pairs of boxers you wear under your tattered cargo pants.

ATTITUDE

Dressing grungy is a great way to draw attention to yourself. And not all of it's the "good" kind. Therefore a little attitude is a must. Snarls, sneers, frowns, and grunts should suffice.

BOOTS

… are good. Beat-up, battered, black boots are better. Laces are optional, as few grungers tie them anyway. (Just make sure to wear socks! Although those don't have to be clean either.)

HAIR?

Long on guys, short for girls. Spikes are good, dreadlocks are great, greasy is better. If your hair is clean, just wear a ski cap for a few days. That should do the trick!

TANK-TOPS

… are another girl grunge gotta-have. Tight is good, tattered is better, and you'll never believe how many shades of army green they come in these days.

PANTS

Anything goes as long as they're baggy.

TURNING THE "TIDE"

You know the grunge look is out. Way out. Over and done with. Medium-well. Fried, even. But, what are you supposed to do now?

After all, you've easily invested over 100 whole dollars in flannel shirts, Pearl Jam albums, Army boots, tube socks, and baggy, pocket-proliferating drawstring pants in various shades of gloomy gray and olive green.

Are you to just dispose of them unceremoniously, only to hop right onto some other lame fashion bandwagon as if grunge never existed? Are you to follow the fickle winds of the fashion industry and let them tell you (yet again) what to wear and what *not* to wear?

And, honestly, what other fashion trend, *ever*, could even begin to compare to grunge—where your primordial instinct, slovenliness, was celebrated rather than denigrated. Where odor was prized over order. Where flannel was a commodity and pallor a priority. Where unemployment ruled, coffee was considered a food group, and a bottle of shampoo could last you an entire year.

After all, grunge was absolutely, positively *perfect* for you!

And now, like anything once hot, it's icy cold and slowly making way for hip-hop, club kids, retro, the mod revival, and who knows what else will eventually take its place as the 21st Century marches on.

And so, on a warm, spring day, with a heavy heart and a nagging girlfriend leering over your shoulder, you face your incense-residued closet and stare at the stained Sonic Youth T-shirts. The black and red check of your favorite lumberjack flannel. The boots you'd trampled many a preppy in. The socks so stiff and worn they look half-ready to up and leave the closet all by themselves.

Just then, reaching for the first

TOP 5 REASONS GRUNGE IS DEAD

5 Huge ozone hole over Seattle caused by citywide B.O.

4 Pearl Jam's recent hit, wait . . . what recent hit?

3 The powerful "lumberjack lobby" was worried about flannel shortages.

2 The Army needed its boots back.

1 Starbucks' new dress code: "No (Oxford) Shirt, No (Deck) Shoes, No Service!"

load to dump inside the empty Glad bag clutched between your girlfriend's clenched fists, you receive what you consider to be a divine inspiration.

An epiphany, if you will.

"What if," you venture out loud, like a death row inmate receiving a phone call from the governor at the very last minute, "What if I *wash* everything. Huh? Think about it. Clean clothes, even if they are grunge-inspired, are not *technically* grunge at all…"

RETRO REVIVAL

Scooby-Doo. The Jetsons. The Flintstones. Gilligan's Island. If it was once old and camp, chances are it is now considered new and cool. And if they're not wearing Shaggy T-shirts or bringing *Land of the Lost* lunchboxes into corporate cafeterias, today's generation is busily combing the local thrift shops for outfits worthy of any Potsie or Ralph Malph look-alike contest.

★AWESOME★ ACCESSORIES

Patchouli. Mood rings. Vests with leather fringes. Protest signs? If you can find it in your parents' old photo albums, you can wear it with retro pride. Your wallet a little light after all of that so-called "thrift" shopping? Why not opt for tattoos? Try '60s staples, such as butterflies, flowers, and, of course, mushrooms!

★BELL★ BOTTOMS

Retro pants are a breeze even for born-again stoners: bell bottoms! Stone washed or corduroy, tight or baggy, denim or rhinestones, you'll be the bell (bottom) of the ball as long as you've got major flare potential happening in your awesome ankle area!

★HAPPENING★ HAIR

Groovy, dude. Long hair is definitely feeling the hippie, retro vibe. Straight is great, a couple of braids never hurt, and even pony tails are fine. (As long you skip the red knee-highs and Buster Browns, that is.)

★HALTER★ TOPS

Until those naked sit-ins à la John and Yoko come back in style, retro ragers still have to wear something up top. Naturally, the '60s and '70s left us the hippie heritage of those greatest two tops of all time: tube and halter. From macramé to Lycra, from fuscia to tie-dye, anything goes as long as it goes in the right place. Naturally, since these top-only toppers leave you with a bare midriff, going retro is not quite as easy as it seems. (Did they do sit ups in the '60s?)

★FUNKY★ FEET

Shoes are possibly the funkiest part of retro shopping. From John Denver desert boots to go-go boots, from Jesus sandals to platform soles, your feet will be loving the way they feel inside these kooky kickers. (And don't forget the socks. When in doubt, a lovely smiley face or peace sign pattern will do in a pinch!)

SIXTIES SHOPPING

Luckily, retro fashion is cheap, abundant, and readily available these days. Whether you pick up a polyester leisure suit for five bucks down at the local flea market or root around in your older sister's closet for her ex-favorite Monkees T-shirt, you're bound to find hidden treasures if you just look hard enough.

But where do you start? Attics are great places to find "ravishing retro rejects." Just past Grampa's war chest and that old Singer sewing machine is likely to be a pile of boxes containing your parents' campy wardrobe from way back in the '60s and '70s. Most likely, this treasure trove will be chock full of polyester, velour, ruffles, peace signs, anti-war slogans, and go-go boots. (What more could you ask for?) Too big? See if that old sewing machine still works. Too small? Wasn't there an article about that new grapefruit and Snickers diet in the *National Enquirer* downstairs?

If you can't find an attic or your parents weren't all that trendy back in the day, why not check out the local thrift shop? Although not quite as "thrifty" as they used to be, these second-hand stores nonetheless carry a wide variety of even wider lapels, ties, sleeves, and cuffs. Materials that haven't been around for decades cram the shelves, relatively wrinkle free thanks to their high amount of petroleum based radioactive products, and hangers galore carry everything from flapper-style tube dresses to platform flip-flops.

Can't find an attic or a thrift shop in town?

Well, there's always that last resort of buying "new" old clothes at one of the zillions of retro inspired clothiers cropping up

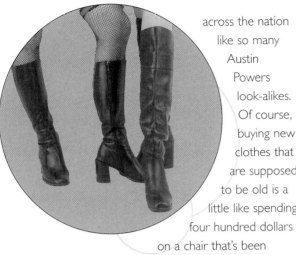

MONKEY BUSINESS

across the nation like so many Austin Powers look-alikes. Of course, buying new clothes that are supposed to be old is a little like spending four hundred dollars on a chair that's been purposely weathered as opposed to just grabbing one that's thirty years old and *really* weathered at a garage sale for a quarter. Still, such new/old stores do have benefits. After all, the clothes are cleaner and the risk of contracting communicable diseases from those *Wonder Dog* Underoos are a lot lower!

But what happens when your "retro revival" goes way beyond fashionable and turns—fanatical? Read on:

Your little brother, not for the first time, of course, is beginning to get on your nerves. It's not those constant loans he's always begging for. Or the way he uses *your* address to deliver his porn club membership orders to so his girlfriend won't get mad.

No, it's his insatiable appetite for all of the old photo albums entrusted to your capable hands by your mother. Not a week goes by lately where he doesn't call you up on Sunday morning, usually just as you've settled in for a relaxing morning of cinnamon java, the Sunday paper, and the light jazz brunch on the radio.

"Dude," he'll say, despite the fact that he's nearly twenty-three. "You've *got* to let me scope out those old photo albums again. I found this trippin' thrift shop on the edge of town last week and I wanted to know what we were into back in the day so I've got some idea of what I want when I go back there. This whole retro thing is so *hot* right now, man, so— are you busy?"

Of course, you've offered to let him keep the moldy photo albums at *his* apartment. But he's not quite ready for the "responsibility," as he calls it, of being the keeper of your family's entire celluloid history.

"Look 'bro'," you remind him in the Retro-speak he loves. "It's a bunch of pictures of dad drunk, mom pregnant, and us crying under the Christmas tree holding last year's G. I. Joes. What's the worst that could happen? You actually lose them and we're spared the embarrassment of ever having to see them again?"

"No way, man," he says seriously. "I can't handle that kind of pressure."

So here he comes, flip-flops flapping, baggies baggy, a faded Twister (the game, not the movie) T-shirt from the late '70s clinging to his pasty, vampire-inspired frame.

He slurps your $12 a pound imported coffee as if it just came from some skanky gas station, barely finishes one of the cranberry scones you bought just for the occasion, and stinks up your apartment with his patchouli and incense "body oil" and his *Brady Bunch Goes to Hawaii*-inspired puka shell necklace.

Rifling through the photo albums, he recalls fondly the times the two of you used to sit and watch all of the shows that have now become his fashion Bible: The *Jetsons*.

Scooby-Doo. Gilligan's Island. The Monkees. The Land of the Lost. Peanuts. Etc.

You remind him that you also used to watch *The Waltons, M.A.S.H.*, and *Chico and the Man* religiously, too, but he just ignores you, such shows obviously not being cool enough to hop on the retro bandwagon. Not just yet, anyway.

"And how about the way we watched *Escape From Witch Mountain* every time it came on TV?" you remind him pointedly. "Why don't they bring those styles back? In case you've forgotten, those black and white checkered corduroys, matching reversible belts, and blue velour turtlenecks with shoulder buckles and neck zippers used to be quite—hip."

"Hip schmip," he mumbles around his $4 mug of coffee. "Now, *this* is what I'm talking about," he exudes, pointing to a chubby, 8-year old you wearing your *Planet of the Apes* T-shirt. The lemon one, too tight and with yellow and green piping on the sleeves. "I would *kill* for a shirt like that, dude. That is my new quest. I am single handedly going to bring the *Planet of the Apes* back into vogue."

"Yeah," you grunt. "Good luck. Just don't show that picture to anybody."

"Dude," he whines, lifting it from the crinkly cellophane protected album page while you're not looking. "I've got to show it to the lady at the consignment shop so she can be on the lookout for me. Peace out."

Your girlfriend, stopping by on the way home from her yoga class later that afternoon, hands you a lime green flyer and points to a towheaded, cute kid wearing a *Planet of the Apes* T-shirt pictured on the front of it.

"Is that *you?*" she asks without shame. "The hair is different," she points out mercilessly. "But the chubby cheeks are still the same. Whoever hung these was quite ambitious. They're all over town!"

You read on to discover that your brother has not only taken the picture but that he also must have zipped right over to Kinko's and run off who knows how many flyers. And each one with your stolen photograph as its centerpiece! Below

your picture are the words: "WANTED: *Planet of the Apes* paraphernalia for new, hot, retro fashion craze. Sort through your closets to find anything similar to the shirt worn by the dork in the picture. Only serious offers please! E-mail me at apeslover@hotmail.com. Thanks. Peace out!"

As per his request, you *do* e-mail your brother. Anonymously, of course, offering an entire collection, in *just* his size, of shirts exactly like that worn by "the dork in the picture." Arranging a time (late at night) and a place (the seediest, most desperate intersection in town) you sign off with a cheery, "Peace Out!" You then act surprised when your little brother calls to tell you the "good news" about his late night adventure. After all, what are big brothers for?

5

YOUR BEAUTY MAKEOVER

Beauty. It's not as elusive as you might think. After all, if beauty is in the eye of the beholder, then the trick is simply to get him (or her) to look at you in the first place. Today, of course, you can get as much or as little help in that desirous department as you feel you require. From makeup to cosmetic surgery, from diet drugs to camouflaging swimsuit cover-ups, beauty is just a nip, tuck, or terry cloth muumuu away. Of course, since we all know that real beauty comes from within (yeah, right), no beauty makeover would be complete without a little soul searching first. After all, there are a few questions one must ask before declaring oneself a bona fide fashion emergency.

For instance, it's not enough to say you want to look like a celebrity. The question is, which celebrity? Will Smith or Willy Wonka? You don't simply claim you want to lose weight. The question is, how much weight? Twenty pounds or two hundred pounds? And, finally, you'll have to answer the ultimate beauty makeover question: Will I still like myself after it's over? Sure you will. As long as you remember that beauty is in the eye of the beholder, that is. And in this case, you are the ultimate beholder!

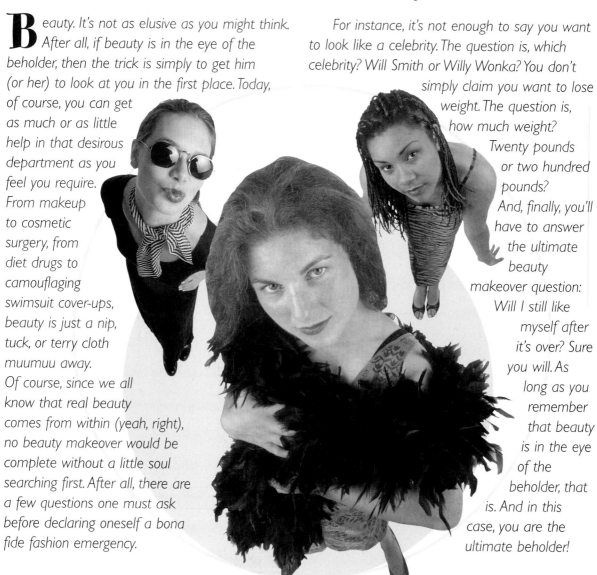

SWIMSUIT
ISSUES

As long as most of the world is covered with water, sandy beaches, and poolside tiki bars, most of the world's inhabitants will be plagued with what are commonly referred to as "swimsuit issues." For while clingy, sheer bikinis are still the norm for today's swimsuit *buyers*, most swimsuit sellers know that the smaller the size, the clingier the bikini.

(NOT ENOUGH) DRESSING ROOM

It is finally May and the summer months you've been waiting for (and dreading) are finally almost here. Of course, as a modern American female, you've been planning for this far-off season since New Year's Eve, when, at the top of your hastily written list of resolutions, you put: "#1: Get your fat ass in shape for swimsuit season!"

January, therefore, was spent investing in an entire new batch of diet books, Suzanne Somers exercise products, and as a backup, a health club membership from a gym that cleverly offered those appealing "New Year's Resolutions Solutions" specials, or, in laymen's terms: lifetime memberships for only $1,500 measly dollars.

You devoured the books in bed each night, surrounded by Light yogurt cups and Snackwell cookie wrappers. You broke the cheap exercise equipment during one overzealous Tuesday night marathon workout session to equal out the Super-

Sized Value Meal you had for lunch that day. And you went to the gym for a grand total of fourteen times, which, of course, sounds great on paper. However, if the truth be known, you went three times a day for one torturous, unforgiving, possessed weekend, then once every Sunday for the next couple of weeks before finally giving up and writing your 1,500 samoleons off to experience. Again.

Since then, winter has slowly turned into spring and your exercise excuses have gone from, "Well, I can't walk/run/bike/swim today, because naturally it's snowing/sleeting/slushing," to "Well, I can't possibly walk/run/bike/swim today, because naturally now it's melting/mudding/sludging…"

Two weeks of Valentine's Day candy gave way to two months of Easter candy and, while you certainly

TOP 5
WAYS TO TELL YOU MAY NEED TO GO UP A BATHING SUIT SIZE

5 The salesgirl is really pushing the optional "cellulite cover-up."

4 Instead of a 2-piece, you now need a 4-piece.

3 You use the handicap dressing room, and you don't have a wheelchair.

2 One size fits all…doesn't.

1 You actually have to ask if the sizes stop at XXXLLL.

haven't *gained* any weight, you've gotten nowhere close to losing any, either. Of course, the annual treks to the beach, resorts, hotels, and backyard pools this summer can absolutely *not* be made in last year's dowdy bathing suit fashions, and so the annual trek to the mall, after the prerequisite two days of fasting, is eventually undertaken.

There, you are shocked to find, last year's swimsuit fashions weren't only dowdy, they were

According To a *Prevention* Magazine Survey:

60%
of women have dieted or are on a diet

44%
of women refuse to be photographed in a swimsuit

37%
of women won't play beach games while wearing swimsuits

downright Victorian compared to this year's! French cut, which formerly only gave you a mild case of "naked nerves," has now given way to "Biblical cut," as in the fig leaf variety.

While none but the fearless (not to mention "fat"-less) eighteen-year olds dare enter the "thong" section, one can't fail to notice that not much separates this year's crop of revoltingly revealing bikini bottoms and the so-called thongs except for the fact that yours have two centimeters more material and thus cost *twice* as much!

And so, fleeing to that staid section in the back usually populated by gray- and blue-haired seniors, despite the fact that you just turned thirty-one, you suddenly realize that bathing suit companies belong to two trains of thought: revealing and—revolting.

You are forced to decide between a slinky little two piece that would show more skin than a XXX movie, and a delightfully baggy one-piece suit the color of an overripe tangerine, complete with a frilly, aqua "skirt" to cover your bulging thighs and a matching rubber bonnet to keep your hair dry.

Naturally, you buy one of each. and, munching frantically on a fresh bag of Mrs. Field's cookies in the food court, carefully compile a list of valid reasons why you might wear the skirted one-piece.

As in: "Would you believe it, the one piece of luggage I lost on the way down here this year contained my real bathing suit. I had to borrow this one from my mother. Isn't it positively dreadful?"

To avoid such swimsuit issues next time, we've come up with a tempting tower of titillating tips to help you avoid a fitting room freak-out:

FITTING FRENZY

Finding the right fit in a bathing suit is often as grueling and unrealistic a task as seeking out the Holy Grail. (In Poughkeepsie!) Either the bottom is too small and the top's too big, or the bottom's hanging around your knees and the top has miraculously turned into a neon green choker necklace.

Surprisingly, several cutting-edge companies (in California, anyway) have actually started to sell their bottoms and tops separately. (Without you having to do the old switcheroo out of view of the surveillance cameras, that is.) Alas, until the rest of the country catches up, this is an eternal struggle that sees no end in sight.

However, if you do find a specialty store offering tops and bottoms à la carte, here are a few suggestions when choosing them separately:

TOPSY TURVY

There are several options when choosing a bikini top today. For starters, the "triangle" style of top offers a variety of pros and cons.

Naturally, it helps if you're eighteen and everything's still standing at "attention." This is because the triangle only covers the actual mammaries in question and leaves everything above, below, around the side, or in the middle to chance. The triangle comes complete with a spaghetti neck and back ties, and, while it "works" for all sizes, the recommended sizes for this top are from B to D cups.

The "classic twist" style of bikini top is nice for tanning because it's strapless. In addition, its flattering curves and sleek lines make smaller-cupped women look larger. (Always a plus.) And, with its back hook closure and snug form, larger-cupped women are held in snugly.

The attractive "butterfly" top features a spaghetti back and neck ties, adjustable sides, and a removable center loop. While this is good for all sizes, it is still best in the medium to large range. However, the real blessings of this beauty are the adjustable sides that allow you to make cups smaller or larger. (Is there anything better in this topsy-turvy world of yo-yo dieting and plastic surgery?)

The versatile "Parisian tie" style of bikini top, like so many others, offers a spaghetti neck tie with a convenient back hook closure and a removable center loop. And, with its center loop and spaghetti strap coming in different colors than the top itself, this unique top makes it possible to mix and match with numerous styles of bottom. Again, a further convenience when back loads tend to widen with age.

BOTTOM FEEDER

While buying the top of a bikini is hard enough, it's absolutely nothing compared to buying the bottom! Nothing evokes fear in a woman's heart more than squeezing her size twelve can into a size ten (or eight) bikini bottom. (Except, perhaps, looking at it in the fitting room mirror.) However, the following guide just might make what you take into the fitting room with you a little easier.

Fortunately, the "Brazilian" style bottom provides full coverage with a helpful "shape-it" seam in the rear. Of course, this sensible seam is meant to shape and lift your rear-end. Naturally, this is an extremely popular bottom and helps to complement many styles of figures, whether you're pear, apple, or peach.

Then again, on the cover-up scale, the "Rio" weighs in at a close second to the Brazilian and does offer some back coverage. At least, compared to the more daring thongs and g-strings. However, the accentuating dip just below your belly button is bound to show off any unsightly bumps or bulges. Still, this may be a small price to pay for having the extra added comfort of a backside that covers, well, your backside.

Another derriere development on the bathing suit brigade includes the tonga. This delightful little number comes in a wide variety of colors and styles and is the answer to the same old French cut or wide bottom routine. Somewhere between a thong and a traditional bikini, the tonga provides some back coverage and dips pleasantly just below your belly button.

Naturally, the thong offers you minimal back coverage and yet another low front dip. Once controversial, these daring little numbers have mellowed somewhat over the years and are now standard fare on beaches and beside pools across the country. Naturally, thongs aren't for everybody. With a backside that's often more revealing than its frontside, a few trips on the step machine might be in order before actually stepping outdoors in one of these skimpy swimsuits.

Of course, the g-string offers no back coverage whatsoever. If you're an exhibitionist who thinks thongs and tongas are for wimps, this veritable Band-Aid with straps is right up your (back) alley. On the other hand, if you've never even considered visiting a nudist colony, you might want to steer clear of this style. On the up side, they are very adjustable and fit most sizes.

Hold on, however. All is not lost. A relatively new kid on the bathing suit block is here to save the day. Trunks without a doubt provide the most coverage while still appearing as an attractive alternative to the all-encompassing one-piece. In addition, these "girl" trunks, which look similar to boy's "baggies," provide plenty of flexibility and are excellent for active women.

ONE IS THE "ONLIEST" NUMBER

Of course, frustrated by tops and bottoms, spaghetti straps and tongas, the good, old one-piece is an option many women (there's a reason we didn't use the word "girls") settle on after numerous fitting room fights with themselves, not to mention their butts and thighs.

Naturally, you should order your one-piece according to your dress size. However, unlike dresses, a one piece should never be

Swimwear Simplicity

As if picking out summer swimwear wasn't already difficult enough, those brilliant bikini builders have gone and made their sizes almost unintelligible. Not anymore! See the chart below (works for most brands) for an itsy-bitsy, teeny-weeny translation:

If Your Dress Size Is:	Your Swimwear Size Is:
1 to 2	XS/Petite
2 to 4	S
6 to 8	M
8 to 10	L
12 to 14	LL
16	1-X
18	2-X

allowed to sag or groan, bunch or droop. After all, just because it's not showing off your belly button and butt cheeks doesn't mean you get to walk around in a Lycra muumuu. Remember that just because you're no longer sixteen and anorexic doesn't mean that you forgo fashion and style for comfort and cover up.

Fortunately, today's bikini builders realize that women still buy bathing suits after their high school graduation. This means that modern one-pieces don't have to be a simple straight up and down affair. Today such frills as buttons, stripes, bows, and mesh necklines are standard on many styles of one-piece bathing suits and don't leave you feeling like such an Olive Oyl each time you dare to dip your foot in the pool or stroll the beach!

C. Y. A. (COVER YOUR ASS)

To provide the finishing touches to one's swimwear decision, don't overlook the oft-neglected cover up. After all, just because your grapefruit and coffee ground diet is working great *this* week, that doesn't mean you won't fall off the wagon with a week-long donut and Budweiser binge later on in the month. In such cases a cover up can mean the difference between hitting the beach and hiding inside.

Today, of course, your cover up options are better than ever before. Black mesh, silver Spandex, tie-dyed wraps, and shimmering Saran Wrap plastic numbers have usurped the old standbys like terry cloth and T-shirts. Funky designs, seashell buttons, and matching flip-flops or carry-alls combine to make this new breed of cool cover ups an attractive alternative to simply wrapping a towel around your sunburned self and sprinting back to your car.

FAVORITE BATHING SUIT COVER-UPS

- Sarong
- Muumuu
- Jean cut-offs
- Mesh cover-up
- Lycra
- T-shirt
- Mini-shorts
- Beach towel
- Terry-cloth anything

CELLULITE PLIGHT

Forget contraception, the remote control, and taking out the trash, the major dispute between men and women during the 21st century will undoubtedly be something much more sinister: cellulite. As in, "Why do women have it, and men don't…"

> **Cell'u•lite, n.** is the name given to the lumpy, irregular fatty deposits that appear as dimpled skin around women's hips, buttocks, and thighs. Cellulite begins to form during puberty, but it's not always noticeable on younger women because their skin is more supple.

HOLD THE (COTTAGE) CHEESE

You have no idea how the big fight started, except maybe for the fact that you walk a little more slowly than your girlfriend of three months does. This, coupled with her decision to wear a surprisingly skimpy pair of aptly named "shorts" for your weekly Sunday stroll around the park, an occasion that usually marked the highlight of your romantic weekends together. Or, at least, of the clothed variety anyway.

"Is it too much to ask that you look at me when I talk to you?" she had snapped, out of the blue, halfway through your week-end-ly constitutional. Although, in fact, you were actually in the middle of telling *her* something about work.

"S-s-sure, hey, great," you had stammered, stretch-walking like a giraffe just to catch up to her. "I love looking at your beautiful face. Can I finish my story now?"

Again, several minutes later when you had once again fallen behind to watch an old man feeding the ducks, she had actually turned around and walked backwards until you caught up with her.

MYTHS ABOUT CELLULITE

Myth: Cellulite only happens to overweight women.
Truth: Even very slim women can have areas of cellulite on their thighs, buttocks, and hips.

Myth: Cellulite is a natural part of aging.
Truth: While it can worsen with age, you don't have to sit back and accept it.

Myth: Cellulite is not serious and it won't get any worse.
Truth: If you don't take any action against it, the appearance of cellulite will usually get worse over time.

Myth: Strict dieting alone will eliminate cellulite.
Truth: On its own dieting cannot get rid of cellulite. In fact, strict dieting is more likely to eventually increase your body fat percentage.

"What is wrong with you today?" she asked, rolling her eyes and waiting until you were even with her to turn around and walk normally again.

"Hey, sorry," you say. "I didn't know this was a race. I thought we were supposed to be relaxing. Geez."

"Yeah, sure," she snaps, now watching your feet and timing hers to recreate the same footsteps, even leading off with the same foot as you do until your pace becomes a perfectly even left, right, left, right. "It must be easy to relax when you're not lugging a carton of cottage cheese around on the back of each thigh!"

"What?" you ask, stopping in your tracks and enraging her all the more, as she has to backtrack again just to keep facing you. "Cottage cheese? Thighs? What are you *talking* about?"

"Yeah, right," she sneers, her hands reaching to tug down at her shorts, which you happen to enjoy if only because they *are* so revealing. "Like you haven't been disgusted by my cellulite all morning. That's why you're walking so slow and being so quiet. You're thinking of ways to dump me!"

You laugh, but only quickly, judging by the hurt expression on her suddenly irrational face, that it was the wrong move. Instead you try to circle around her and get another look at what you had always considered her long, slender, exceptionally firm legs.

Of course, like the proverbial tiger chasing its tail around a tree, she counters your every move until the two of you look like you're performing some energetic mating ritual.

"Just stop it," she shouts, finally tiring of the cat and mouse games and sitting down on a patch of grass. "It's not my fault I haven't done the laundry yet this week and these were my only pair of clean shorts. Otherwise I would have worn the longer pair and you wouldn't have to be subjected to my disgusting fat pockets!"

You deny, you encourage, you console, you compliment, you soothe, you even lie, yet none of these sensitive tactics serve to calm her paranoid delusions that she is freakishly obese, if only in the all-important area of the backs of her thighs.

Carefully, you point out the fact that, after more than several lustful tumblings across the landscape of

HIP TIPS

Follow these tips to improve the appearance of your cellulite . . .

Drink water:
A steady intake of water helps to flush out toxins from your body and generally improves your metabolism.

Eat fiber rich foods:
Fiber is essential for healthy digestion and plays an important role in eliminating wastes. Make fruit, vegetables, and whole grain cereals a major part of your diet.

Reduce dietary fats:
While some dietary fat is essential to a healthy body, we all know it is all too easy to have excessive amounts in our diet.

her studio apartment, in various stages of undress and complete and utter nakedness, you've seen every inch of her well-proportioned body in sunlight, moonlight, and even mood lighting. And despite all of this, never once have you found an inch of her to be anything less than perfect.

"Oh, God," she groans, missing the point entirely, "don't remind me! It's just not fair. You can wear anything you want and never have to worry about it. Guys just don't *get* cellulite. It's like a curse on women. And for what?

"What did we do to deserve it? Menstruation, menopause, and childbirth weren't enough? We had to be blessed with lumpy, fatty, dimpled deposits on the most visible part of our anatomies as well?"

By now folks nearby can hear and her lips are trembling in what, through several tear-jerking dinners and sad movie dates, you have come to realize are her "pre-crying jag" jitters. In a moment of sheer panic, you suddenly heft up your favorite T-shirt and pinch the slowly widening "love handles" you'd noticed creeping over your belt loops lately.

"What about *these*?" you point out, pinching the frighteningly flabby patches for emphasis. "I don't notice you lugging any of *these* around on that tiny waist of yours, now do I?"

Going you one better, she quietly extends her arms and jiggles them slightly, expecting you to be shocked by the nearly invisible way the fleshy part of her arms only slightly, ever-so-slightly, wiggles.

"Oh, yeah," you one-up her, still raising your shirt and bending over just enough so that your tiny beer belly creases into several fleshy, unflattering wrinkles,

TOP 5

SIGNS YOUR CELLULITE PROBLEM'S GOTTEN OUT OF HAND

You've quit wearing "support hose" and gone straight to duct tape.

Borden asks you to pose nude for their new cottage cheese poster.

The sound of your thighs rubbing together is much louder than your stomach rumbling.

"Garter belts? Try fan belts!"

Titleist is doing research on your thighs for their new line of golf ball dimples.

• • • • • • • • • • • • • •

and finally evokes the tiniest of laughs from her adorable little face.

"And what about *this*?" you ask before turning around and wiggling your decidedly ample, of late, backside.

"And how about *this*?" you continue to query, arching your face into your neck and exposing more chins than you have fingers.

By now your girlfriend is rolling with laughter, all thoughts of cellulite gratefully erased from her short-term memory. Only now it's *you* who is depressed. After all, you've never actually taken the time to examine the many unflattering ways your body has changed since you quit playing college ball and settled down into a sedentary job in a towering office building downtown.

"Let's go eat," you announce sullenly, pulling her now-smiling form off of the ground and suddenly realizing that you are winded from the effort. "And don't you *dare* walk behind me."

Reduce salt intake:
Salt contributes to water retention, so avoid foods that are high in sodium.

Exercise regularly:
Focus on exercise that is using your whole body such as walking, swimming, and sports such as tennis. Simple exercises to tone your cellulite "problem areas" can also help.

DISASTROUS DIET DRUGS

So, worn down by your lifelong war with the "Battle of the Bulge," you've finally decided to circumvent the enemy's left "flank" and resort to "chemical warfare" in the form of those ever-present, ever-available, ever-promising diet drugs. But before you're two sizes smaller than your current one, try reading the fine print on the *back* of the pill box instead of admiring the scantily-clad hottie in the string bikini on the front…

SLIM (NOT SO) FAST

"That's it," you have finally decided (again) after yet another weekend of dining out, dining in, and dining "in between" before trying to slip into yet another pair of business slacks that don't quite fit anymore come Monday morning. "It is time to go on a diet. Once and

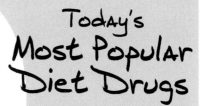

Today's Most Popular Diet Drugs

Acutrim (phenylpropanolamine)
Dexatrim (phenylpropanolamine)
Tenuate (diethylpropion)
Mazanor (mazindol)
Sanorex (mazindol)
Fastin (phentermine)
Ionamin (phentermine)
Preludin (phenmetrazine)
Bontril (phendimetrazine)
Plegine (phendimetrazine)
Adipost (phendimetrazine)
Dital (phendimetrazine)
Dyrexan (phendimetrazine)
Melfiat (phendimetrazine)
Prelu-2 (phendimetrazine)
Rexigen Forte (phendimetrazine)
Didrex (benzphetamine)
Prozac (fluoxetine)

for all. Period. End of story. I mean it—this time. I'm serious!

"And, now that I've made such a healthy decision, I think I deserve to have one last 'breakfast blowout' à la Dunkin' Donuts. Now, does one dozen equal a blowout, or should I make it two?"

Of course, you have no cause to feel all alone. Dieting in America is big business. Big with a capital "B." Fitness magazines, diet books, workout videos, Lycra, Spandex, weight loss drugs, and free weights all combine to form a multi-billion dollar industry whose coffers are growing "fat" off of corpulent citizens just like yourself.

And, while most diet products, all the way from

> *"One cannot think well, love well, sleep well, if one has not dined well."*
>
> — Virginia Woolf

fat-free shakes to Thigh-Be-Gone Cellulite Removal Cream and Stain Remover implore you, as required by most state laws, to "...consult a physician before beginning any new weight-loss plan," most are betting, and betting "heavily," that you won't.

After all, any doctor with a medical degree from any place other than The Quack and Grifter School of Licensed Doctorology will gladly give you the "skinny" on diet pills, with relish. In fact, most will tell you in no uncertain terms that taking a handful of diuretics in the morning and washing them down with a mouthful of laxatives at night is not exactly a prudent way to shed pounds. Let alone keep them off for any reasonable amount of time.

Which is precisely the reason why most diet pills are sold over the counter these days. No messy, i.e. legal, prescriptions needed here. Just cold, hard cash and the willingness to shed excess pounds. (Not to mention—money.)

Gone are the days when pharmacists proudly referred to a single cramped corner of one lowly shelf crammed with Dexatrim and Tab as their "One-Stop Diet Center." Nowadays the competition for Slim-Fast shelf space is as fierce as that once reserved for breakfast cereals.

In fact, modern department store Diet Centers often overflow from one bowling lane sized aisle into two, hawking everything from Slim Fast bars to weight belts, with everything from laxatives, stimulants, and cotton balls crammed in between.

The centerpiece of such aisles, however, is without a doubt the gleaming, shimmering, prepackaged rows (and rows and rows and rows) of diet pills. Like lollipops in a candy store, they scream at your slimline sensibilities with high-resolution pictures gracing their glossy covers. And, whether their box-top model is a 98-lb. weakling holding up his former pair of tent-size pants or a streamlined sister sporting legs for miles and poking ribs, their claims of "magical," "extraordinary," and "miraculous" weight loss are nothing less than

TOP-10 CDs
TO LISTEN TO BEFORE DIETING

10. Mos Def – *Ms. Fat Booty*

9. Bill Cosby – *Fat Albert*

8. Bullocks – *Fat, Old & Useless*

7. Paul Woodcock Band – *Fat White Weirdo In A Cadillac*

6. Beauty School Dropout – *Teasing The Fat Kids*

5. Shawn Colvin – *Fat City*

4. Rev W. Leo Daniels – *Too Fat To Get To Heaven*

3. Toy Dolls – *Fat Bob's Feet*

2. Hot Damn – *Big Fat Lover*

1. Skulker – *Too Fat For Tahiti*

TOP-10 CDs
TO LISTEN TO WHILE DIETING

10. Kingpin Skinny Pimp – *Skinny But Dangerous*

9. Robby & Friends – *Skinny Dipping*

8. Mephisto Odyssey – *Catching the Skinny*

7. Joe Tex – *Skinny Legs & All*

6. Three Crosses – *Skinny Flowers*

5. Big Boys – *Skinny Elvis*

4. Kofy Brown – *Skinny & Tight*

3. Skinny Boys – *Skinny Boys*

2. Taylor Barton – *Skinny Kat*

1. Strung Out – *Skinny Years (Before We Got Fat)*

amazing in themselves. Yet what lies inside of these Pandora's boxes full of so much hopped-up hope? The answer, unfortunately, is not very much.

Not much that can help you lose weight anyway:

For most over-the-counter products are a hodgepodge of diuretics, stimulants, and laxatives that, if anything, lead to a temporary loss of water weight—and a good case of the jitters—but won't lead to any long-term changes in your weight or metabolism. More important, many of these weight loss aids have dangerous side effects.

For instance, caffeine, a major component of many such drugs, is actually a diuretic and central nervous system (CNS) stimulant. It increases urinary output, heart rate, and blood pressure. Of course, caffeine does have some positive effects. For example, it enhances the effect of analgesics such as aspirin. However, the only way caffeine will help you lose weight, and only temporary water weight at that, is by the fact that you may urinate a bit more often than usual. In fact, if you exceed two cups of coffee a day, you may experience increased heart rate and palpitations.

Benzocaine, another diet drug diva, is a local anesthetic that alters taste sensation by numbing taste buds (and everything else) in the mouth. Period. All you can expect from this drug is a temporary (as in, a few minutes) suppression of the urge to put something in your mouth. Not to mention a numb tongue. If all you want is something in your mouth, go for sugar-free gum instead.

Ephedra, otherwise known as Ma Huang, is a plant that contains the active ingredient ephedrine, another CNS stimulant. Ephedrine acts on the appetite control center of the brain, the hypothalamus, suppressing the desire to eat. Like all CNS stimulants, ephedrine stimulates the heart and causes blood vessels to constrict, increasing blood pressure and heart rate.

Among its most common side effects are nervousness, headaches, insomnia, and heart palpitations. All you can expect from this disastrous diet drug is a temporary suppression of appetite, a racing heart, and clear nasal passages and lungs. (Ephedrine is also a decongestant and bronchodilator.)

Don't fall for the "all-natural" sales pitch, either. Ephedra's active ingredient is still a drug, and shouldn't be used as a weight loss aid or energy booster.

While there are certainly more scientific-sounding diet drugs out there, and surely new ones will continue to plague Diet Centers in the future, this brief sampler of today's main diet drug ingredients should serve to convince you that, in dieting as in everything else, moderation is the key.

After all, if "breakfast blowouts" consisting of donuts, pastries, or entire Kentucky Fried chickens are a tradition at the start of every single one of your diets, you might want to consider not dieting at all.

You're sure to lose some weight that way….

TOP 5 SIGNS YOUR DIET DRUGS MAY BE WORKING TOO WELL

You just don't have the energy to throw up after every meal like you used to.

Your 7-year-old niece is tired of you borrowing her outfits.

The DMV keeps calling to ask if you want to become an organ donor "before it's too late."

You call a breath mint "dessert."

Sally Struthers wants you for her next commercial.

COMMON SCENTS

In the ever-heady world of over-the-counter beauty products, as opposed to those found on the black market, that is, perhaps no experience is as petrifying as searching for a new perfume. For it's not just the idea of plunking down most of a hundred dollar bill for a beauty product that will change the way you and, indeed, others will think about you. At least, until you change your mind and choose another one, that is. Indeed, it's the actual purchasing of perfume that gives modern day scent-shoppers the cosmetic chills!

After all, it's not as if one can simply run out to the local convenience store and zip into the perfume aisle as if picking out a gallon of milk on the way home. Oh, no. Shopping for perfume is an event, much like buying a new car or home.

Indeed, the competition for your perfume purchase is often just as fierce. Cosmetics counter clones working on commission and clad in faux-doctor's cloaks vie for your attention as intensely as any real estate broker or car salesman (not to mention carnival barker) would. It's just that their high heels, nametags, and sophisticated airs serve to make you feel even more intimidated.

It doesn't help that throughout your scent-search you are surrounded by glossy, glowing, well-lit, airbrushed, touched up, and life-size images of stunning models like Estée Lauder's Elizabeth Hurley, who subliminally warns you that, if you choose *not* to buy the scent she's hawking, you'll never get another date again.

Add to this the extremely secretive tactic of not putting price tags on (naturally) the most pricey perfumes, such as Chanel No. 5 and Calvin Klein's newest unisex experiment. Not only does one appear to be the consummate amateur by having to ask, "Yes, excuse me, how much is that bottle of Dior's latest scent? No, uhhm, not that one. The one right there.

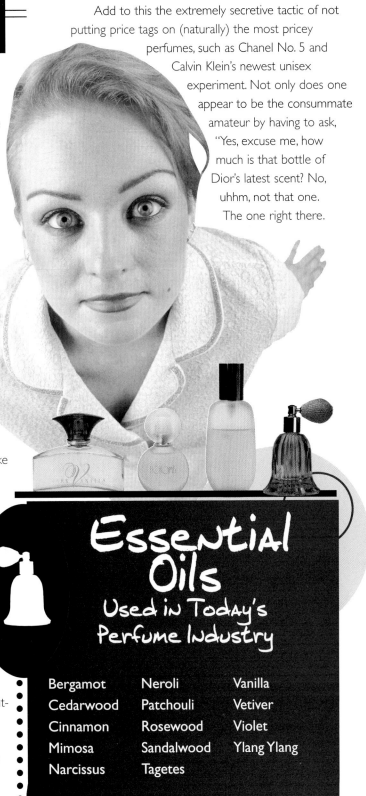

Essential Oils
Used in Today's Perfume Industry

- Bergamot
- Cedarwood
- Cinnamon
- Mimosa
- Narcissus
- Neroli
- Patchouli
- Rosewood
- Sandalwood
- Tagetes
- Vanilla
- Vetiver
- Violet
- Ylang Ylang

"complimentary" gift package for another ten or twenty bucks.

Of course, modern technology has started to work for the savvy cosmetics consumer in a variety of ways that combine to make purchasing perfume slightly less petrifying than in previous years.

For one thing, e-commerce and cosmetics super-sites like eve.com and ibeauty.com allow you to shop for cosmetics from the comfort of your own home. Naturally, this means no snobby salesgirls, no sneeze-causing samples sprayed up your nose on a continual basis, and no shame in asking for a perfume's price, since it's labeled right there in blue and white hyperlink.

However, unlike department stores that have earned the major cosmetics conglomerate's trust over years of dependable treatment, not all perfumes are available on all sites, and some of the biggest names aren't available anywhere except the traditional department store or boutiques.

Naturally, this is subject to change and the exponentially evolving nature of the Internet might make the above sentence obsolete faster than you could read it. Still, this revolutionary form of cyber-scent-shopping might just leave you surprisingly—unsatisfied. After all, conditioned to the cruel realities of the cosmetics counter, shopping with ease might be a little too—easy.

No, no—the *smallest* one."

But when the price still amounts to what you paid for your last dishwasher, you're either forced to buy it and starve for the next fiscal quarter, or decline and slink over to the clearance aisle for a go at last year's Everaude holiday gift set.

Naturally, most perfume buyers enlist common "scents" to help them budget for just such a periodic purchase, but even then they resent being treated like "working girls" when they don't choose the biggest bottle or opt for the

Perfume, according to all of those artsy ads anyway, is supposed to be all about emotion. And where's the emotion in clicking a few cute icons and keying in your credit card number?

Mail-order catalogs have always been an option for wardrobe-weary perfume shoppers. And, unlike the Internet, they actually involve living human beings at the other end of those convenient 1-800 phone numbers. The catalogs are attractive, well-organized, easy-to-understand and often include those handy scratch and sniff samples for private smelling.

Still, pictures are often deceiving and, unless you're willing to actually measure out ounces or liters, you might just get stuck with a lot less perfume than you bargained for.

Finally, of course, there's the unspeakable act of running into some low-rent, chain department store and picking up a bottle or two of your favorite designer rip-off, imitation perfumes at a mere fraction of the cost of the real thing.

Surprisingly, imitators do a passable job of cloning colognes and, for the price of just one of the "real" bottles of perfume, you can snap up a year's supply of

the knock-off. Naturally, this practice is anathema to the vain world of the fashion conscious, but the fashion "unconscious" don't seem to mind all that much and therefore the rip-off business is doing rip-roaring numbers.

Of course, there is always the fear, even among the so-called fashion fearless, that one's friends or even worse, one's date, might discover those numerous and jumbo bottles of Chanel No. 15 and Mrs. Vanilla Fields scattered across one's nightstand or vanity. Yet, with a simple purchase of just one of the real bottles (either that, or a quick trip to the dumpster behind the local Saks Fifth Avenue) a quick refill of an actual empty is a super scent solution.

This, of course, is the adult version of buying generic cereal and pouring the $1.99 Crispy Crunchies or Citrus Rocks into the old Captain Crunch or Fruity Pebbles boxes. But isn't fashion all about staying young anyway?

Regardless of how one chooses to solve this perplexing perfume problem, however, never lose sight of the fact that, when it comes to consuming cosmetics, never lose sight of your common scents.

> "To attract men, I wear a perfume called 'New Car Interior'."
> —Rita Rudner

MAKEUP MATTERS

Blush. Lip Gloss. Mascara. Foundation. Eyeliner. Lipstick. Rouge. Where would we be without any of them? Besides cowering behind closed doors with the lights off and a paper bag over our heads, that is…

Makeup is as integral a part of fashion today as any designer, synthetic material, diet pill, high heel, Wonderbra or supermodel could ever hope to be. After all, if we can barely get out the front door without a full hour at the well-lit, magnified vanity mirror, what good are any of those other things anyway?

Naturally, not everyone looks at the matter of makeup in quite the same way. Need proof? One quick trip to the DMV or ER should prove this hypothesis out thoroughly and without dispute. For while some women view makeup as a "means to an end," others' lengthy makeup sessions don't "end" until they look downright "mean"!

We all know that some women can

get through an entire day with nothing more than a clutch purse containing a simple compact and a tube of lipstick.

But why do others need a shopping cart full of Revlon's finest just to tiptoe out the door in the morning to snatch the Early Edition off the front stoop?

Many believe that one possible reason for this dimple dichotomy is upbringing. For while every little girl experiments with mommy's cosmetics case during her first session of "playing makeup," reactions to the experience vary from girl to girl. For instance, getting made up for the first time can be as fun and exciting for some as playing with dolls or having a tea party, while for others just cleaning all of that goop off of their face can nip that face-painting practice in the bud for evermore.

And while some mothers allow girls in junior high to go to school looking like streetwalkers straight out of last night's episode of *Cops*, other girls aren't allowed to wear makeup until they travel off to college and end up rooming with Avon's future Salesgirl of the Year.

Factors outside the home are often just as influential to future facial femme fatales as those inside, however. Naturally, the Brownies, 4-H, and Catholic schools all tend to frown on the practice of applying makeup before the age of, say, 47 or so. And few supermodels accepting their "Face of the Year" awards are ever heard thanking their high school soccer coach for "—helping me perfect my blush stroke."

Conversely, young members of the "He-Woman MAN Hater's Club" have little else to do but perfect their lipstick longings and cover-up curiosity together in their tree forts turned cosmetic counters.

Peers are another big Max Factor factor. Few schoolgirls are confident enough to go it alone through the hallowed halls of academia, and most necessarily fall into one Clinique clique or another. And, while the library might be their first choice when doing a report on George Washington, teen magazines are *de rigueur* for finding out the latest fashion facts, the first of which is often makeup.

Top Makeup Companies

Cover Girl	Max Factor
Maybelline	Bloom
Revlon	Neutrogena
Clinique	Avon
Elizabeth Arden	Merle Norman
Lancôme	Oil of Olay
Coty	Mary Kay
Estée Lauder	Wet 'n' Wild
L'Oreal	

Then, of course, comes the entire reason for wearing makeup in the first place: boys. And, just like adults, there will always be the girls who opt for the "less is more" philosophy and rely on their inner charms to attract the boy of their dreams. Yet there are even more who dip into their beauty bag of tricks to snag their man, painting on buckets of blush and eye shadow in the hopes of attracting that all important second, third or fourth look.

As women mature, one would hope, so does their facial fashion sense.

However, television stars such as Mimi from *The Drew Carey Show* are proof to the contrary. And while it's relatively simple to remind a female friend that her suede tennis shoes "might not" match her satin evening gown, it's quite another

TOP FIVE MOVIES TO AVOID WHEN APPLYING MAKEUP

Big Top Pee Wee
Circus Boy
Clownhouse
Circus of Horrors
Killer Clowns from Outer Space

to let a beauty buddy know that her face looks like something straight out of a Ringling Bros. Circus poster.

Naturally, old age does not have to be a factor in matriarchal makeup matters. No one who has ever visited a nursing home can deny that, quite to the contrary, makeup seems to accumulate along with one's years and broken hip bones. Which is not necessarily to suggest that the makeup-wearer learns to apply it any better in their golden years, either!

So there you have it. The facts are in: makeup matters! After all, we've all seen those "Actors Exposed: Candid snapshots of celebrities first thing in the morning" issues of *National Enquirer* in the checkout line down at the grocery store. And while we've all felt grossed out that anyone would actually go out in public looking like that, at the same time, we've all been secretly pleased that even the "beautiful people" look like crap in the morning. Now haven't we?

SURVEY

EVEN MEN ADMIT TO APPLYING MAKEUP WHILE DRIVING

A new survey of car owners reveals that many drivers are doing everything but driving while behind the wheel. The survey conducted by Pennzoil reveals that:

- 46 percent of women and 4 percent of men say they've applied makeup while driving.
- 42 percent of drivers admit to reading a book while driving.
- 26 percent have changed their clothes while in motion.
- 25 percent of drivers have actually styled their hair while the car is in motion.
- 8 percent shave while driving.

And now for the gross stuff: 10 percent of drivers pluck their nose hairs while driving and 7 percent floss their teeth!

TOP 5

SIGNS YOU USE TOO MUCH MAKEUP

5 You recently sold your king-size bed to make room for your king-size vanity.

4 People keep asking if it's true you were the inspiration for *Memoirs of a Geisha.*

3 You're getting a little sick of hearing, "A little early for Halloween aren't we?"

2 Revlon calls to thank you for "last quarter."

1 People keep asking, "How's Drew Carey?"

FASHION MAGS: VICIOUS OR VICTIM?

Fashion magazines have long been the scourge of the fashion industry. Especially those directed at young girls. For while the grown women who read *Cosmo* and *Elle* know that they're never going to look like Cindy, Tyra, or Nikki, the hormone-impaired teenyboppers who read *Seventeen* from cover to cover don't. Yet. (After all, they still think The Backstreet Boys can dance.)

The debate is simple. On one hand, you've got a bunch of hormone-engorged teenyboppers wanting to look like Sarah Michelle Geller and willing to do anything, with a capital "A," to do it. On the other, you have a bunch of corporate-run periodicals whose readership is well into six figures cashing in on their dreams, hopes, desires, and dietary imbalances.

And, in the middle, you have a lot of parents, relatives, teachers, social workers, and generally caring people who want to keep these two as far away from each other as possible.

An impossible feat, to be sure. After all, if today's teens can't cadge enough money out of mom's purse for the latest issue of *Teen*, then they'll just boost one at the local five and dime or, better yet, spend a few hours in the library taking notes on how to survive on nothing but celery and cotton balls or how to attract guys by acting dumber than them.

Of course, the publishers of teen "fashion" magazines state that they're doing nothing wrong. And, legally, they aren't. After all, they're providing a service. Teenage girls *want* to know how to dress, how to do their makeup, how to do their hair, how to date, how to use sanitary products, etc. All of which these magazines provide. Indeed, ad nauseum.

Naturally, it's not the actual content of the magazines that all of those parents, teachers, and socially conscious activists resent. (Although with titles like "How to Land the Stud of Your Dreams" and "Pimple Popping 101," what adult can read them?) No, it's the ads the magazines run, not to mention the models they use in their "bikinis of summer" or "sundresses of spring" layouts.

Girls so thin you can read the print on the opposing page through their rib cage. Girls with flawless (airbrushed) skin, flowing locks (all morning with a hairdresser), and breasts far beyond their years (not to mention cup-size).

So what effect do these fashion magazines have on our teenage girls? Time will tell. But for a glimpse into today's famished fashion future, read on to see how things could go differently with just a little *Teen Beat* debate:

SASSY SHENANIGANS

So it's a Friday night and your older sister, the "responsible" one, has asked you to baby-sit for her 13-year-old daughter, affectionately referred to in your family as "The Brat."

You tried to tell your sister you had a date, but that hasn't happened in over four months and she didn't buy it for a second. Besides, her marriage is on the rocks, again, and she thinks that if she and her husband could just have a nice, quiet dinner together without Eloise, "The Brat's" real name, they could finally patch things up. At least for another six months, anyway.

In short, girls whose beauty is unrealistic. (Not to mention unattainable for 95 percent of the teenyboppers admiring them.)

Still, here are all of these thin, airbrushed, flawless-skinned, beautifully dressed girls shopping in the mall with their similarly thin, airbrushed, flawless-skinned, beautifully dressed friends. Or fighting off hunks, studs, and dream boats at the school dance. Or winning the big cheerleading competition. Or graduating with honors.

Meanwhile, the girls reading them are at one of the most awkward stages of their lives. Taller than the boys. Chunkier than the models they adore. Smarter than the boys they long for. And doing their best to look like somebody, anybody, other than themselves.

you're quite sure that she will do just as much damage in that room as she had to your family room, but at least she'll be out of earshot for upwards of an hour or two, if you remember your teen years correctly.

Besides, you can finally turn off the excruciatingly dismal music videos she'd turned on, at full blast of course, two seconds after she walked in.

Surprisingly bored with the sudden silence, save for the demonic cackles coming from your bedroom (no doubt The Brat has discovered your "secret sensuality" compartment under your bed and is describing each and every sordid item in hilarious detail to her boyfriend), you decide to do a little snooping of your own.

Expecting to find crack cocaine in The Brat's rumpled backpack, you expose instead a source of so much comfort during your youth: simple, innocent, teen mags.

"Well," you say sarcastically, "When you put it that way…"

Ten minutes later your older sister is downstairs in the parking lot honking as you wave to The Brat, who promptly gives you the finger before trudging up the three flights of stairs to your Brownstone apartment. Naturally, you do the same to your sister as she gleefully peels out to meet her husband at some cheap motel rendezvous across town, no doubt.

The Brat pops her bubble gum, drinks all of your soda, and manages to turn your entire apartment upside down, all in her first five minutes upstairs. What once used to look like a print ad for Pier One Imports now just looks like a plain old pier, as in dock, and you pour yourself a stiff one in preparation for one very, very long night.

Finally, The Brat asks to use the phone to call her boyfriend and, despite the fact that he could live in Singapore for all you know, you gladly volunteer the phone in your bedroom. Of course,

"Oh, how sweet," you think to yourself as glass shatters in the other room. "She *is* normal after all."

Settling in, you open up a glossy copy of *Teen* and sigh contentedly. Until you run across the first, full page print ad, that is. For a moment, you're so shocked by the anorexic model wearing a pair of Hi-Tops (and not much more, you add prudishly!) that you flip to the front cover just to make sure you're not reading some story about world starvation in *National Geographic!*

But, as you delve further, you realize that almost all of the ads feature young, barely pubescent girls who look to be teetering on the verge of starvation. Knowing that The Brat might not appreciate your direct comments

BOYS! SEX! CLOTHES! DIETS! MAKEup! MOVIES! SHOPPING!

on the subject, you reach for a pen.

Quickly, without guilt, but instead with a sense of parental righteousness you've never actually felt before, you start adding your own comments to the all-but anorexic perfume, jewelry, fashion, and feminine hygiene ads.

"Not normal!" you scribble next to one particularly emaciated modelette.

"Too, too thin," you write next to the sunken cheekbones of another.

"Belongs in a hospital."

"Gross!"

"Unbelievably unhealthy."

"Is this what boys want? A swizzle stick

in a prom dress? Not any worth their salt."

The admonishments pile up in the magazine's margins like so many dirty jokes in a junior high textbook until, finally, you hear the phone slam down in the other room and The Brat's surprisingly heavy footsteps clomping toward you. Hiding the pen behind your ear and slipping the glossy teen fashion mags back inside her battered backpack, you do your best to look casual.

"Mom buzzed through on your call waiting," she announces, snatching up her pack and zipping it tightly. "She said that the date's a bust and dad's bringing her home early.

"It's too bad, too," she adds sarcastically. "We were just starting to bond! I'll wait downstairs. Don't get up, I can show myself out."

With that, The Brat heads for the door. Before she gets there, you add one last hopeful, parting shot: "Listen, sometimes…when you're upset about things, it helps to read those silly teen fashion magazines. Sometimes…what they say between the lines…can really show you the light."

Not even bothering to turn around, she flips her hair in your direction and exits in a flurry of tennis shoes and fresh bubble gum. You watch from your balcony, waving when your sister pulls up tearfully and grudgingly lets her unsympathetic daughter inside the car. Peeling away without a backwards wave, you lock the window and retire early, grateful for the comfort of your own glossy, fashion mags to put you to sleep.

Settling in, you open your new Cosmo, only to find it defaced by, who else, The Brat.

"Yeah, right," your niece has scribbled using the expensive Parker pen by your phone, which, you suddenly realize, is missing! "Who expects us to look like *this*?"

"Has she eaten this week?" The Brat has scribbled next to another model who, indeed, looks like nothing more than a well-dressed, airbrushed internment camp survivor.

The list of scribbled comments continues through to the end of *Cosmo* and on into the other magazines by your bed: *Glamour, Elle, Bazaar*, etc.

"I guess we have more in common than I thought,"

you think, hoping The Brat is safe in bed by now and perusing her own graffiti'd glossies.

And, if not, there was always tomorrow night. You are sure your sister will want one more chance at that loser husband of hers. Maybe, if you volunteer to baby-sit, you and The Brat can talk about the fashion industry's unrealistic expectations of modern women.

At least, it was worth a shot.

Chances are, you might even get your pen back!

TOP

5 SIGNS TEEN FASHION MAGS MAY HAVE HAD A NEGATIVE EFFECT ON YOU WHILE GROWING UP

Your constant use of the word "sassy."

Your unexplained crush on every member of Duran Duran.

Your irrational fear of quizzes.

You still think "Chachi" is hot.

You still buy a prom dress each spring.

6 SIX
ACCELERATED ACCESSORIES

Belts. Buckles. Shoes. Purses. Barrettes. Bow ties. No outfit, no matter how stunning or expensive, would be complete without the right accessories. Does this tie match this jacket? Are these earrings too much? After all, what's more fun? Spending a week shopping for the drop-dead dress? Or spending two weeks shopping for just the right pair of shoes to go with it?

Why, the need to accessorize dates all the way back to Biblical times.

What? You think Adam and Eve didn't check out the olive, plum, and apple leaves before they settled on the fig leaf? Naturally, buying accessories is a little like eating potato chips: It's hard to stop after just one.

Fortunately, today's funky fashions not only encourage artsy accessories, they practically demand them! From zebra-skinned sandal straps to beetle broaches, from chain mail handbags to temporary (or permanent) tattoos, the world of accelerated accessories has finally shifted into overdrive.

So now all that's left to do is pick out the perfect seatbelt! Hmm, let's see: satin or silk?

PERPLEXING PIERCINGS

Gone are the days when one could tell another's sexuality by whether or not their right ear was pierced (or left, depending on which rumor you'd heard last). In fact, many look back on the days of "above-the-neck-only" piercing as sheer nostalgia, as in, "Remember when little Billy only had his tongue, lip, ears, eyelids, and nostrils pierced? Boy, were *those* the good old days."

TOP SIGNS YOUR LOVER'S THINKING ABOUT PIERCING HIS/HER GENITALS

5 You keep finding your missing earrings in his underwear.

4 Her sudden interest in your wallet-chain.

3 He's replaced all of his zippers with Velcro.

2 She keeps asking you if you know any pirates.

1 His sudden fascination with magnets.

NAVEL ACADEMY

As a modern, free-spirited, twenty-something female, you have finally decided to take the plunge. As a devout follower of modern fashion, you feel you are duty-bound to join the ranks of the perkily pierced and endure, er, enjoy the boundless benefits of a sterilized piece of silver-plated metal sticking out of somewhere very sensitive upon your body. Voluntarily.

POPULARLY PIERCED PLACES (Don't try this at home!)

Eyebrow (middle, corner, whatever)
Earlobe (top, bottom, whatever)
Bridge (of the nose)
Nostril
Septum (cartilage separating the nostrils)
Lip (upper and lower)
Cheek (either side, both sides, whatever)

Tongue
Navel
Nipple (guys and girls)
Penis (guys only, ouch)
Labia (double ouch)
Clitoris (triple ouch!)

It's not because you want to, of course. But all of your friends have, most of your neighbors, everyone at work (whether they wear them into the office or not), and you're feeling most definitely unfashionable with only your six ear holes and their corresponding loops, spirals, studs, and crosses.

And so, calling in sick to work on an average old Wednesday, you look up "body piercing" in the yellow pages and, surprisingly, find several columns full of reputable "piercing practitioners."

Undaunted, you read between the lines and cross out those establishments A.) in the rougher parts of town, B.) with questionable names such as "Prickly Phil's Peter Piercers" and C.) that display young, nubile, seductive, half-naked temptresses with lead pipes sticking out of their ears in their quarter-page phone book ads.

It's not easy, but eventually you narrow your choices down to "Grandma's Attic: Body Piercing and Crocheted Planters" and "Two Tin Tiny's: Body Piercing for the Faint of Heart."

When a man who sounds more like the demon from *The Exorcist* than the wizened grandmother of seven answers the phone at "Grandma's Attic," you grab your purse and head to "Two Tin Tiny's" instead.

Nervously navigating the streets of downtown, you find Tiny's on the second floor of an old brownstone that boasts a dance class and a Korean grocer.

Surprisingly, there are no derelicts roving the streets with MD 20-20 in waxy paper bags, no hookers turning tricks in the alley, and no cop sirens heard during the four minutes that it takes you to find a decent parking space.

You walk upstairs and find a perfectly normal sized man named Phil in clean jeans and a denim shirt who asks you a few medical questions, makes you sign a brief release form, and then offers you his "portfolio" as he calls it, of his "work."

You browse through hundreds of semi-tasteful Polaroids boasting perfectly pierced belly buttons, nipples, lips, noses, eyelids, cheeks, vulvas, and two decidedly flaccid penises. Cringing at the latter, you admit to Phil that you're not quite sure *what* you want pierced.

"Are you gay?" he asks quite conversationally. "Do you want to be?" he continues when you shake your head emphatically. "Okay then," he sighs. "We'll skip the breasts, nose, lips, vulvas and, obviously, the penis. Unless—you have one? No? Didn't think so."

"Well, what's left then?" you ask him. For an answer, he pats your belly.

"Trust me," he says. "It's the least painful, the least obvious and, if you wear the right kind of peek-a-boo teddy—the *most* sexy."

Smiling shyly, you pay Phil up front and follow him out back. In a sterile "office" with hardwood floors and vertical blinds, he sets to work and talks about his pet cat, "Tiny," while you wince in anticipation.

Minutes later, he does something quickly with something sharp. Of course, owing to the fact that your eyes have been closed ever since he said the dreaded words "trust me," you have no idea what just happened.

As a result, however, you sit up slowly to feel a slight pulling sensation in your stomach region as you look down to see a glittering, inexpensive silver hoop dangling tastefully where once before there was only lint and a tiny, moon-shaped birthmark.

"All done," says Phil gently, handing you a mimeographed sheet of hygiene instructions, which you follow religiously until the one-month time period is up and you venture out on the town for your first post-piercing ladies night out.

The effect is instantaneous and—unsettling. Guys you would formerly have Maced (or at least pepper sprayed) upon first sight are now asking you to dance, boogie, mambo, and have their love child. Vampire boys and biker babes literally fight for your affections and, after half an hour of experiencing what you're sure it must feel like to have large breasts, you disappear into the crowded ladies room and quietly un-pierce yourself.

Temporarily, that is. Meanwhile your silver belly button ring rests innocently in a wad of tissue paper just inside your purse. (Until you get home, that is. Wouldn't want the hole to cave in so that you had to go back to Tiny's all over again!)

Returning to the dance floor as if invisible, just like the good old days, you enjoy the rest of the evening and write yourself a quick note before turning in for the night several hours later: "Shop for 'the right kind of peek-a-boo teddy'— A.S.A.P!"

No sense wasting your newfound popularity on the masses. Let them get to know you first before you hit them with your belly button boy magnet!

TATTOO
YOU!

If those salty sailors of old only knew what personal hygiene hell they'd wrought on today's modern parents, they might have smiled a lot more and pillaged a whole lot less. For tattoos have long since passed the point of fashion fad and have become instead a "fashion fixture." Indeed, tattoos are now something of a right of passage for today's modern youth, and even not-so-youth.

TATTOO
TIMELINE

Throughout history, tattooing has had a rather "checkered" past. The Greeks used tattooing for communication among spies and the Romans used tattoos to mark both criminals and slaves. Polynesians developed tattoos to mark tribal communities and rank, while the Japanese used tattoos to mark criminals.

As the 20th century dawned and brought with it a string of world wars, tattoos became known as travel markers. You could tell how many places a soldier had been by his abundance of, or lack of, tattoos. And, while today's proliferation of gang-bangers and Hells Angels continue to use tattoos to

Naturally, such tattoos tend to fall into several categories. Like their highly individualistic owners, no two tattoos are ever really alike. And, like samples in a do-it-yourself T-shirt store, they range in taste from extremely cute to just plain extreme. Some are downright cheap, while some cost as much as a Hepatitis-B vaccine. Some make Mom proud, while others are only suitable for more—intimate—viewing.

For instance, one tattoo titan has always been the "rebellious" tattoo. This brand of impish ink art is most often reserved for amateurs who yearn to brag about their tattoo, yet don't actually want it to ever interfere with future job interviews, marriage proposals, or appearances on national television.

This is typically the owner's first, and often only, tattoo. And, while it may represent something as dangerous as a fire-breathing dragon or as innocent as a smiley face, its owner will consider it the finest work of skin art this side of a 1980's Rolling Stones album cover. Until, that is, his rebelliousness wears off and he begins investing in those greeting card sized Band-Aids to cover it up with.

Accountants, bored housewives, and lifetime librarians, however, most often prefer the "secret" tattoo. Naturally, such skin stamps have a rather limited area of their owners' epidermis on which they can actually appear. Generally they are placed somewhere rather "private" and easily covered by most unmentionables, notably a conservative bra, tube sock, or pair of jockey briefs.

Secret tattoos range from the popular "rose and daisy" variety to the perverse "copulating aliens" ilk. While the buttocks would appear to be a natural place for such secretive tattoos, most "secret" tattoo wearers prefer somewhere more easily viewed by themselves, say in that hidden mirror in the secret compartment over that bed they keep down in the basement.

TODAY'S MOST POPULAR TATTOOS

Barbed wire around the forearm (à la Pamela Anderson)

Lightning bolts

Hearts

Celtic Symbols

Tribal armbands

Tweety Bird

Skulls

Oriental symbols (i.e. yin-yang, etc.)

Those damn Grateful Dead bears

Unicorns

Snakes

The "drunken" tattoo is another popular standby that never quite manages to lapse into extinction, thanks to the abundance of both alcohol and temporary insanity present in the world. While tattoo artists prefer to weave their creative craft on owners who truly appreciate and understand their underrated art, drunken tattoos are nonetheless a great way to pay the bills and still have a little fun at the same time. For not only are drunken tattoo-ees less critical of the finished product, but they're not bitching, wincing, wining, and moaning the whole time they're getting stuck by that scary electric needle, either.

Besides, it's a lot easier to convince an inebriated ink recipient to "shoot the works" and purchase the entire Loony Tunes collection of tattoos than it is the sober "victim."

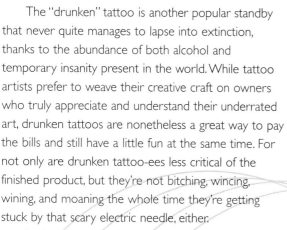

and erotic tattoos that allow the artist to explore his innermost feelings and desires, but he gets unlimited access to explore bare, naked flesh for hours at a time. Obviously, the recipient of a sexy tattoo enjoys it as well. Where else can such exquisite pain and beauty be experienced at the same time, and under such bright lighting to boot?

While some rednecks actually consider the Confederate flag a "sexy" tattoo, especially when it waves over the ever-widening expanse of their broadening butt-cheeks, most recipients are considerably more discerning. As its name implies, both the tattoo and its placement are equally sexy. Breasts, pubic regions, buttocks, and even genitals are the most popular areas to receive a sexy tattoo. Meanwhile, the

While the previous tattoos are more popular with their wearers, the "sexy" tattoo, however, is a favorite of the tattoo artist. Not only does it usually involve intricate

tattoos themselves are just as alluring.

Men tend to go "phallic" with their sexy tattoos, whether it's a pulsing python extending from their navel to their kneecap, or a fiery dragon carrying a nubile Amazon warrior and her huge sword. Women, on the other hand, gravitate to the softer side of sexy. A viny thorn wrapped around a rosy nipple, perhaps. Or a pastel Tweety Bird on the inner thigh. Either way, only the most special and intimate viewers, not to mention gynecologists, prison guards and rescue technicians, ever get to see the "sexy" tattoo.

The "artsy" tattoo is only sought after by the most cerebral of skin painters. These wondrous works of living art are usually elaborate affairs consisting of glorious full-color masterpieces produced by endless hours of blood, sweat, and tears. Literally. Since most sessions involve intense pain and concentration, they can't last too terribly long. Therefore, numerous sessions are often involved to complete these human masterpieces.

Not content with mere bicep billboards or barefoot broadcasts, artsy tattoo seekers usually get intensely inked on more expansive parts of their body, generally using their entire back, chest, or sometimes both, as a free-flowing flesh canvas.

Naturally, more skin means more ink, and often such elaborate tattoos become quite personal for both the tattoo-er *and* the tattoo-ee. Jungle scenes with roaring tigers, landscapes boasting of life-size palm trees, and dream sequences involving alien abductions are all popular

fodder for the "artsy" tattoo.

The "tattoo in progress," naturally, is a patchwork pursuit that evolves over time. Such tattoos often involve normal, everyday scenes from the wearer's life, such as a nasty divorce or particularly good ice cream cone. Naturally, such scenes aren't exactly "documentary," as often the wearer is depicted as a muscle-bound barbarian or glamorous fashion model cavorting through life in slinky negligee. Nonetheless, such personal paintings are a passionate affair that begin shortly after adolescence and continue until wrinkles, walkers, and hospital gowns begin to cover up all of that beautiful skin art.

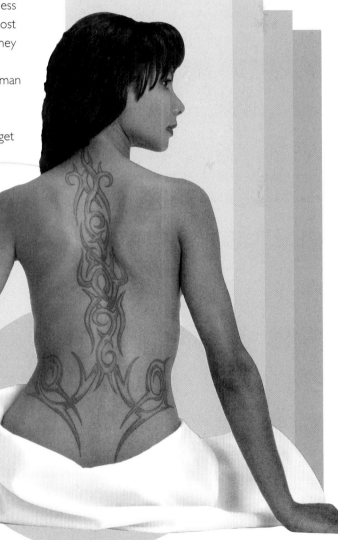

The "hardcore" tattoo is a variation of the "tattoo in progress," just with a little less commitment and a *lot* less consistency. For, while tattoos in progress represent a planned, lifelong commitment to telling a story, albeit with one's arms, chest, buttocks, and legs, the hardcore tattoo is a much more emotional, spontaneous undertaking.

Hardcore tattoos are not so-called because of their graphic nature, although such skin art often takes the form of bloody skulls or horrible monsters, but more from the intricacy involved in the tattoo itself. Anyone willing to sit through the pain involved in recording such intricate affairs as say, the infinite detail in the bark of a tree trunk or the tread of a monster truck tire, is naturally considered a "hardcore" individual.

Hardcore tattoos often take the form of dark, sinister canvasses involving snakes, skulls, bats, and other creepy things, but are portrayed so realistically that they tend to give the wearer the very same qualities as the art. For instance, a skinny, wizened biker with an old man's white beard and arms the size of toothpicks nonetheless becomes a sinister character when said arms contain graphic images of death, mayhem, menace, and destruction.

Of course, while few believe that the future of tattoos can possibly sustain the bright spotlight they currently enjoy, no one disputes the fact that tattoos, for better or worse, are here to stay.

HIPPER ZIPPERS

Once a modern generation's answer to the antiquated chastity belt, zippers have long since become yet another fashion accessory for the new millennium. From go-go boots to fanny packs, leather to lace, zippers have found their way onto places once considered formerly zipper-less.

In the old days, of course, we had buttons to keep our pants *up*, and zippers to keep our pants *closed*. But then came those darn button-flies and unemployed zippers had to find somewhere else to go. But where? How about on Michael Jackson's *Thriller* jacket? Or maybe the Boy Scouts could use some help keeping all of their pocket knifes and matchbooks zipped up. But then sandwich bags needed zippers, as did money belts, purses,

and even those funky new khaki pants that, with one zip (on each leg, of course) turn into those funky new cargo pants!

Nowadays, the zipper has more work than it can handle. So much work, in fact, that few zippers are even of the old school, stainless steel variety anymore. Modern zippers come from durable plastic that is more and more being upgraded to waterproof, fire proof, and, eventually, *There's-Something-About-Mary* proof.

But what happens when our love for zippers goes a little *too* far? Zip through the following story to find out:

Modern Zipper Materials

Brass

Oxide

Aluminum

Nickel

Polyester

Nylon

Molded Plastic

Delrin (a new type of plastic)

ZIP IT! ZIP IT GOOD!

You're not quite sure what to make of your most definitely modern girlfriend's most definitely modern birthday gift to you. You're quite sure, (she's dating *you*, isn't she?) that she's got a brain in her head. What you're unsure of is where she left it when she walked into whatever horror shop she chose to buy your birthday present in.

"I love it," you say dutifully, the candles on your cake still glowing. "What *is* it?"

"It's the hottest new thing," she shouts, pulling it out of the fancy gift box and displaying it across her outstretched arm like a waiter with an expensive bottle of wine in some fancy restaurant. "They're called Z-jeans. 'Z' as in zipper. There are zippers on the pockets,

zippers instead of buttons, zippers on each thigh, zippers behind each knee, even zippers along the sides in case you're wearing big boots and need to slip them on quickly."

"Super," you joke. "They'll go great with my *Thriller* jacket. How thoughtful."

"Listen, you," she says, throwing a lighthearted punch that almost blows the candles out on the cake. "This is *the* fashion trend this year. In fact, it's so hot, it even came with a zippered baseball cap, a zippered wallet, and a zippered fanny pack."

"Awesome," you say sarcastically. "Did it come with a zipper for your mouth? Because if you say 'zipper' one more time I'll throttle you!"

She laughs and insists you try them on right away.

"All the hot, male models are wearing them," she insists, cutting the cake in the kitchen while you change out of your perfectly acceptable, one-zippered pair of old jeans into this newfangled zipper explosion. "I saw them on the *E! Fashion Report*," she goes on in between licking her fingers free of frosting. "And on MTV's *House of Style* and they're *all* over the Internet. I'm telling you, you'll look so hot in those things you'll be irresistible. Which reminds me, why did I buy them for you?"

"I have no clue," you mutter to yourself from the other room, having just finally found a temporary combination of quickly forgettable zippers that actually lets you inside your gift. "They're the stupidest things I've ever *seen*!"

"What's that, dear?" she asks amid the clatter of plates and forks.

"I said," you recover quickly. "I think I saw them in a *magazine*!"

"Oh, wow," she squeals as you zip your way out into the living room, the clatter of teeny, tiny zipper handles nearly deafening when combined with her squeals of delight. "Those are *hot*!"

"They *are* hot," you agree. "Literally. There's so much more metal than denim in these crazy things— it's like wearing a frying pan around your hips."

"Oh, quit complaining," she groans. "When the rest of the world catches up to you, everyone will be

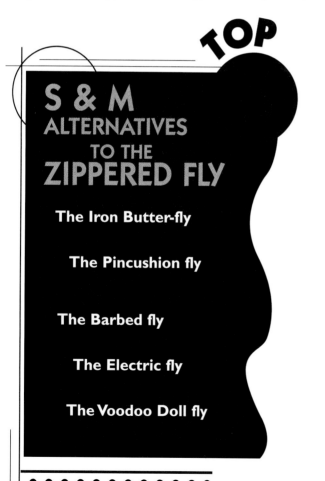

S & M ALTERNATIVES TO THE ZIPPERED FLY

TOP

The Iron Butter-fly

The Pincushion fly

The Barbed fly

The Electric fly

The Voodoo Doll fly

wearing these things."

"That's just it," you counter. "And when they do, all any enemy superpower will have to do to subdue us is lob a giant magnet into each of our state capitals. We'll all stick together and be rendered defenseless!"

She is no longer listening to your lighthearted complaints, however. All thoughts of cake long since forgotten, your zipper-happy girlfriend is tinkering with several of the seven hundred zippers on your new jeans at the same time.

"I never knew you had a zipper fetish," you whisper longingly in her ear as she unzips one zipper after another, still nowhere near the only zipper you actually care about.

"Me either," she coos, revealing your naked knees, naked calves, and naked ankles, but none of the more vital parts of your still zipper-enclosed anatomy. "But these Z-jeans are driving me crazy."

"Me too," you counter. "Get them off of me!"

"I'm trying," she grunts, her hands unzipping faster than the speed of light, all to no avail. "But, I can't find any that actually *open*."

"Well," you say, lending a hand. "Look harder."

"I am," she grunts amid the sound of her continuous unzipping. "Don't you remember how you got them on?"

"No," you admit truthfully. "After the first 50 zips, I just lost track."

In vain, the two of you try to free yourself from your birthday present to reveal your birthday suit, with little, then no, success.

The zippers at your side are just for show, the zippers on your backside reveal only your zippered wallet, and even more zippers waiting inside. The zippers on your pelvic region are all designed for much smaller things, i.e.

tic-tacs, Swiss army knives, and Chapstick. And, you soon discover, the only zipper worth having, the one that usually covers your BVDs, was apparently left out of the designer jeans' design altogether.

"Just pull the Z-jeans off," your girlfriend suggests.

"I can't," you admit. "One zipper's stuck to my boxers, another zipper's stuck to my shirt and, if I'm not mistaken, a third zipper has disappeared up my backside. I'm *trapped*!"

"So you are," she sighs, eventually losing interest and returning to her slice of birthday cake for her endorphin rush instead.

Joining her, your only alternative is to eat as much birthday cake as possible, hoping that the eventual carbo-bloat will stretch your jeans to the point that, once digestion finally kicks in, you will be able to slip out of them and their newly stretched capacity. Naturally, this could take hours of cake-smeared celibacy.

Until then, you casually remind your girlfriend that *her* single zipper should be in perfect working order.

BUTTONS & ZIPPER TRENDS IN YOUR FASHION FUTURE

- Invisible zippers that conceal the teeth with integrated designs
- Detachable and interchangeable zipper pull-tabs
- Delrin, aluminum, and brass zippers
- Zippers made from fire- and water-resistant materials
- Printed teeth and tapes, or transparent teeth, slider and pull tabs
- High-end laser-designed shell buttons
- Customized buttons in a range of materials including polyester, nylon, acrylic, wood, resin, brass, shell, nut, nickel, marble, zinc, and gemstones
- Molded, laser-engraved, or electroplated buttons

SOLE SEARCHING

Shopping for shoes. Is there anything better? (Besides sex, that is.) The smell of fresh leather. The thrill of the hunt. The crinkly feel of those pesky silica gel packs under your toes. The sexiness of those sleek designs, those high heels, and that hunky sales boy with the big, caressing hands. The styles, the colors, the sales, the ringing cash registers, the overdrawn credit card(s). Ahh, such is the splendor of shoe shopping success.

But why is all of this so—thrilling? After all, these are just shoes. Right? Foot coverings. Toe toppers. Sole slippers.

(No one gets even near as excited about shopping for socks, do they?) By rights, shopping for women's shoes should be the least exciting activity on the planet. After all, they're expensive, they're uncomfortable, those darn boxes never fit in the kitchen trash can, they take up way too much room in the closet, they smell (eventually), and, dammit, they last about as long as a sensitive boyfriend.

Yet, still, few women are able to resist the siren call of a new pair of Ferragamos in a department store window during the throes of a full-bore shoe shopping spree. Heck, let's be honest. Few women are able to resist the call of any pair of shoes, in any window, anywhere, at any time of day. (Or night, for that matter. Put down that crowbar!)

So, if you've just gotta have 'em (and you do) here's a handy reference guide to help you stay in control (and under budget) the next time you let your feet do the walking:

KNOW YOURSELF

Let's face it, shoes are sexy. But then, so are you. (Come on, admit it.) Naturally, so much sexiness in one little shoe department is one big time bomb just waiting to go off.

This is why you go into your local department store needing a simple pair of un-sexy Keds to do the

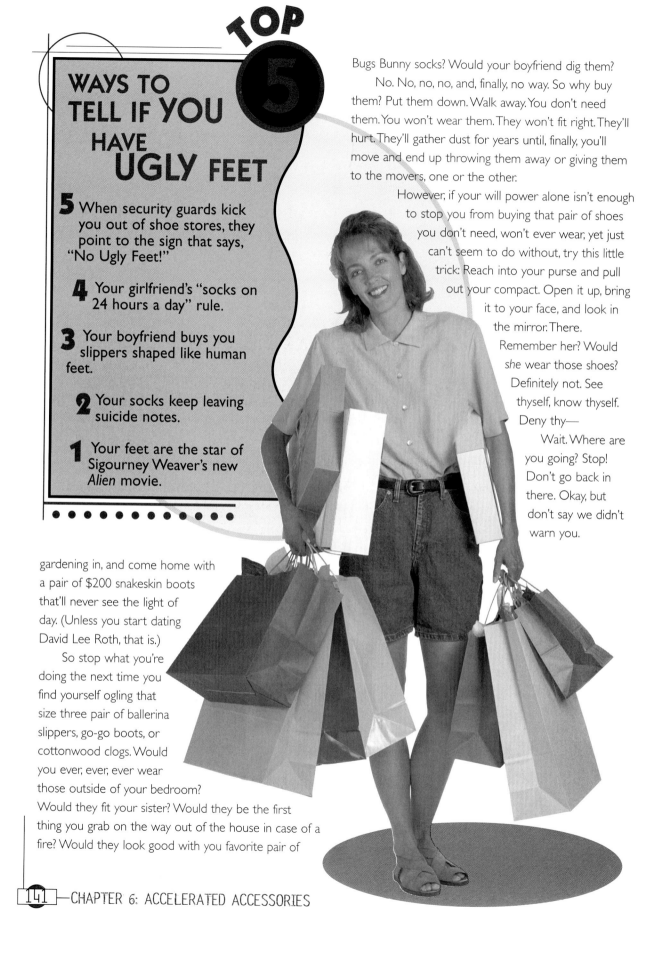

WAYS TO TELL IF YOU HAVE **UGLY** FEET

TOP 5

5 When security guards kick you out of shoe stores, they point to the sign that says, "No Ugly Feet!"

4 Your girlfriend's "socks on 24 hours a day" rule.

3 Your boyfriend buys you slippers shaped like human feet.

2 Your socks keep leaving suicide notes.

1 Your feet are the star of Sigourney Weaver's new *Alien* movie.

Bugs Bunny socks? Would your boyfriend dig them? No. No, no, no, and, finally, no way. So why buy them? Put them down. Walk away. You don't need them. You won't wear them. They won't fit right. They'll hurt. They'll gather dust for years until, finally, you'll move and end up throwing them away or giving them to the movers, one or the other.

However, if your will power alone isn't enough to stop you from buying that pair of shoes you don't need, won't ever wear, yet just can't seem to do without, try this little trick: Reach into your purse and pull out your compact. Open it up, bring it to your face, and look in the mirror. There. Remember her? Would *she* wear those shoes? Definitely not. See thyself, know thyself. Deny thy—

Wait. Where are you going? Stop! Don't go back in there. Okay, but don't say we didn't warn you.

gardening in, and come home with a pair of $200 snakeskin boots that'll never see the light of day. (Unless you start dating David Lee Roth, that is.)

So stop what you're doing the next time you find yourself ogling that size three pair of ballerina slippers, go-go boots, or cottonwood clogs. Would you ever, ever, ever wear those outside of your bedroom? Would they fit your sister? Would they be the first thing you grab on the way out of the house in case of a fire? Would they look good with you favorite pair of

TIME YOURSELF

If knowing yourself didn't exactly work out so well, try another tip that usually works a little better. (Unless you're a particularly fast shopper, that is.) Don't save your shoe shopping until you have plenty of time. For instance, avoid weekends and holidays if at all possible. Likewise, shopping for shoes on vacation is a real no-no. Nighttime shoe shopping, unless you're late for a movie, isn't so great either.

Instead, try shopping for shoes on your lunch hour. This way, you only have a certain amount of time (usually less than sixty minutes, unless you *work* in a shoe shop) in which to do a certain amount of damage. If you absolutely, positively *can't* control your girlish gushing over that new pair of Gucci pumps, at least you won't have enough time to try on each and every color and style in your size. (Hey, it's a start.)

Limiting your in-store shoe shopping time has other advantages, as well. For instance, once you find the pair you were looking for (you *did* have something specific in mind, didn't you?), you're more than likely to have run out of time. No time, no more shoes. Unless you blow off the rest of the work day altogether and rack up the rest of your credit card limit on those Gucci pumps and several other pairs of new shoes you just have to have.

In which case, you'll probably get fired. Which will mean you won't be able to pay your credit card bills. Which will mean the bank will repossess not just your brand new pair of shoes, but all of your other worldly possessions as well. Naturally, you'll soon be homeless. Which, unfortunately, will leave you plenty of time for shopping. Window shopping, that is.

PACE YOURSELF

If you must shoe shop, without the aid of a self reflection and the time restrictions of a lunch hour, at least do yourself the favor of pacing yourself. Fine. Super. Go ahead. Shop 'til you drop. Just don't *buy* anything. Yet. Admire those flats, those sneakers, those heels, those thongs. Pick them up. Try them on, even. Then just walk away. Of course, we know how hard that is. (After all, if you were in control of your shoe shopping, you wouldn't be reading this!) But, in the words of the

POPULAR STYLES OF SHOES

- Pumps
- Running shoes
- High-heels
- Sneakers
- Elevator shoes
- Loafers
- Bowling shoes
- Hi-tops
- Ballet shoes
- Cowboy boots
- Flats
- Moccasins
- Stiletto heels
- Hiking boots
- Cleats
- Clown shoes
- Topsiders
- Sandals
- Flip-flops
- Slippers
- Clogs
- Platform soles
- Tap shoes
- Go-go boots
- Golf shoes

world's most famous shoe slogan, "Just do it!" Walk out the door and enjoy a nice, long cup of coffee or a bag of cookies in the food court. Browse a bookstore. Run home and take a cold shower, whatever. Just pace yourself so that you have time to consider the ramifications of yet another pair of lemon yellow flats.

Now, if you're still thinking of the darn things an hour later, you're either really hooked or really like lemon yellow flats. Either way, you might need professional help.

OKAY, TREAT YOURSELF

No one is suggesting you give up shoe shopping altogether. Okay, maybe your boyfriend is. And your mother. And your boss. Certainly your therapist is, but, they're not in the shoe store with you right now are they?

So, the solution to your shoe fetish is quite simple: If you can afford the shoes, buy the shoes. Period. Only *you* know what your bunion budget can handle and what it can't.

Besides, it's often just a matter of priorities that keeps you from that new pair of shoes anyway. As in, would you rather dine out on the weekends and skip the shoes, or just eat peanut butter and sandwiches for 48 hours in order to shoe shop come Monday evening? What's more important at this point? Food, or your feet?

So, when you have an answer, treat yourself. Just make sure you don't overdo it. After all, it's only a treat if it's not something you do every day. (You're not shopping every day are you?)

SPECTACLE HEALING

While UV rays are certainly damaging to the eyes, if sunglasses didn't look so darn cool, today's fashion-conscious faces would do a lot less spending and a lot more squinting. After all, sunglasses have had a long history of "coolness" in the popular media. Why, everyone from Audrey Hepburn to Jackie Onassis, from Tom Cruise to Corey Hart, have worn their shades proudly. (Not to mention, coolly.)

So why can't the rest of us get into those snazzy Hollywood premieres? Could it be because we don't take the time to treat sunglasses with the proper respect? After all, there's no sense wearing shades unless they look cool.

To help you in this eyeball endeavor, here are a few sunglass tips you might want to keep in mind next time you pass one of those cute little salesgirls at the sunglass shop:

• Make sure to buy the best. After all, sunglasses aren't supposed to just *look* cool. They're actually designed to protect your precious eyes (remember them?) from all of those pesky UV rays. Consult our handy list for some of the country's best sunglass manufacturers, and then go to it.

Don't let the salesperson tell you what's "hot." Find out for yourself. Check out the latest surfing, skateboarding, snowboarding, or other boarding magazines. They're sure to have a plethora of sunglass ads and product reviews designed to inform sunglass buyers like yourselves. Ask for the "hottest" brand when you approach the sales counter, and no one will have time to treat you like a sunglass sucker!

• Make sure they fit! Just because they cost a lot and come with their very own lens shammy doesn't mean they're not going to fall of your noggin' the first time you lift up your head a little *too* fast. Spend time in front of one of the twenty display mirrors scattered around the store. (That's what they're for!) Look to see that the glasses aren't crooked or ride too high or too low. Also, make sure they cover your eyes! (Hey, you'd be surprised. Some of today's slimmest models barely do this.) Coolness aside, this is probably the biggest factor in deciding on a pair of new sunglasses. If they're not comfortable, you won't wear them. Period. So not only will you not look cool, but your eyes won't be protected either. Flare your nostrils. Wink. Smile. Laugh. So what if the salesgirl gives you back your phone number. At least your shades won't fall off on the way home!

So, do you feel confident enough to actually go out and buy yourselves a good pair of shades now? (Not the kind you can get for $4.99 at the drug store, either. Although they'll do in the event of a solar eclipse.) Well, before you get carried away, why not strain your eyes over the following "true" story about one guy who took his love of sunglasses just a little too far:

TOP
5
MOVIES WHERE TOM CRUISE AND HIS SHADES SHARE TOP BILLING

5 *Top Gun*

4 *Rain Man*

3 *The Color of Money*

2 *Mission Impossible 2*

1 *Risky Business*

SUNGLASS SHENANIGANS

Your boyfriend, you've finally decided after months of careful and sensitive consideration, is a complete and utter moron. There is no other way to explain his complete and unadulterated obsession with, of all things, sunglasses.

He has, you suspect, many more pairs of overpriced, overrated, overexposed shades than he does underwear, clean *or* dirty. They litter his dashboard, his nightstand, his backseat, his bureau, his coffee table, and his kitchen counter. You find them in laundry hampers, kitchen drawers, gym bags, briefcases, luggage, magazine racks, and medicine cabinets.

Compulsively, throughout the day and well into the evening, or at least just before the sun goes down anyway, he must slip on one pair or another before stepping foot outside. You've even seen him put them on to stick his hairy arm out the front door and retrieve the Sunday paper from its perfectly centered position on the miniscule front stoop!

Of course, in true obsessive-compulsive, anal-retentive, i.e. *jackass* style, he must breathe on both surfaces of each lens twice, "huff, huff, huff, huff," and then wipe them gingerly with one of the miniature shammy cloths he special orders each month. To do so, of course, he must huff and puff, wipe and re-wipe, un-glass and re-glass, a process that can take numerous minutes.

Minutes that, naturally, you'd prefer to spend wringing his neck instead.

Around which, of course, dangle that inevitably ridiculous pair of red and black foam Croakies!

He claims the sunglasses prevent "damage from UV rays," a well-rehearsed line you are quite certain he borrowed from one of the lavishly rich and sumptuous brochures that come with each outrageously expensive pair, usually tucked inside their faux-leather or, often, *real* leather carrying cases.

This UV protection malarkey comes straight from a man who claims that only "gays, girls, and grannies" wear sunscreen. Like it's so "macho" to breathe heavily all over inanimate objects and then rub them languorously over your untucked golf shirt while closing your eyes in rapturous ecstasy?

You wouldn't mind, of course, if they were actual eyeglasses to correct medical conditions such as myopia or nearsightedness. That would be completely different. His sunglass obsession, on the other hand, is sheer and utter vanity. Pure and simple.

His obsession is so bad, of course, that it has caused you to acquire one of your own. It's not quite agoraphobia, since you're certainly not *afraid* to leave the house. It's more like embarrassment-at-

future-ex-boyfriend-a-phobia.

A disease so complex that its symptoms include suggesting Blockbuster nights each Friday, college ball all Saturday and pro ball on Sunday! Yes, it is that bad! You'd actually *prefer* to watch televised sports than go out in public with your boyfriend, the buffoon. For now, anyway.

Lately, you see, you've been trying a new tactic. Far from throwing out all of those ridiculous pairs of sunglasses, you've been donating them, at a rate of three or four per week, to the local Lion's Club and their "Shades for Seniors" campaign.

TOP

5 REASONS TO WEAR YOUR SUNGLASSES AT NIGHT

5 Your yellow *Thriller* contact lenses really freak out the honeys.

4 You'd prefer your date not to know you're a blood-sucking zombie until it's much too late.

3 Hey, it worked for Tom Cruise in *Risky Business*.

2 You're too cheap to buy mascara.

1 The guy from *America's Most Wanted* keeps looking at you funny.

Your boyfriend, in between cleaning his current pair of glasses as well as the backup pairs in each rear pocket, "just in case," noticed an elderly gentleman in front of him wearing an extremely expensive, not to mention familiar, looking pair of shades.

"Excuse me," he said inquisitively to the elderly *Odd Couple* fan. "Could I ask where you got those sunglasses? I used to have a pair just like them and I'm interested in replacing them."

"Why, take a look for yourself, young man," said the helpful old geezer, much to your chagrin. "I got them down at the Lion's Club. Some durn fool donated 'em, believe it or not."

"I see," he said, turning momentarily shadeless eyes in your direction with a glare so hateful you were quite sure you needed protection from UV rays! "That's odd. You see these initials scratched into the left earpiece right here? Those are *my* initials. I scratch them into each pair of sunglasses I own the day I buy them. How strange that some, 'durn fool' has the same initials as I do."

As he hands the glasses back to the helpful old codger, you watch your ex-boyfriend search for you in vain from your safe spot in the taxi-stand line three theaters down.

"Oh, well," you think. "He was bound to find out someday." Besides, you're absolutely positive he'll feel pretty guilty when he returns home to find the X-tra large bottle of sunglass cleaner wrapped in a big, red bow waiting for him on his kitchen counter.

At least, he'll feel guilty until he reads the gift card resting nearby. The precious one that will read, in a rather feminine yet frustrated hand, "Take your glasses and stick 'em where the sun don't shine…"

A program in which donated sunglasses go to needy retirees and other older folks who can now enjoy the sunshine again, without any "danger from UV rays."

Of course, your clueless boyfriend had no idea this was going on at all, until the day you actually agreed to go to a twilight movie with him, in public, and arrived behind a busload of senior citizens waiting in line for the latest Jack Lemmon and Walter Matthau cinematic romp.

PERSONAL PURSE SPACE

Whether it's a sequined matchbox with straps barely big enough to hold much more than a tic-tac and an aspirin or a trendy male "organizer" full of business cards and Trojans, today's purses have a lot more to do with fashion than they do with function.

Take the mini-backpack purse, for instance. Is it particularly pretty? Not likely. Does it lend itself to evening gowns, frilly dresses, or other formal wear? Not unless you're Angelina Jolie. Is it particularly feminine? Nope. Does it say, "I am woman, hear me roar?" More like, "I am lazy, watch me pack." Ah, but does it hold a lot of junk? You bet.

For far too long, women have had to put up with purses. It's a common misconception, therefore, that women *like* purses. (Yeah, right. Like they like tampons, tweezers, Neet, and breast exams.) Actually, women have grown accustomed to purses in their everyday (not to mention every night) life and so are simply trying to make the best out of a bad situation with their endless trips to the purse department at the local mall.

Generally, despite the number of actual purses a woman owns, there are three main types of purses: work, play, and evening. Period. Naturally, there are

variations of each. For instance, the "nice" purse you take to your big job interview isn't necessarily the same purse you schlep into work with on some rainy Wednesday morning three years later. Likewise, the shimmering, heart-shaped number you dazzle your blind date with on Valentine's Day night isn't the same purse you take out on an evening with the girls.

Of the three types of purses, naturally, work purses are the least attractive. (Unless you work at a strip club, that is, and then it's the biggest piece of your wardrobe. Literally.) Most work purses are functional, yet frumpy. Big enough to hold makeup, money, and Mace, but small enough to fit inside of your filing cabinet. (Thank God!) Very few are exceptionally colorful, let alone pretty. Most are used for business-like purposes, everything from shielding one's self on the subway to transporting hidden candy bars to and from your weekly Weight Watchers meetings. All in all, a purse to put up with.

Play purses, however, are probably the most flexible. These are the purses you bring with you to the mall, to the theme park, to the gym, to the movies. Cuter than work purses, they are usually smaller and considerably more fashionable. Most are still functional, but often more frivolous. Shiny metallic, for instance. Braided trim. Denim. See-through plastic. In short, your work purse is probably what your mom still uses. Your play purse is also what your mom still uses. (If your mom's Madonna.)

If women *do* have a favorite purse, however, it will most likely be one of their evening purses. Of the three, these are the fanciest affairs. Reserved for only the most elegant functions, such as dances, balls, anniversary dates, and weddings, evening purses are often the smallest purses in a woman's closet. This is because they're only supposed to carry a simple tube of lipstick, a compact, house keys, and a spare quarter for a phone call home in case of emergencies. Often shaped like clamshells, pill boxes, or wallets, evening purses can be made from all kinds of materials. From beads to gold lamé, from chain mail to silver rhinestones, anything goes as long as it's small and easy on the eyes.

Which is all well and good, in theory. Of course, most women have considerably more than three purses. (Try, three hundred.) So what's a poor girl to do when she has too *many* purses? Read on and find out:

HANDBAG TRENDS IN YOUR FASHION FUTURE

- Calf hair and leather handbags
- Wood beaded bags
- Bowling handbags
- Brocade handbags
- Skinny baguette bags
- Handbags with beaded straps
- Clutches
- Small hand or tote bags
- Animal print handbags
- Raffia handbags
- Snakeskin print totes
- Straw bags
- Bamboo handbags
- Silk patchwork handbags

SHE SAID

It was bound to happen. After all, it was just a matter of time before that extra business card or last box of breath mints pushed your current every day purse beyond all physical limits and caused it to explode like so many Roman candles on the 4th of July. (But did it have to happen while you were standing in the express aisle with a quart of Rocky Road and the new *Enquirer?*)

Returning home with a seamless purse, one grocery bag full of ice cream and tabloids and another full of what *used* to be in your purse, you decide that, instead of watching the *Mary Tyler Moore* marathon on Nick-At-Nite, you are going to clean out your "purse shelf." (After a heaping dish of Rocky Road, of course.)

And so, fortified with chocolate fudge, walnuts, and caramel (not to mention the latest on Liz and Hugh's big breakup) you forge into your closet, push aside your winter coat, your three ex-bridesmaid dresses, and that neon green terry cloth robe your younger brother gave you last Christmas. There, stacked like so many dirty dishes after Thanksgiving dinner, are what you like to refer to as the "purses of your past." From the fanny pack you bought on

that cruise last year to the navy blue handbag your grandmother gave you from what you're quite sure was her personal collection (owing to the balled up tissues and prehistoric lipstick you found inside), your entire handbag history, the story of your life, rests upon that shelf.

That leather Aigner number you just had to have your senior year in high school. That pink plastic contraption your old college roommate gave you as a graduation present. That nautical-themed cinch bag with the anchors and lifesavers. The funky red lips with a handle you picked up on the clearance rack after Valentine's Day. Your Liz bag. All of them stuffed to the gills with the remnants of your life.

Like an archaeologist at a dinosaur dig, you delve into the stratus layers of your sagging purse shelf. A trashcan at the ready, you scour through old movie stubs, matchbooks, lipstick tubes, and perfume samples. Moldy tic-tacs, unused panty liners, and foreign coins. There are keys to locks you no longer own, not to mention monogrammed keychains, pictures of old boyfriends, travel size bottles of mouthwash, and receipts from romantic dinners (and some not so romantic). There are pay stubs, ATM receipts, and phone numbers on cocktail napkins, coasters, and matchbooks.

Before you know it, memories are racing past you at a staggering clip and your trashcan is still empty except for a stray tic-tac and that novelty condom you won at your old job's last Christmas party. Your purses are still bulging with the detritus of your life and not one is appealing enough to replace the one that exploded in the grocery store. Yet none are quite bad enough to throw away, either.

"Oh, well," you think, returning for another round of Rocky Road and a few more pages of tinsel town trash talk, "I needed a new purse anyway."

Now, if you can just find another novelty condom.

HE SAID

Despite what Jerry Seinfeld might think (Jerry who?), today's modern man is *not* afraid to carry a purse. Well, why should he be? After all, sexual equality has given him the unprecedented freedom to cook without being accused of being henpecked. He can likewise do dishes, vacuum, and even dust without fear of reproach.

He can play with dolls, or, as they're called in layman's terms, "Star Trek Action Figures." He can actually cry without being considered gay. (Unless his Dad or old football coach is around, of course.) Why, he can even do Tae-Bo in public, without fear of being seen in tights. After all, it's the new millennium.

Still, armed with all of this newfound freedom does not automatically mean that modern man is ready to actually call the item he is now free to carry a "purse." After all, it's really more like a "personal organizer" anyway. Or, let's say, a miniature briefcase. How about a large Rolodex? With a zipper. A convenient carry case for the fast-paced executive (or mid-level assistant manager, anyway) on the go?

Besides, if it has a built-in calculator, a flap for your checkbook, a slot for your pen, a zippered pocket for spare change in case of emergencies, and even two handy flaps for your extra house and car keys, does it really deserve to be called a purse? After all,

does your regular, everyday *purse* have all that?

Okay, so even if it does, modern man is nothing if not ingenious when it comes to disguising his true intentions. After all, there are many ways around admitting that the virtual handbag slung across one's shoulder is, in reality, a purse.

Even if it looks like one, feels like one and, in all actuality, is one.

In fact, for those men wanting to carry a purse, but not quite ready to admit that they're actually *that* in touch with their feminine side, there is a vast array of options available to them in the form of cheap, but passable, imitations.

For instance, there is the inevitable backpack. This fresh fashion accessory, once restricted to die-hard campers and college freshmen, has pockets, zippers, and room galore. There are handy, padded straps for comfort during those long morning commutes or walks to lunch. There's even a convenient hook on top for that first trip to the restroom after your morning cup of coffee. Why, the latest models even come with a matching water bottle in case your car breaks down and you're stranded on the side of the freeway for an hour or two!

Still, it takes a certain type of personality to pull off the whole backpack look. For one thing, they don't come in gray flannel or tweed yet, so finding one to match your three-piece suit is always a hassle. And, while they're great for sneaking Twizzlers and bottles of soda into the movie theater, your date might get a little upset when you toss it in *her* lap at the first sight of an usher or security guard.

Guys who *do* opt for the backpack look are often closet surfers, beatniks or skaters who enjoy lugging around flip-flops, sex wax, Fruitopia, and girly mags just in case their office building blows up overnight and they get an unexpected day off to "hit the beach." There's the odd professor who can get away with this look, of course, but inevitably a briefcase or shopping cart becomes much more convenient for those in academia.

Of course, there are less bulky options than the backpack. One such alternative is the cassette tape case. These are roomy, padded affairs intended to store up to 12 cassette tapes (remember them?) when you need them on the go, in the car, on the boat, etc. They usually come with a handle, which is convenient for carrying purposes, but they're boxy and unattractive, often coming only in gray or black.

Guys fond of cassette case purses often drive around in so-called "classic" cars, which most often translates into a 1982 convertible K-car. They're also fond of Hawaiian shirts and aviator sunglasses and, inside of their cassette-tape purses you're most likely to find an abundance of Chapstick, breath mints, and free Burger King coupons.

Then there's something known as the "man tote," which is little more than one of those canvas recyclable shopping bags "duded up" with pictures of sailboats, duck decoys, or fishing lures. A pair of simple straps and a pocket or two make this option a convenient carryall, however, no one but male librarians or secretaries ever take this armbag version of "Le Car" seriously.

The zipper tote is a much more acceptable version of the man purse. A cross between a shaving kit and a junior briefcase, a simple handstrap and a zipper make this nearly the perfect option for the man on the go who's moved beyond the wallet but not all the way to the handbag. Affordable, masculine, and

accessible, it should by all rights be a hit with the modern man.

If only it had a belt loop, leash, or collar so guys wouldn't forget them on the tops of cars, desks, sinks, or urinals… Finally, of course, there is the tried and true Crown Royal bag. Ever trendy, ever regal with is royal colors of purple and gold, this option works on so many levels. With plenty of room for matchbooks, nose hair clippers, wads of cash, and the odd cough drop, it is small enough to be unobtrusive yet large enough to accommodate a wallet and key-chain. You can hang onto it with its fancy drawstring or, if you're feeling particularly "dandy," toss it over your shoulder with a "devil may care" grin.

Not to mention, if you ever find yourself up against six thugs in a darkened alley conveniently standing next to a soda machine with a roll of quarters in your pocket, you can always buy four or five cans of Diet Dr. Pepper, toss them in your bag, and come out swinging à la Sean Penn in *Bad Boys*.

Of course, women seem to have a problem with the Crown Royal bag and this, naturally, throws the "bag balance" quite off-whack. After all, what's the point in having enough room, not to mention all of that purple camouflage, to hide a full roll of condoms when no girl worth her salt will come near your convenient cocktail container? Not to mention…you?

And so the battle for the ever-elusive male purse market rages on. For until someone comes up with a purse that looks, acts, and feels more like a…beer cooler, men will continue to stick with that famous fallback, the wallet.

Come to think of it, the beer cooler thing just might be the way to go. Insulated, attractive, practical. Shoot, add a shoulder strap and a vanity mirror and you might just be on to something.

7

UNDERWEAR
AFFAIR

As long as men and women have roamed the earth, there have been records of that most basic of fashion necessities: underwear. From the earliest models that involved leaves and fur, to the revolution of the cotton gin, underwear has been as much a part of human history as wedgies and panty raids. Bloomers. Knickers. Skivvies. Drawers. Unmentionables. Boxers. Briefs. Tighty Whities. Whatever you want to call them, underwear has become much more than mere bun huggers or pocket protectors in this comely culture of "be all, bare all."

Nowadays mega-monopolies like Fruit of the Loom and Victoria's Secret have built billion dollar businesses around our insatiable need to cover up down under. Forget fig leafs and potato sacks, today's modern underwear has more in common with evening gowns and sporting equipment than they do diapers or girdles. From Calvin Klein bikini briefs to robin's egg-blue Wonderbras, is it any wonder that briefs keep getting briefer and thongs keep getting— thongier?

MENTIONING THE UNMENTIONABLES: UNDERWEAR COMES OUT OF THE CLOSET

A BRIEF HISTORY

Ahh, underwear. Where would we be without it? (Besides walking around constantly chafed.) From boxer shorts to "classic" Fruit of the Looms to fruit colored edible thongs, America's love affair with underwear has retail icons like Victoria's Secret and Hanes feeding our fascination with an endless variety of product that is generally meant not to be seen—except by the right person.

Almost from the beginning of time, early people began to wrap leaves, furs, and skins around their waists and between their legs to stay warm, to keep off bugs, and to protect themselves from unwanted advances by members of the opposite sex. (Not to mention some randy beast out roaming around.) Naturally, these early variations catered more to comfort than style.

Eventually, however, even these simple loincloths evolved into fancier versions that provided better support and fewer restrictions. Some were lined with fur. Some were tailor made, as opposed to one size fits all. Some were even designed to attract the opposite sex. (What a concept!)

As centuries passed and loincloths slowly gave way to underwear that wasn't made from palm fronds or mammoth skin, modern attitudes about underwear changed as well. It became a societal standard in cultures everywhere that people, those currently walking on two legs anyway, were to wear underwear. Period. Like eating, drinking, hunting, pillaging, and plundering, wearing underwear had become a "pre-historic" must.

Eventually, thoughts about underwear changed along with the materials used and number of pairs one owned. As techniques for costuming advanced and newer and better materials became available, function gave way to form and animal skin gave way to style. At many times throughout history, people became dissatisfied with the human shape, and sought to change it to a more "idealized" form. About 2000 B.C., in early Crete, depictions of a ravishing serpent goddess show her wearing an outfit that was belted around the waist, making her breasts protrude in that tempting way that goddesses have.

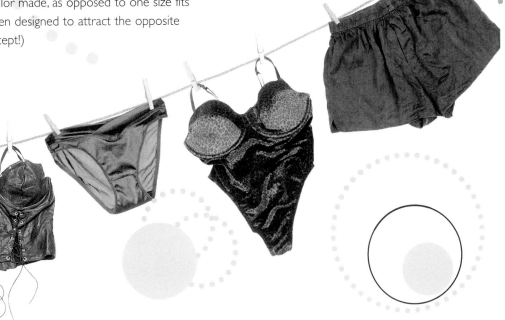

The first bra or "breast band" was actually worn by the ancient Greeks. It was called a mastoeides, meaning, "shaped like a breast." Those crafty ancient Greeks were also the first to wear "girdles." However, they called them "zones." A band of linen or soft leather was bound around a woman's waist and lower torso to shape and control her mid-body.

The iron corset was devised in 1579 and was worn by women for long, painful years. Lighter-weight corsets and girdles were seen as a vast improvement and first worn on the outside of clothing. In Florence during the Renaissance, Catherine de Medici decreed it bad manners to have a thick waist and designed a hinged corset that narrowed the waist to thirteen inches.

In fact, until laces were later shifted to the front, it was impossible for the corset-clad to lace themselves up without assistance.

The first modern corset appeared in Britain in the 1700s. Still, there wasn't much cause for celebration. After all, a so-called "modern" corset was still an uncomfortable, blood-restricting device that advanced fashion but at a torturous price.

THE REAL SKIVVY

However, with advances in everything from whalebone corsets to silk lingerie, the 20th century has seen a bona fide revolution in underwear. Men started the century in the famous one-piece outfits known as "long johns" or "union suits." Today's T-shirts, briefs, and boxers hadn't even been invented yet. Women didn't fare any better, however, consistently wearing sagging slips, clingy chemises, and baggy undies. Overall, underwear still had light years to go before becoming the national obsession we so thoroughly enjoy today.

With the industrial revolution, however, underwear became readily available for the first time, as it no longer needed to be custom-made. Bust improvers, otherwise known as padded bras, were slowly becoming popular by as early as 1840. And while historic images of these classic cups reveal them to be somewhat less than daring, at least their names were fun. After all, these bras have been called falsies, cuties, bosom friends, waxen bosoms, gay deceivers, lemon loves, and pneumatic breasts! European women did not generally wear underpants until the early 1900s. A short and light corset was made in America in 1911 in order for women to have the freedom of movement needed to dance the tango.

Men, meanwhile, slowly grew tired of their one-piece union suits and were thankful for the rise in popularity of "brief" underwear after its design in the 1930s.

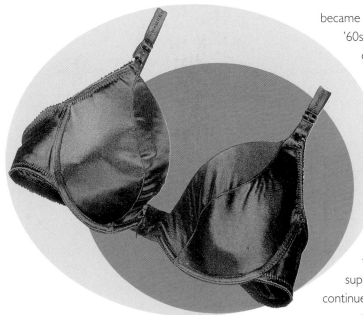

became a fad on American college campuses in the '60s. Boys (as in "frat") would storm women's dormitories and steal their underpants as silky souvenirs. And, while briefs were once considered men's underwear only, in the 1970s women began wearing them, too. Then, much to their boyfriends' delight and their mothers' chagrin, men's boxer shorts became outerwear for women in the heady days of the 1980s.

Finally, the push-up bra was introduced in the 1990s. As an added bonus, it made women's breasts look larger than they actually were and gave them support *and* comfort as their workaday world continued to demand both form and function.

ÜBER UNDERWEAR

After women threw out corsets, the new feminine ideal became younger and thinner. Men gave up the one-piece union suits as T-shirts slowly came into vogue. Rubber girdles made bodies look thinner. The modern form of the bra was finally invented to support, lift, and enhance, much to the relief of women everywhere. Men's briefs were invented, and are still the best-selling item of underwear for men.

It wasn't until 1935 that bras were made with both cup and band sizes. The British called the cup measures "junior," "medium," "full," and "full with wide waist," while American bra manufacturers would eventually assign a more detailed system of sizes with letters of the alphabet, ranging from A to K.

After this surprising turn of events, the manufacture of bras soon started an explosive period of growth. Strapless bras were introduced in 1938 and were finally popularized in the 1950s. At around the same time, the form fitting "sweater girl" bra was manufactured. Its cups were shaped to points and looked a lot like cones, which naturally made it easier to both attract boys and then repel their advances all at the same time.

In other areas of female underwear, "panty raids"

Synonyms For Underwear

Drawers
Unmentionables
Skivvies
Jockeys
BVDs
Step-ins
Tighty Whities
Scanties
Underpants
Briefs
Grape
  Smugglers
Loincloth
Knickers

Bloomers
Inside clothes
Fig Leaf
Indescribables
Underoos
Ball Huggers
Underpinnings
Boxers
Undies
Banana
  Hammocks
Shorts
Unwhisperables

"A lady is one who never shows her underwear unintentionally."
-Lillian Day

NOW IT'S OUTERWEAR

While much of history saw a strict division between men's and women's underwear, today both men and women can use underwear to express their deepest fantasies. The lines have been blurred almost to the point of invisibility. Women wear jockeys that, while possibly pink or potentially purple, are still just as sturdy and rugged as a man's pair of cotton Fruit of the Looms. And, thanks to those Chippendales dancers, men are finding it more and more acceptable to wear bikini underwear with decorative animal prints.

In fact, with a little help from celebrities like Madonna and companies like Joe Boxer, what was once simply a means of warming one's sensitive areas and protecting from bug infestations, is now worn as both underwear and outerwear. It may still be used to protect and keep warm, but today it is increasingly used for self-expression and to attract. Whether it's leather or Lycra, silk, mesh, or nylon, if you can dream about it, you probably can wear it.

TOP 5 SLOGANS YOU DON'T WANT TO SEE ON YOUR BOYFRIEND'S UNDERWEAR

5 "Property of State Correctional Facility."

4 *Batteries not included.

3 "I'd rather be wearing panties."

2 "Yes, this is as good as it gets."

1 *Magnifying glass not included.

BRIEF vs. BRIEFER
A SHOPPING GUIDE FOR
(DARING)
MEN

There has always been the boxer vs. brief dilemma, but today's man now faces an even greater challenge, brief vs. briefer. For while jockey shorts used to be one of the most mentionable of unmentionables, today's briefs are becoming (much, much) briefer.

DRAWER
WARS

You're not sure whether to laugh or cry, so of course, you do both. You've just lost the last working strip of elastic in the last decent pair of underwear in the very last corner of your barren sock drawer. Naturally, there's nothing left to do but go *au naturel* and start "swinging," or break down and buy some more.

And since you've started taking over three minutes just to zip up ever since you saw *There's Something About Mary*, you decide to break down and go shopping. Of course, it's been a while since you've shopped for underwear. In fact, your last six pairs lasted you so long they still had your initials written in permanent marker by your

mother's hand on the day she sent you off to college.

It doesn't take you long to notice that quite a few things have changed since then.

First of all, as you wander through the department store wondering whatever happened to good old Fruit of the Loom with their big fat grape and apple models, you can't quite decide, once you finally find it, if

you're standing in the underwear aisle, or the "alternative" section of an adults-only bookstore smack dab in the middle of San Francisco.

Pre-teen, hairless boys who aren't quite men lean back provocatively in artsy black and white photographs on slim, phallic-like boxes as their six-pack abs and sock-stuffed underwear leap out at you from the daring covers. Their cheekbone-abundant, pouting faces seem to say, "Of course I'm gay. But even though you're not, you'll *still* want to get in my pants."

When your blushing recedes to the color of ripe pomegranate seeds, you realize that there's actually a method to the underwear advertiser's madness. Certain sizes of underwear have different sizes of models on their blatantly boastful boxes. For instance, Size-S has the anorexic boy with greasy hair and long fingernails. Size-M has the athletic, tanned jock who looks like he just stepped out of the locker room. Size-L has a hairy, beefy guy so ugly that he scares you straight into the XL section, where none of the masculine models have anything in common except the cucumber they obviously passed around during the photo shoot.

Naturally, despite the fact that you have a 32" waist and could technically shop in the "young men's" section, you reach for a couple of boxes of XL, only to find that underwear is no longer simply underwear anymore.

There are so many different shapes and sizes, you might as well be in the shoe department four aisles over. There are bikini briefs, whose boxes show more hairless butt-cheek than a baby album. Nearly thongs, these leopard skin and tiger-patterned briefs take their name quite literally.

I'M TOO SEXY! FOR MY UNDER-WEAR!

Briefly Speaking: Underwear Types (And Then Some)

Low-Rise Briefs
Hipster Briefs
Hip Briefs
String Bikini
Sport Briefs
Mid-Rise Briefs
Hi-Rise Briefs
Pouch Briefs
Knit Boxers
Button Fly Boxers
Boxer Briefs
Midway Shorts

Midway Boxers
Full Size Boxers
Tapered Boxers
Snap Fronts
Boxers
Silk Boxers
Nylon Boxers
Thongs
Long Underwear

Laughably small, even in the biggest sizes, you seem to remember the very same Band-Aid sized items on the gag gift counters when you went shopping for your best friend's bachelor party. To further add insult to injury, they only come in a tube of ten and range from animal skin to every other color of the red-hot rainbow. The pretty-boy posing on the cover may as well not be wearing anything at all, but at least you'd be buying so many in one pop, you wouldn't have to go through this unbearable underwear ordeal for another five or six years. At least.

Knowing your girlfriend would laugh you straight out of the bedroom should you buy such a pair of drawers, you realize that even if you break up, there would still be the "bank robbery" factor. As in, "Everybody in this here bank needs to hand over their wallet and strip to their skivvies. Hey there, Clem, lookie-here. We've got us a boy wearing women's panties over there. Is that *real* tiger skin, boy? Whaddya say, Clem, I think we just found ourselves a hottie for a hostage."

Tossing the "tube of T-backs" into your basket anyway and moving on, you find yourself in safer waters, although still there are more choices than a candy store across from a school ground. Thigh-high, clingy, loose, relaxed fit, "room to breathe," and "next-to-nothing" are descriptors that blare out at you from the relatively few words adorning the bulging box covers. None of them even closely resemble what your mom sent you off to college in, and you wonder if "swinging" wouldn't be such a bad idea after all.

Maxing out your credit card, just in case your zipper paranoia is a lifelong affliction, you buy one box (or tube) of each style. As she rings them all up, of course, you blatantly hit on the salesgirl, even though she's old enough to be your grandmother, just so she doesn't think that you're buying them for the petulant pictures on the boastful boxes.

Back home in front of the mirror, with the phone off the hook and the shades pulled down in case any of your neighbors should think you've started filming amateur porno movies right under their noses, you quickly dispose of the offending boxes and arrange the underwear on your bed like some sort of an ass-covering assembly line. On go the thigh-highs, which are too restricting and remind you too much of those back-flap lumberjack drawers the menfolk wore on the *Beverly Hillbillies.* Then the "relaxed fits," which provide about as much support as a pillowcase and are only slightly less flattering. On and off go the other selections you made, until finally you are at the end of the line.

The bikini briefs with the animal prints are, of course, laughable. On the other hand, they are surprisingly comfortable, and might make a good Valentine's day gag gift for your current lady friend. Then again, as you strut

TOP 5

BENEFITS OF INVISIBLE UNDERWEAR

5 The box covers would be much more interesting.

4 Finally, an end to the boxer vs. brief dilemma.

3 No more "skid marks."

2 "Clean? Dirty? Who cares?"

1 No more complaining when your girlfriend drags you to Victoria's Secret.

around the house feeling entirely too comfortable and eerily at ease, you realize that the briefest briefs of all have the distinct advantage of making you feel like a swinger, without any of the "danger" of actually swinging. Tossing the rest of your underwear menagerie into a bottom drawer for emergencies only, you step back into your button-fly jeans and quietly vow to avoid banks from now on. But what if you have a car wreck?

THE **THONG** DILEMMA: A SHOPPING GUIDE FOR (DARING) WOMEN

In Florida they arrest you for selling hot dogs in one, but they won't let you on the *Howard Stern Show* without one. But as bikini bottoms, for both men and women, gradually decrease in size year after year, are they making the once controversial thong a thing of the past?

THONG (SWAN) SONG

It's finally your fifth date and he's been giving off all of the signals that, in the words of the perpetually horny toad Rod Stewart himself, "…tonight's the night." Of course, your outfit for the upcoming, all-important date has been picked out even before the restaurant or the bottle of wine back on your first. However, when it comes to the big day, you can't find a single pair of underwear that's appropriate for what might happen mere moments after you ask him up for a nightcap.

Your comfortable, fruit- and butterfly-covered "period panties" are

all much too baggy and, while perfect for concealing an absorbent pad the size of a Sumo wrestler's diaper, not quite what you'd call the sexiest thing alive.

Your holiday panties, given to you by your eccentric aunt each year, are actually rather comfortable and of course only slightly used, but you're afraid the Santa, Easter Bunny, and Jack O'Lantern patterns might give off a little too much of the sedate school marm vibe.

Your collection of satin's slinkiest are always nice, but you're afraid in the heat of the passion that he, or possibly you for that matter, might just rip them off in a moment of frenzied monkey lust, and they're almost $12 a pair, so that's entirely out of the question.

Finally, with hours to spare before you have to get ready, you head down to the local lingerie store to treat yourself to a little petticoat present. There, in a room that smells more like Jackie Collins's bubble bath than a retail outlet, you let your manicured fingers run through silk and satin, leather and lace. All the while, your fantasies run the gamut from good girl gone bad to just plain—bad.

Then, just as your sensibilities are swinging back from nympho to nun, you run across a lovely little lavender number marked "one size fits all." Which, of course, you believe entirely because the literal "stitch"

of cloth in your trembling hands is barely enough to cover what it's supposed to, not to mention what you'd *like* it to.

Still, passion is in the air and the distant drumbeat of hot, jungle love is calling louder than the soul music playing ever so smoothly over the in-store Muzak. And so, not even trying it on, you plunk down your first real thong, blush-free, on the sales counter, glad for the snooty, striped, handled bag with complimentary tissue paper the salesgirl buries it in.

"Oh, good," you blurt, your sensibilities momentarily overriding your impishness. "Now I won't have to wrap it up before the bachelorette party tonight." The salesgirl flashes a too-quick smile, signifying that she's heard this line one too many times before.

Later, the classy bag opened like a ripe plum to expose the passion-colored fruit inside, you hear your date's corny "shave and a haircut" knock on the front door to your apartment and slip quickly into your scandalous purchase. Only to find that, with mere moments to spare and despite the reassuring words on its tiny label, "one size" definitely does *not* fit all.

Or, at least, it certainly doesn't fit you!

Too late to return to the cozy confines of your underwear drawer and the luxuriant comfort of your fall-back period panties, you flex your thighs to try and make them smaller and suck in your gut, finally deciphering the curves, bumps, ridges, and bulges of your pelvis and posterior until the tiny little thong arrives over its intended erogenous zone with an audible "snap."

Waddling like a mermaid on dry land, you hobble over to the front door and open it just in time for a gust of wind to lift up your sensible skirt and expose *all*

of you, save for the 2 ½ centimeters covered by your recent purchase, to your date.

"Wow," your dumbfounded date says admiringly, flowers and candy dropping in an unceremonious heap at your feet. "How did you know purple is my favorite color?"

Moments later, limbs entwined and all thoughts of dinner replaced by a more immediate, primal hunger, you have just one thought as you tumble, arms and legs akimbo, onto the sofa: "How am I going to get this damn thing back off?"

Of course, in order to avoid getting yourself into such "tight" situations, on the next page are ten timely tips to help you in your endless quest for that "not wrong" thong:

TOP 5 SIGNS YOU SHOULDN'T BE WEARING THONG UNDERWEAR

That "no thong" symbol on your driver's license.

People say things like, "You shouldn't be wearing a thong."

You have to tell the cashier you're buying them for someone else before she'll ring them up.

You have to buy them from the "Big & Tall" store.

"One size fits all" doesn't.

THONG

1. Be realistic about your body. Even with today's flattering fabrics and computer-generated lines specifically designed to lift and enhance, there's only so much a little old thong can actually do. To avoid disappointment, don't expect miracles. (As in, "If you want a better thong, bring a better ass!")

2. Keep in mind that most thong manufacturers size up, so if you wear a size medium in your period panties, try on a size large thong. It's more important to get a good, comfortable fit than a flattering, albeit mythical, size. (Besides, if anyone's admiring your backside in a thong, you can pretty much guarantee they're not looking at your tag!)

3. Don't just stand there—move it! Sit down, bend over, reach up, twist around. How does the thong feel? Is it comfortable? (Yeah, right!) Does it stay in place or ride up? If so, how far up? (Then again, it is a thong.)

4. Despite what you may think, thongs *are* supposed to be comfortable. Try several different brands to get the fit you want before settling on something that feels like what those popular girls did to you back in the locker room all those years spent in junior high (i. e., a "wedgie").

5. Check thongs for construction. After all, your average thong sees a lot more "action" than those cotton bloomers your grandmother used to wear. The seams should be well sewn with tight stitches and there shouldn't be any wrinkles or puckers in the crotch. (Unless you put them there, that is.)

6. Not all thongs are created equal! So don't limit yourself to a single style. In fact, try several to find the most flattering for your figure. Some thongs rise higher, some go lower. Depending on your body shape, you may be pleasantly surprised to find which type is more flattering.

Lingerie

Baby dolls	Bustiers	Garter belts	Robes	Teddies
Body	Camisoles	Gowns	Sleepshirts	Thongs
Stockings	Chemises	Nylons	Slippers	Top &
Boxers	Corsets	Panties	Stockings	bottom
Bras	Crop tops	Pantyhose	T-shirts	sets

TIPS

7. Once you do find the right size and style thong for you, invest in several different colors to suit your mood. After all, in the vibrant world of tempting thongs, red doesn't always mean "stop" and the girl in black isn't always the "bad" girl. Besides, everyone knows some colored thongs are "cheekier" than others!

8. While there's not as much space on a thong as there is on other styles of underwear, don't forgo a simple pattern or print just because you can't see much of it. Vertical stripes are still slimming, even on two square inches of Lycra, and depending on your personality, zebra skin might suit you better than daisies. Or vice versa.

9. Check the elastic. Sure, nobody wants their thong to creep down their thighs during the evening's pre-festivities, but you don't want those telltale elastic prints on your tummy, either. For the best test results in the quickest amount of time, try thong shopping after a Chinese meal. The MSG and sodium bloat is sure to put any elastic to the test, and if your thong of choice doesn't leave a "ring around the waist" after an all-you-can-eat bonsai buffet, chances are it won't leave it after anything else either.

10. Last, but certainly not least, have fun! After all, you've already made it past the, "Ohmigod, I'm actually buying a thong stage." Now that you're finally in the dressing room, let that kinky little devil on your left shoulder be your guide. Shiny glitter? Sure. Those funny little lips? Super. Why not try both? After all, someone might see them one day. You don't want him to think you only own one pair do you?

"It's only when the tide goes out that you learn who's been swimming naked."
-Warren Buffett

VICTORIA'S
NOT SO
SECRET

Can anyone even remember a time when Victoria's *was* a secret? Certainly those who do are as few and far between as those who heard about the Hindenburg crashing *live* or who used to know why a refrigerator was called an "icebox." From television commercials to chain outlets in massive shopping malls, Victoria's Secret is now anything but.

Indeed, to think that corporate America, even really *hot* corporate America, can commercialize and McPantie a shopping experience as personal and intimate as shopping for lingerie is absurd in the first place. After all, this is underwear we're talking about. Not oil changes, hamburgers, or soda.

Besides, most women know that they only really need two types of lingerie: Those they wear everyday and those they wear on special nights. (Of course, there is that special breed of women who doesn't need any lingerie, ever, but that's a whole other chapter.)

Everyday lingerie, of course, includes a boyfriend's T-shirt, that Garfield nightshirt you got last Christmas, boxer shorts, sleepers, jumpers, rompers, and anything else you know no one else will ever see you in. The only real exception to everyday lingerie (if it can really be called that) is if your aunt from Poughkeepsie is in town for a week and too cheap to spring for a hotel room. In that case, of course, you'll run out to the local department store and buy something appropriately perky, most likely cotton, with little hearts or clouds on it, that at least goes down to your knees. (This is what's commonly referred to as "unwanted houseguest lingerie.")

Lingerie for special nights, on the other hand, involves a little more thought and creativity. Vibrant colors, daring styles, revealing tops, and bottomless bottoms are all fair game for that upcoming "special night." Whether it be a one-year anniversary, Valentine's night, or just a mid-week treat to yourself, all of the above will do quite nicely. Naturally, this is the kind of self-gift buying we all stream into Victoria's Secret and even Frederick's of Hollywood for.

However, what happens when a mega-chain's specialty takes a backseat to its marketing department? Read on to find out:

LINGERIE LESSONS

It's your two-year anniversary and you know he'll forget so you decide to treat yourself first and avoid the disappointment later. You don't want chocolate or flowers, music, or books. You have enough candles and bath beads. What you don't have enough of, you realize all of a sudden at lunch one day, is ribbons and bows and things that are pretty, dainty, and not for public knowledge.

Therefore, you drive over to the mall after work shortly after your revelation and head straight for Victoria's Secret, a company known entirely for what goes *on* in the bedroom. Or more important, what comes *off*.

TOP 10

THINGS NOT TO SAY IN THE LINGERIE STORE

10 "Does this come in children's sizes?"

9 "No, thanks. Just sniffing."

8 "I'll be in the dressing room going blind."

7 "Mom will love this."

6 "Oh, the size won't matter. She's inflatable."

5 "No need to wrap it up. I'll eat it here."

4 "Will you model this for me?"

3 "The Miracle What? This is better than world peace!"

2 "45 bucks? You're just gonna end up NAKED anyway!"

1 "Oh, honey, you'll never squeeze your fat ass into that!"

(Courtesy of *TopFive.com*)

Ten-feet-tall glossy photos of scantily clad supermodels greet you from display windows the size of your living room as you wipe the mustard from that hot dog you just had to have in the food court off of your lips. You hate these obviously genetically engineered women, but admire them and trust their inbred fashion sense, so what they wear, you must wear. Or at least, wear a likely facsimile of it.

A salesgirl who looks much more like you than a supermodel offers you a new perfume bearing yet another supermodel's name and smelling just like all the other scents in the world. Another cashier offers you complimentary Victoria's Secret bath beads if you purchase a Victoria's Secret loofah scrub and facial blackhead mask in a matching Victoria's Secret backpack. You decline politely, the image of a slinky negligee still foremost in your mind as you navigate

the intricately detailed Victorian sales floor, dodging faux-antique settees and finding Victoria's Secret T-shirts, bathrobes, slippers, hair ties, candy bars, and even CD's strewn in strategic, perfectly eye-level locations along your primrose-scented path.

Like a woman dying of thirst yet surrounded by a beautiful saltwater ocean, you race desperately through franchised, trademarked, and well-researched accessories only to find that Victoria's *real* Secret is that she's almost stopped carrying lingerie altogether. Or, at least, in your neck of the woods anyway.

What few panties, bras, teddies, and negligee you find are either size 2 or size 22, and obviously the stockgirls are much more interested in ordering more loofahs and lighters and flip-flops and shower caps, all emblazoned with the sassy yet sexy Victoria's Secret logo.

You sigh, finding nothing that floats your boat *or* creams your Twinkie, and leave the lingerie mega-store with nothing but the scent of cheap perfume in your nostrils.

Across the way is a dime store specializing in do-it-yourself T-shirts and those booths where you and a friend take goofy pictures that come out in black and white strips of four. Canned Elvis oozes from the Muzak and there, in between the housedresses your grandmother favors and the motor oil is a tiny rack of frilly, lacy, cheesy teddies with boas sewn in and crotches left out. You laugh at the ridiculously low price and high waistline, and with the change leftover from a $20 bill buy a cheap bottle of champagne at Circle-K on the way home.

When your boyfriend comes home from the office, he hasn't forgotten after all. Bearing loofahs and sponges, bath beads and visors, he dumps them all and their accompanying Victoria's Secret bag on the bed next to your reclined form.

Sipping your champagne before pouring his, a tear collects in one of your eyes at his thoughtfulness.

`"I looked all over for something like—" he stammers, in awe of the cheap yet classy combination spread-eagled before him, "for something I-I-like *that*, but all I got were these free samples. Where did you get that thing so I'll know next year?"

You smile, stifling a sneeze from the damn feather boa, the only thing covering your tingling cleavage, and whisper the answer as you draw him nearer, "Shhh," you say, "It's a secret."

THEY DON'T CALL IT A "WONDERBRA" FOR NOTHING

There are certain ideas that make the American public sit up and wonder, "Why didn't someone think of that before?" The recent rise in popularity of the Wonderbra is surely one such invention. After all, this modern answer to stuffing your bra with tissue paper (or oranges, cantaloupes, whatever) is now as common as the regular old, un-Wonderbra. There's certainly no more shame in admitting that you'd like to be a little more endowed than, say, Olive Oyl. So be free. Buy one. (Heck, buy one . . . for every day of the week!)

Of course, there are numerous benefits to the Wonderbra. (Besides the obvious, that is.) For instance, with advances in recent technology and the refinement of form, texture, and materials, Wonderbras are now as natural as, well, the real thing. (Only bigger.) No more unsightly bulges, folds, ripples, or clasps poking out of your blouse or sweater to give away the fact that your new bust came out of a shopping bag.

Heck, now they even make tank tops and bathing suits with built-in Wonderbras. Why, as long as no one ever sees you naked, you can be a D-cup until they're wheeling you into the local nursing home!

Before the Wonderbra, of course, a woman considering enhancing her breasts had two options: the aforementioned tissue or melon route, or cosmetic surgery. While the tissue and melon route was fine back in high school, cosmetic surgery appeared to be the answer for every girl who ever looked in a Hollywood tabloid and asked herself,

BEFORE

AFTER!

let 'em think it was luck.

not just push-ups anymore. **Wonderbra**

physical contact. Not that you don't want it. Close, physical contact, that is. It's just that, you feel a little bit like an imposter these days and don't want your boyfriend to feel, well, cheated. (Not to mention, empty-handed.)

After all, is it *his* fault you walked into your new job that first day wearing a brand new Wonderbra under your Liz sweater and Gucci scarf? Of course, you've been kicking yourself ever since. But it seemed like such a good idea at the time. You'd moved to an entirely new city after graduating from college, were recruited by one of the best companies in town, and in a fit of celebratory exuberance, walked into a downtown department store and purchased your very first Wonderbra.

"What the heck?" you figured. New town, new job, why not grab yourself some new

"Why can't I look like Jane Mansfield?" At first, anyway.

After hearing numerous horror stories about leaks, tears, and silicone poisoning, many women resigned themselves to the fact that they'd be shopping in the juniors section from now until they started shopping in the seniors section. Of course, the famed Wonderbra changed all of that.

But what happens when the Wonderbra has its desired effect and you actually get to the point of contact? As in, sexual contact. For unless he prefers the lights out, a blindfold, and you can convince your well-endowed girlfriend Betty to stand in for the sex scene, your frisky boy toy might just notice the way you walked into the bedroom a D-cup and ended up an A-cup. Read on:

WILL WONDER (BRA)S EVER CEASE?

Well, it's been a whole month now and somehow, some way, you've managed to avoid any type of close

TOP 5

SIGNS YOU MIGHT NEED A WONDERBRA

5 Women get offended when you walk into the ladies room.

4 The guys at work look surprised when you don't know the scores on Monday morning.

3 People keep mistaking you for Leonardo DiCaprio.

2 You keep getting Old Spice from your "Secret Santa" at work.

1 You got your last bra in 6th grade.

WHAT THE HECK IS MY REAL BRA SIZE ANYWAY?

(Come on, admit it. You always wanted to know!)

Begin by measuring directly under your bust (i.e. around your chest and under your arms) to obtain what is known in the mammary marketplace as your "band" measurement. Next, measure the fullest part of your bust. This is what's known as the "bust-line." The difference in inches between your band measurement and your bust-line is, ta da: your cup size. And now, to answer one of life's biggest mysteries, refer to the chart below:

If the difference between your "band" and your bust-line is:	Your Cup Size is:
Zero to 1½ inches	A
1 to 2½ inches	B
2 to 3½ inches	C
3 to 4½ inches	D
4 to 5½ inches	DD/E
5 to 6½ inches	F
6 to 7½ inches	G
7 to 8½ inches	H
8 to 9½ inches	I
9 to 10½ inches	J
10 to 11½ inches	K

breasts while you were at it? After all, shopping in the training bra section for the last seven years hasn't exactly been what you'd call "empowering." And besides, no one except your new landlady and next door neighbor, and he was blind, knew what your real rack looked like anyway.

Naturally, the repercussions were instant. You had more free drink offers that week alone than you had in, say, the past, oh, seven years! People stared, and it wasn't just because you had lettuce on your lip. Women were less catty (to your face, anyway), and men were less coordinated. (To date, you'd caused two near misses and one genuine three-car collision.) Like the song says, it was "a whole new world."

And you liked it. You also, you've come to realize, like your boyfriend. Very much. Too much, at this point, to be able to deal with what his reaction might be later that evening. After all, every sign was pointing to this night being *the* night. He'd made reservations at the finest restaurant in town, had flowers delivered to your door, and had

belt buckles.

"I know, I know," he breathes into your ear. "I like you too."

"Not that," you pout. "I haven't been entirely honest with you."

"Me either," he pants, standing before you in boxer shorts and dress socks. "I *really* like you!"

Since this line of conversation isn't really moving you forward (although now you *really* like him, too), you decide to let actions speak louder than words. Specifically, you unbutton your blouse, unclasp your strapless Wonderbra, and let the truth hang out. (Then again, maybe hang is not the right word. Stick out? No, no. How about, poke out? Okay, better . . .)

"Wow," sighs your soon-to-be ex-boyfriend, not taking his eyes off of your boyish physique.

"Well," you explain, "I'm tired of living a lie." Preparing for the inevitable good-bye, you reach for the silk robe lying across your bed. Oh, well, it was fun while it lasted.

been bragging all evening about his "world famous" omelets. (And unless he was talking about whipping one up for dessert, you were pretty sure he was intending on staying the night.)

Your suspicions are confirmed when, before walking you upstairs, he reaches into the backseat for a Land's End backpack and gives you a peevish smile. Smiling yourself, you give over to your passion and find yourself entangled before you even make it through the front door.

"What the heck?" you think as clothes (mostly his) litter the carpet to your bedroom like so many cup sizes you are about to reduce in the next several minutes. Now's as good a time to come clean as any.

"There's something I want to tell you," you murmur around stolen kisses and fumbling

"Thank God," he groans, smacking his forehead. "I thought I was going to have to put up with those big hooters for the rest of my life. I was really starting to get worried."

"Big hooters?" you exclaim, stopping just short of the robe. "But you only paid attention to me when I wore my Wonderbra!"

"Honey," he smiles, "I started paying attention to you the first day I saw you. I didn't know you were wearing one of those god awful things. I just thought you had some type of mammary dysfunction. You know, elephantitis of the breasts or something. Phew, what a relief."

"Relief?" you ask. "But I thought all guys dig big breasts."

"Hey," he explains, moving forward. "Some guys do, *this* guy doesn't."

Smiling, you embrace and don't stop smiling until he whispers in your ear: "Besides, now I don't feel so bad about stuffing my jockey shorts!"

> "I think it's about time we voted for senators with breasts. After all, we've been voting for boobs long enough."
>
> —Clarie Sargent

BALLOT BOX

BOXER REBELLION

Once the undergarment of choice for traveling salesmen and science professors alone, boxer shorts have exploded of late onto the modern fashion scene. From the walk-shorts of choice for the college crowd, to the middle-third of most junior high and high school students' outfits, even the marketing of boxer shorts has changed forever:

TOP 5 SIGNS YOUR BOXER SHORTS ARE TOO LOOSE

5 Your neighbor's sudden interest in binoculars.

4 No need for that convenient fly when using the bathroom.

3 Sudden draft whenever you walk.

2 "Swinging" has taken on an entirely new meaning . . .

1 . . . so have "blue balls."

BOXERS, ETC.

You've just taken a part-time job at the local Boxers, Etc. store to make a little extra cash for the car payment, electric bill, your drug habit, etc. From the whole application and interview process, you know that Boxers, Etc. is an underwear chain as big as any other retail or fashion mega-outlet—complete with hip, happening, with-it tunes pumped in over the noisy Muzak and other fresh, young faces like yourself standing patiently behind the gleaming rows of eight constantly chattering computerized cash registers.

You show up for work on your first day, looking respectable in your khaki Dockers and powder blue, button-down Oxford, ready to don the traditional Boxers, Etc. apron, hat, or nametag. However, Tad, your brand new, 22-year old manager fresh from the MBA program at the local state university, instantly informs you that all Boxers, Etc. employees, except for himself, of course, are expected to wear the actual product out on the sales floor.

"It was my idea, actually," he gloats, fingering the weak goatee on his even weaker chin. "It's cheaper than buying those cheesy

mannequins *plus* you don't have any of those employee-stealing-uniforms-when-I-fire-them issues like we did when I interned at Burger King."

When you politely protest, he points casually to those gleaming cash registers and illuminates the fact that, if you look closely enough beneath the counters they sit upon, all of the cashiers, male and female, are in fact wearing boxer shorts of varying shades, sizes, and shapes. You mention how convenient it was of Tad not to point this fact out the day you accepted the job. He simply replies, "If I had, would you have come back?"

"I do not believe in an afterlife, although I am bringing a change of underwear."
—Woody Allen

Point made, he gives you an entire ten minutes to pick out five pairs of boxer shorts, one for each shift you work a week. Then you are to report to his broom closet-sized office to sign your W-2 forms and, hopefully, *not* have to model your five choices in private.

As you scour the store in record time, you suddenly realize how big it actually is. Boxer shorts, it seems, are no longer just plain "underwear." In fact, boxer shorts are hardly even boxer shorts at all anymore.

This fact becomes even more apparent as you peruse through the "silk" section, where brand names like Tabasco and Budweiser adorn garments that look more like lengthy, clingy Speedos than the plaid and striped baggy unmentionables your Dad used to wear around the house on lazy Sunday mornings.

You reach out to touch their delicate, clingy, almost sensual material and imagine yourself wearing a pair on the sales floor, swishing seductively to and fro as you aid female customers who can't help noticing your "enthusiasm" for the job, no matter how far you bend over to give them change.

Skipping silk, you head for the "flannel" section next, where pockets and buttons proliferate and mere lumberjack plaid has been replaced by purple, paisley, fuscia, and burnt umber. A college freshman grabs a size Large covered in smiley faces and slips them on over her Spandex biking shorts in the middle of an aisle. You watch in awe as she saunters off casually to pay for them before wearing them out—in public.

Maybe your manager isn't such a pervert after all. After making only the polite attempt at the Denim, Sweat Pant, Tan-through, See-through, Muslin, Polyester, and Velour boxer aisles, you finally find Cotton stuck in a corner at the very back of the store. Here the pickings are slim to none, but you somehow manage to grab five XL pairs that, thanks to the current "retro" trend, aren't all that dissimilar to what your dad wore "back in the day."

Filling out paperwork in Tad's entirely too-organized-for-a-22-year-old's office, he glances at your selections and grunts, "The company pays for them, you know. You didn't have to scrounge through the 'Clearance' aisle."

You smile, excuse yourself, slip on a pair in the restroom, and wander onto the sales floor, your naked, hairy legs exposed for the whole world to see between your polka-dotted, retro boxers and your old man's dress socks and penny loafers.

An 80-year old spinster gives you the eye in between searching for her nephew's birthday present and fanning herself with the day's sales brochure, and you finally understand how it feels to be a Hooters waitress!

How many skivvies can you make with a bale of cotton?

A bale of cotton weighs about 480 pounds. One bale of cotton can make 1,918 work gloves or 313,600 $100 bills. Here are some things that are made from a bale of cotton.

Handkerchiefs
8,347

Brassieres
6,460

Knit panties
6,436

Boxer shorts
2,104

Men's T-shirts
1,217

Jockey shorts
2,419

Mid-calf socks
4,321

Sleeveless undershirts
1,943

Nightgowns
780

Shorts
733

Diapers
3,085

[Source: *National Cotton Council of America*]

8
HAIRY CONCLUSIONS

What started out as a simple body covering intended to keep us warm and safe from mastodon mosquitoes and saber-toothed tiger flies has blossomed into a cultural obsession and multi-billion dollar industry that has made the likes of such follicle icons as Paul Mitchell, Vidal Sassoon, and Jose Eber household names. For hair is much more than a necessity in these days of air conditioning and mosquito repellant. Indeed, follicle fashion is right up there with haute couture and Tommy Hilfiger when you get right down to it. And God forbid you should lose a little. You might as well invest in a lifetime supply of overalls and move to Siberia, as far as follicle focused America is concerned.

That said, at least all of this hair-raising hijinx leaves you choices. Lots and lots of choices. From dreadlocks to bobs, crewcuts to Caesar, your hair can say as much, or as little, about you as you choose to reveal. But why stop with your natural hair itself? Today there are extensions to make it longer, weaves to make it fuller, and everything from butterfly barrettes to chopsticks to top it all off.

Don't like the color? Dye it. Sick of that ornery cowlick? Braid it. Why not? After all, it's only hair.

HAIR AFFAIR: OUR LOVE FOR LOCKS

Throughout history, human beings have had a bona fide love affair with their hair. While body hair slowly shed as we evolved and pubic hair quickly became an embarrassment to cover up with fig leafs and loincloths, the long, luxurious hair on top of our heads continued to mystify and delight us. From those charming pterodactyl bones sticking out of Betty Rubble's prehistoric "do," to the fake powdered wigs of Victorian England, to Farrah Fawcett's tumbling locks, hair has been the one truly portable fashion accessory. After all, humans came with hair included!

Despite the lack of blow dryers or butterfly clips, hair still managed to be a driving force in Biblical times. (Remember what happened to Samson when he let Delilah mess with his?) Naturally, thanks to the lack of scissors or razors, long hair was all the rage

HAIR TRENDS in your Fashion FUTURE

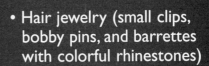

- Hair jewelry (small clips, bobby pins, and barrettes with colorful rhinestones)

- Full and voluminized long hair

- Glitter

- Bobby pins in pairs (with colorful rhinestones or jewels)

- Flowers made of faceted crystals and faux pearls

- Braids

- Fancy scarves (like your grandmother wore)

- The "blown away" look for guys

- Wraps (look like scarves)

- Frog, fish, and sea horse clips and barrettes

- Black or brown tortoise shell clips with rhinestones

- Tiny sparkles

TOP 10 TIPS FOR BETTER HAIR

10 Use salon brands. (They're worth it.)

9 Stay out of tanning beds! (Or use a sunscreen on your hair, or wrap your hair with a towel if you do).

8 Take TV ad claims with a grain of salt!

7 Ask your stylists questions about what they are using to achieve your style.

6 Use a moisturizer with UV protectors.

5 Use a shampoo with a pH of 4.5 to 5.5.

4 Blow-dry your hair on "cool."

3 When combing out tangles, use a wide toothed comb.

2 Don't do color at home, see a good stylist instead.

1 Don't spray lightening products on your hair.

throughout much of history. Men and women alike toyed with such longhaired styles as ponytails, buns, braids, and piles atop their heads.

Much of ancient writing reveals the historical concept of hair as a symbol. A symbol of strength, comeliness, virility, and power. Long hair kept warriors' heads warm on long, winter nights and kept their women busy while they waited for their return from battle.

As civilization grew more "civilized," additions were made to hair to enhance its beauty and add variety to the boring drudgery of hunting and gathering, foraging and pillaging. There were the aforementioned bones, followed closely by flowers, sticks, leaves, vines, oak branches, wreaths, and beads.

Before soap, shampoo, or even beer, egg, and mayonnaise concoctions, both women and men used a heady combination of blended herbs like rosemary, chamomile, ginseng, lemongrass, nettle, lavender, and sage to keep hair clean and smelling fresh. Eventually, of course, the Iron Age dawned and humans quickly realized that all of those swords, daggers, and blades could be used for something other than battle or the sacrifice of virgins.

Peruvians, Africans, Greeks, and Romans alike all dabbled in the finer arts of "barber"-ism and created the famously fabulous hairdos that still abound in history textbooks throughout elementary schools across the world. Naturally, each ancient culture had its own unique style. But as modes of transportation improved and trade routes opened, civilizations were eventually introduced to each other and, accordingly, each other's fab fops.

But hairstyles were not the only things traded along these routes. Silk scarves, jade hairpieces, turquoise combs, and other exotic accessories soon crossed the beehive boundaries to give follicle fashion a real kick in the pants. And if silk and other fabrics could be dyed, why not hair?

Why stop there? Tired of being a leprous beggar? Sore from hoeing the fields all morning? Aching from participating in the world's oldest profession? Why not sell your hair? Whether it be doubloons, coquina shells, or drachmas, human hair soon became a commodity as more progressive civilizations began the manufacture of wigs from human hair. Whether it be for business or pleasure, the business of hair was here to stay.

Since then, of course, the planet's love affair with hair has "evolved" into worldwide obsession. Fortunes have been made (and lost) on the manufacture of hair products, cleansers, dyes, and accessories. Modern

TOP 10 CDs EVERY HAIRDRESSER SHOULD OWN

10 Skip Rats
Let Your Hair Down

9 Kimberli Ransom
Living With Her Hair On Fire

8 Barney Kessel
Hair Is Beautiful

7 Weird Al Yankovic
Bad Hair Day

6 Cement
Man With The Action Hair

5 Steve Goodman
Artistic Hair

4 Annalise
You Can Dye Your Hair But Not Your Heart

3 Nazareth
Hair Of The Dog

2 D C Parkinson
Don't Let Your Hair Grow

1 Original Broadway Recording
Hair

inventions didn't hurt, either. Scissors revolutionized hair care all the world over, and were soon followed by hot irons, curlers, and those little levers the barbers use to raise and lower their chairs.

Electricity not only brought us further inventions like curling irons and blow dryers, but radio, TV, and the movies as well. Rock bands like the Beatles, politicians like Henry Kissinger, activists like Angela Davis, movie stars like Bette Davis, TV heroines like Lucille Ball, punkers like Sid Vicious, and even baldies like Michael Jordan all gave us daring dos and happening hair to emulate and imitate.

Naturally, the booming business of barber shops, beauty parlors, and full-service salons didn't hurt. After all, revolutionaries like Vidal Sassoon, Paul Mitchell, and José Eber became just as famous as the celebrities, movers, and shakers they so cleverly coiffed. And what does the future hold for hair? A cure for baldness, perhaps? (Extra-double-super strength Rogaine?) New hair colors for the young and old alike? Or perhaps computerized clippers? While it's still too soon to tell, one thing is certain: our love affair with hair is in no danger of fizzling out anytime soon!

DREADLOCK HOLIDAY

Dreadlocks. Locks. Dreads. Nattys. Whatever you want to call them, the hairstyle dating back to the founding of a uniquely Afro-Caribbean religion called Rastafarianism in the 1920s is definitely making a comeback. The name, dreadlocks, was originally coined in response to nonbelievers who were surprised by the decidedly "earthy" hairstyle, as in "Gee, I really dread those long locks."

However, not all of this decidedly recognizable hairstyle's wearers are as socially conscious as its originators. After all, the origin of dreads is a Biblical one. "They shall not make baldness upon their head," reads Leviticus 21:5, and taking this as their spiritual guide, true Rastas outlawed the combing or cutting of their hair. As a result, it formed natural strands, or locks, of rich, long, curly hair as a testimony of their wearer's faith.

When Bob Marley sang "Natty Dread" (i.e. "knotty dread") in the mid-1970s, the term dreadlocks found its way into the international vocabulary. Since then, of course, the peace, love, and harmony vibes of the Rastafarianism religion have found their way to America, where the pleasantly jammin' reggae we hear on the radio makes us feel "Irie."

Of course, it doesn't hurt that dreads look so darn cool and are a massive babe magnet! Thus, dreadlocks as a fashion statement are apparently here to stay—whatever the wearer's religious beliefs (or non-beliefs). Need proof? Read on:

Rastafarianism

"They shall not make baldness upon their head."
Leviticus 21:5

TOP 5 REASONS TO GROW DREADLOCKS

5 One shake of your head makes your dreads deadly weapons.

4 Great camouflage when hiding in the broom closet.

3 You and your girlfriend always have something to talk about.

2 Gives you that "just got back from a cruise" look all year long.

1 Perfect for hiding your extra house key.

NATTY DREAD(HEAD)

It's nights like this one that make all the hard work of keeping your dreadlocks up to snuff worth it. 'Cause it's not easy, mon. The extremely detailed washing vs. non-washing schedule posted next to your bathroom window. The myriad of hair products scattered hither and yon in your medicine cabinet, on top of your toilet tank, under the sink, and even spilling onto your kitchen counter. The rubber bands, the beads, the cowry shells, the gaily-colored knit caps. Why, it's downright never-ending.

In fact, all of the hard hair work is exactly what you picture being a girl must be like, only without the attractive, topless (not to mention bottomless) reflection staring back at you in the mirror each morning.

Still, on a night like tonight, all of the hard work and effort, the cost and the time, fade kindly into the woodwork as you sip your Corona and enjoy the jammin' sounds of a passable, if predictable, reggae band.

The lilt of steel drums tinkle in your ear, relaxing you as you order another beer, careful to shake your head dramatically for the Jewel look-alike who's

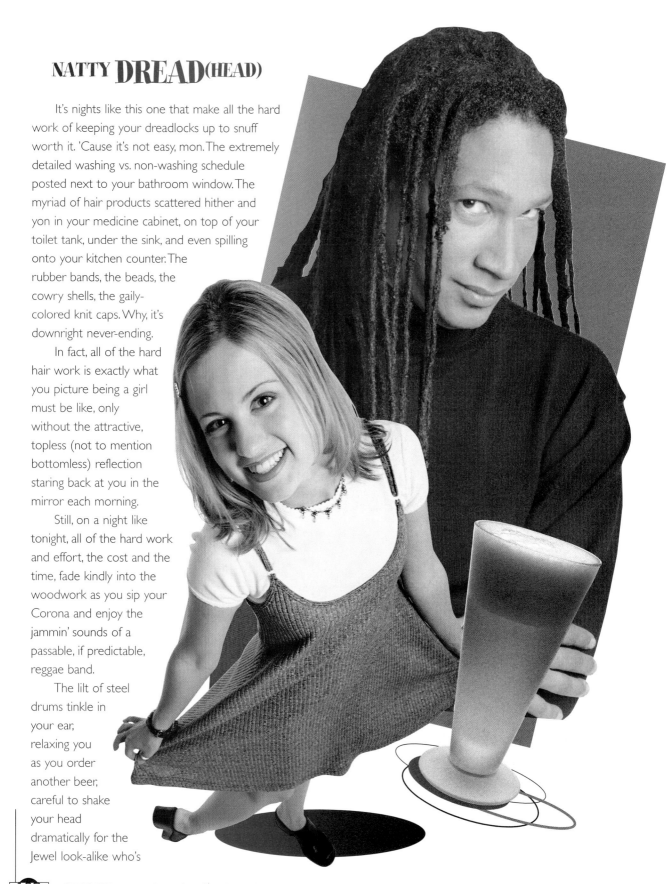

been eyeing you for the last three songs. You can tell she's into the whole "Jamaican Me Crazy" vibe and hope you can fake enough Irie and "Yah, Mon"-s to get her phone number by the band's last, inevitable version of "Redemption Song."

Surprisingly, it doesn't even take that long.

"What are you doing here?" she exclaims, sliding several barstools over and toying seductively with the fresh-squeezed lime on your cocktail napkin.

"Same thing you're doing here," you reply. "Just chillin'."

It only takes a few minutes of "Stir It Up" small talk before she tentatively reaches out to touch your long, luxuriant hair.

"Do you mind?" she asks, curling one, long lock around her mood-ring-covered finger.

TOP 10

REGGAE CDs

(TO LISTEN TO WHILE CARING FOR YOUR DREADLOCKS)

10 Steel Pulse
True Democracy

9 Burning Spear
Reggae Greats

8 Black Uhuru
Chill Out

7 Various Artists
Reggatta Mondatta

6 Gregory Isaacs
Night Nurse

5 Ziggy Marley
Spirit of Music

4 Third World
96 Degrees in the Shade

3 Inner Circle
Speak My Language

2 Peter Tosh
Legalize It

1 Bob Marley &
The Wailers
Legend

"Not at all," you mutter. "Knock yourself out."

Closing your eyes and enjoying the female attention for a change, you're surprised when a sharp "yank" jerks you back into rasta reality.

"Oww," you cry, reaching instinctively to protect your skillfully scalped skull. "What'd you do that for?"

"My friends would never believe I met you," she gushes, admiring the fractured follicles clasped in her hand. "I needed some proof."

"Proof of what?" you say, nursing your scalped scalp.

"Duh," she explains succinctly. "How often do you run into Ziggy Marley at some boring, old nightclub? I hope you don't mind, I just couldn't help myself. I loved your last album."

"Me too," you agree. "Only, I'm *not* Ziggy Marley. I'm a bike messenger. Now I think you owe me a beer."

Disappointed, your lady friend nonetheless complies with your Corona court order, although you notice that your larcenous locks now reside unceremoniously inside a bar top ashtray instead of in her superstar scalp scrapbook. By way of apology, she offers to dance with you, only to realize you weren't playing hard to get when you tried to beg off a total of twenty-three polite, if insistent, times.

"You can't even dance?" she exclaims loudly next to one of the band's speakers, rubbing her damaged toes. When you nearly poke her eyes out with a shake of your legendary lion's mane, she gives up and returns to her former seat at the end of the bar—alone. Until the band's next break, that is.

"Oh, well," you think, heading home, alone, minutes later. "I can't blame the dreadlocks. It's not their fault the rest of my body's not as cool as my head."

GOBS OF GOATEES, THICK VAN DYKES, AND FU MANCHU TOO

When speaking of hair, one must go below the forehead to paint an accurate picture of today's facial hair fashions. While the bushy lumberjack look has slowly faded away, many forms of the half-beard are more popular than ever, much to the delight of weak-chinned men, and much to the chagrin of whisker-chafed women.

WHISKER WISDOM

In ancient times the bearded chin was considered a sign of strength and virility, a symbol of manhood and confidence. Highly prized, its removal was regarded as a degrading punishment. At least, that's the historical spin. More than likely a furry chin was simply the byproduct of the extreme

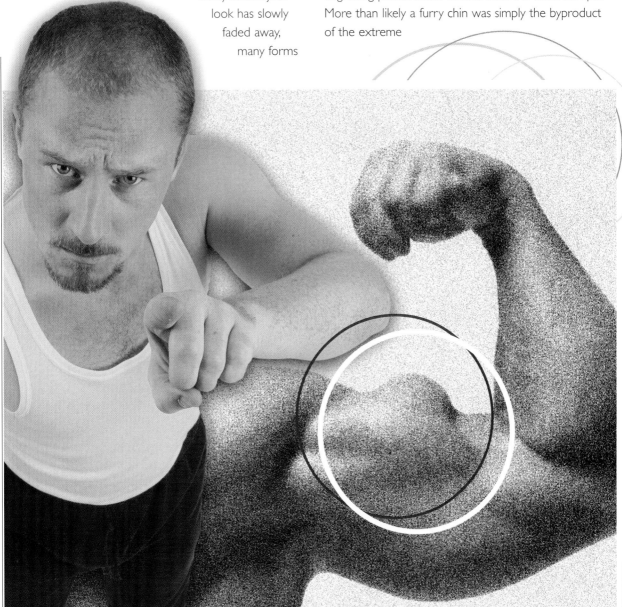

inconvenience it must have taken to shave back then.

With today's grooming utensils literally on the "cutting edge," however, modern men have never had it so good. From the recent Mach 3 razor to cordless electric shavers that come complete with reservoirs that automatically release a soothing skin balm, technology is shaving time off of a man's morning bathroom routine.

So, naturally, they don't use them and grow a wide variety of hairy facial crops. What exactly are the many types sprouting on men's faces these days? Ranked in order from shaggiest to most sparse, here is a sampling of scruff:

First let's consider what many refer to as the "hermit" beard. This whisker wonder shows exactly what can happen when you leave people by themselves for too long. Its scruffy, uneven length reveals an apparent uncaring attitude for the beard or appearances in general. However, one's homeless status is not a requirement for a follicle faux pas of this magnitude. Many wannabe hippies, granolas, and performance artists, not to mention the odd cult leader or Unabomber, cultivate just

Hermit Beard

Patchwork Beard

such a beard to further cement their images as reckless individuals not likely to conform to society's standards anytime soon. Naturally, such extreme fashion

TOP 5

SIGNS YOU'RE NOT READY TO GROW A BEARD

5. Your mom keeps trying to wipe it off with a washcloth.

4. Your barber says, "Trim what?"

3. You begin to hear the words "peach fuzz" more than twice a day.

2. Your girlfriend keeps telling you to wash your face.

1. What you thought was a moustache was really just your nose hair.

Goatee

beliefs, the chunk is all about overcompensation. It is intended to exude undeniable masculinity, virility, and lack of timidity. "Look," some chunk wearers are really saying, "I may be 42 with male pattern baldness and feet the size of a Barbie doll, but look how thick my beard is. Who's the man now, you wispy whiskered punk?"

The "patchwork" beard, while more manageable than the hermit and less prominent than the chunk, is a nonetheless unique follicle fashion statement notable for its incongruence with the hair on the same owner's head. The most common occurrence of this is the man with strawberry blond hair but a full on, Valentine's heart-red beard.

Then there's just the plain, old regular beard, which consists of simple facial hair on the cheeks, lips, chin, and neck. Often known as the "full beard," this is the most recognizable (and boring) style of beard throughout facial hair history.

statements are prone to their own unique set of pitfalls. Dangers of the "hermit" beard include, but are not limited to, thriving colonies of small insects forming in the middle of one's own face and replies such as "sorry, you can't be seated without a reservation" even though the restaurant is half empty.

A slight variation of the hermit is "the chunk," so named because of its chunkiness, fullness, and ability to hold chunks of food in and around the mouth for later consumption by the owner. While this bulging beard is often just as full and thick as the hermit, the chunk stands apart because it is actually relatively well groomed despite its ridiculous thickness.

While the hermit is most often either a comment on one's laziness or radical social

Full Beard

The goatee is an extremely popular style of modern facial hair achieved by only growing the beard and moustache directly around the lips and sometimes below the chin, much like its namesake, the goat. This style is extremely popular with those hipsters on the outer cusp of their age

Spit Catcher

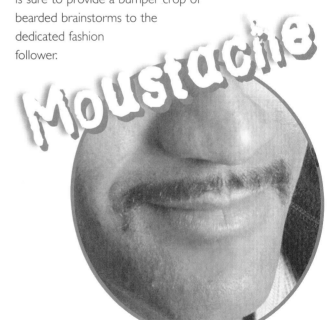

Velcro. This style of beard is also known as an "imperial" and is sometimes called a "mouche", which is French for fly.

Of course, there is always the plain old moustache, that simple component of facial hair that grows above the upper lip. However, notorious lip hair notables such as Hitler, Oliver Hardy, and Wyatt Earp have done little to reinvigorate the moustache's once heady heyday. However, if a moustache-wearing Brad Pitt stars in the next summer blockbuster, all bets are off.

Finally, of course, comes that under-appreciated form of beard otherwise known as the "sideburn." While often mistaken for a part of one's real head of hair, sideburns are actually a part of the beard that just happens to grow in front of the ears instead of around the mouth. The sideburns generally connect the hair on the scalp with the rest of the beard, but many "closet" bearders prefer to grow just their sideburns while the rest of their face remains clean-shaven.

Naturally, such a simple scruffy style is a function of time and space. New styles, hybrids, and variations are always a simple razor stroke (or lack of one, as is the case with mutton chops) away.

However, should facial hair inspiration fail you in your search for the perfect style, a quick stroll through any crowded bus station, rock concert, or DMV office is sure to provide a bumper crop of bearded brainstorms to the dedicated fashion follower.

bracket, many of whom find themselves dealing with premature baldness and are therefore taking advantage of the only possible way to retain their coolness and dignity. (At least from the front, anyway.)

Modern variations of the goatee are plentiful. For instance, the famed Fu Manchu and the Van Dyke have both made comebacks as artsy alternatives to the standard moustache or beard. Yet even these standards are too tame for some, who have somehow managed to find alternatives to the alternatives.

One such whisker whimsy takes the clean shaven look and caps it off with a lengthy wisp of hair on the tip of one's chinny, chin, chin. Like a ponytail on the wrong side of one's head, these wisps of hair are urged to grow as long as possible and then braided or augmented with colored rubber bands. This look is often accessorized with tattoos, clove cigarettes, a glazed look in the eye, outstanding warrants, skull rings, B. O., and pierced lips.

Another beard variation is often referred to simply as the "soul patch" or the "spit catcher." This is the minimal beard style that covers only a small area below the lower lip, like a miniature carpet sample or patch of

Moustache

THE MULLET:
WILL IT EVER GO
EXTINCT?

Oh, the power of the Internet. The power to emulate, speculate, regulate, and denigrate. The power to humiliate, regurgitate, exfoliate, and intoxicate. Where else can one find everything from pickled herring to porn, purses to pinball machines, all in the comfort of your own den?

And now you can also find, right there on the Internet, an entire subculture, cult following, and Web ring devoted to, what else: the mullet! Not that mild-tasting, inexpensive, gray scaled, spiny vegetarian fish that inevitably gets slivered into fish sticks for mass consumption when the kiddies are hungry and even flounder is out of the question. No, the only swimming this mullet is doing is when its wearer takes a bath or, better yet, a long walk off a short pier.

For this mullet is a hairstyle so ludicrous, so white trash, so ridiculous, so ugly, so odd, so aggravating, that one can't tell whether to hate it or—love it.

Don't quite believe it? The Beastie Boys sing about it: "One on the sides/don't touch the back; Six on the top/and don't cut it whack, Jack . . ." in "Mullet Head," the B-side of 1994's single "Sure Shot."

So, what's up with the name? "Mullet-head" was apparently a 19th-century English term for a cretin or fool. A 1932 edition of Webster's

TOP 5 SIGNS YOUR HAIRDO IS OUT OF STYLE

5 Your grandmother's never been more proud of you.

4 Quentin Tarantino wants you for his next film.

3 The Smithsonian keeps leaving annoying messages on your answering machine.

2 Your girlfriend enrolls you in the "Hat of the Month" club.

1 Donald Trump asks where you got the new 'do.

dictionary defines mullet as a verb, "to curl or dress the hair." It is also an old French word for "dim."

One common myth is that the Mullet hairstyle gets its name from the like-named mullet breed of fish. Legend has it the fishmongers of Iceland cultivated the hairstyle to keep their necks warm and dry against the frigid North Atlantic spray. Another stems from the Paul Newman flick, *Cool*

Hand Luke, where one prisoner calls another prisoner with short/long hair a "mullethead." Either way, the name is here to stay. Unless, of course, you choose to call this abominable haircut by its other numerous names, such as Neckwarmer, Ape Drape, Sphinx, Hack Job, Mud Flap, Boz (as in Brian Bosworth), Schlong (short on the sides, long in back), S&L crisis, and Long Island Iced "Tease."

So, what caused a long dead hairstyle to suddenly resurge in "popularity?" One theory proposes that the catalyst for the revival was perhaps the marriage of Elizabeth Taylor to so-called "Mullet Czar," Larry Fortensky. Another, and more popular, school of thought is enough to break your heart, as in, Billy Ray Cyrus's well-publicized mullet cut during his entire "Achy, Breaky Heart" rise to fame. (Not that he's stopped wearing it, by the way.)

And, while both of the above short-lived celebrities have long since come and gone, other clueless coiffeurs have remained around just long enough to perpetuate their hard-headed hairstyle. Leading the pack was tennis star Andre Agassi, that is, until he began thinning on top and shaved his head in the mid-1990s. Then girlfriend Brooke Shields was reportedly "thrilled." Wrestler Hulk Hogan chose to keep his mullet while losing it on top, so that he now sports a "skullet" or "fading glory."

The look, however, is not just for white males. Eddie Murphy was mulletized in *The Vampire from Brooklyn*. Satin-voiced soul singer Barry White and even the black activist Rev. Al Sharpton have also gone long and short at the same time. Furthermore, tennis legend Martina Navratilova and folk rockers the Indigo Girls sport female mullets, just to prove it's not just a guy thing.

So, there's the mullet hairstyle, all wrapped up for you in one big fish net.

Celebrity Mullets

(at least at one point in their career)

Billy Ray Cyrus
singer

Kyle Petty
race car driver

David Bowie
singer

Nick Kershaw
country singer

Jerry Seinfeld
comedian

Mike Awesome
pro wrestler

Travis Tritt
country singer

Patrick Swayze
actor

Alan Jackson
country singer

The Indigo Girls
singers

Michael Flatley
Lord of the Dance(r)

Martina Navratilova
tennis player

Barry White
singer

Gallagher
comedian

Mel Gibson
actor

Jeff Foxworthy
comedian

Eddie Murphy
actor

Randy Johnson
baseball player

Dwight Yoakam
country singer

Larry Fortensky
husband

Michael Bolton
singer

Hulk Hogan
pro wrestler

HAIR TODAY, GONE TOMORROW

After an extreme amount of soul searching, and an even more extreme amount of money spent on hair growth products, thickening agents, and knit caps, you have come to a major life decision. That premature bald spot (why is nothing that starts with the word "premature" ever positive?) that you've been obsessing over for the last year and a half has finally gotten the better of you.

Of course, you gave Rogaine its best shot. You also bought the $40 vitamin-H (for Hair) shampoo your gum-cracking, pregnant, smoke-infested hairdresser raved about. You've gone the Ron Howard/ball cap route. You've even considered, then quickly *re*considered, hair plugs.

However, to your credit, you never did let the rest of your "good" hair grow extra-long only to use the lengthy wisps to comb across it.

Nonetheless, none of it worked, and the other day, while patting your head absently at a red

TOP 5
POLITE WAYS TO GET YOUR MAN TO USE ROGAINE

5 "You know, I wouldn't have to wear sunglasses so much if that glare off the top of your head wasn't so blinding."

4 "When I said I wanted to date a celebrity look-alike, I didn't mean Ron Howard."

3 "Does your bald spot ever get cold? I was thinking of knitting it a sweater for Christmas."

2 "Don't you think you're a little old for a baseball cap collection?"

1 "Dang, I forgot my compact again. Can I use your head?"

light, you were surprised to discover that that cold patch of bare—something— wasn't a tennis visor, yarmulke, or the plastic cover somehow fallen from your dome light. It was skin! Real, live, actual skin with no hair covering it whatsoever.

Nada. None.

Sure, it was only the size of a quarter, (okay, maybe more like a 50-cent piece) sitting there in the middle of your otherwise bushy head of perfectly good hair. But you were quite sure that by the end of the year it would be the size of a tea saucer, and beyond that, who really knew. Either way, you weren't having it. And so, heading straight from the red light to the mall,

BEST SONGS TO LISTEN TO AT THE BEAUTY PARLOR

10 Robyn Hitchcock *"August Hair"*

9 Louis Jordan *"(You Dyed Your Hair) Chartreuse"*

8 Nick Cave & The Bad Seeds *"Black Hair"*

7 Chenille Sisters *"Big Hair"*

6 Robert Klein *"100% Undetectable Hairpiece"*

5 Skunks *"Big Hair Girl"*

4 Dave Evans *"Be Proud of the Gray in Your Hair"*

3 Elvis Costello *"Baby's Got a Brand New Hairdo"*

2 Hair (Soundtrack) *"Hair"*

1 Jon Rose *"At the Hairdresser"*

you invested $30 in one of those do-it-yourself electric razors and raced directly home to the bathroom mirror before you could chicken out.

"If Satan ever loses his hair, there'll be hell toupee."

—Anonymous

Then, like something out of *Platoon* or *Full Metal Jacket* (only without the graphic battle scenes to follow) shorn locks of your thinning hair fell into the sink like so many leaves clattering to the ground from the fall trees.

TOP 10

WORST SONGS TO LISTEN TO AT THE BEAUTY PARLOR

10 Mary Ann Farley
"Better Haircut"

9 Indigo Swing
"Big Hair Mama"

8 Candyskins
"Bad Hair Day"

7 Morrissey
"Baby Let Your Hair Grow Long"

6 Charlie Parker
"Another Hair-Do"

5 Crosby, Stills, Nash & Young
"Almost Cut My Hair"

4 Finn
"Bullets In My Hairdo"

3 Screaming Lord Sutch
"All Black and Hairy"

2 Mick Turner
"Beautiful Hairy Cow"

1 Ike Willis
"Blond Hair, Blond Teeth"

Resisting the impulse to save them and glue them back on later, when you finally came to your senses, you threw them quickly away instead. After all, you'd come this far.

With a regular razor, you lathered up your head like some human ice cream cone and shaved the stubble left by the clippers off of your now entirely bald head, ever so gingerly, of course, not wanting to look like a skull-shaped pizza for the rest of the week.

You then decided, after careful consideration and several shots of tequila, that, actually, it didn't look so bad. It was rather chilly, considerably shiny, and not entirely disgusting as you rubbed your head over and over, back and forth, again and again.

Naturally, to compensate, you immediately began a month long program to grow the fullest, thickest beard you possibly could.

After all, you'd need some excuse to go visit that little cutie of a hairdresser who'd been hired to replace your old one while she was out on pregnancy leave.

Types of HAIR LOSS

Alopecia Areata:
Generally thought to be an autoimmune disorder. Causes "patchy" hair loss, often in small circular areas in different areas of the scalp.

Alopecia Totalis:
Total hair loss of the scalp (an advanced form of alopecia areata).

Alopecia Universalis:
Hair loss of the entire body (also an advanced form of alopecia areata).

Traction Alopecia:
Hair loss caused by physical stress and tension on the hair such as prolonged use of hair weaving, corn rows, etc. Done too tightly on weak hair, these can cause permanent hair loss.

Telogen Effluvium:
Usually temporary hair loss. Causes: Physical stress, emotional stress, thyroid abnormalities, medications, and hormonal causes normally associated with females.

Anagen Effluvium:
Generally due to internally administered medications, such as chemotherapy agents, that poison the growing hair follicle.

Treatments for HAIR LOSS

—Learning to live with hair loss. Often the assistance of a professional counselor can be helpful in coping with hair loss.

—Hair styling and cosmetic techniques such as permanent waves and hair colors. The proper haircut alone can make a vast difference in diffusing hair loss.

—Rogaine, the only FDA approved topical treatment for male or female pattern hair loss. Although Rogaine is not effective in stimulating new hair growth in many males, it appears to be more effective in retarding hair loss in a substantial amount of both male and females.

—Hair Additions have made many advances in both appearance and more secure attachment methods.

—Hair Replacement Surgery has also made many advances toward more natural appearing results.

—A combination of Hair Additions with Hair Replacement Surgery.

(Courtesy of *The American Hair Loss Council*)

9
FASHION NET-IQUETTE

Parking spaces. Malls. Food courts. Clearance racks. Snooty salesgirls. Ah, shopping! Forget what you thought you knew about that most hallowed of all purchasing pastimes. The Internet, combined with your handy home computer, has made your most secret wish and hidden fantasy come true: Yes, it's true, you can finally shop in your underwear! Or not. It's up to you. Either way, the World Wide Web has changed the way Americans shop.

From lipstick to lingerie, toupees to taupe tube tops, your Web browser is your new best friend in the cutting edge world of fashion e-tail. Sure, shopping from home may take some getting used to. (Especially if you're overly fond of escalators!) But where else can you put on your own Muzak, down a dozen donuts, and clip your toenails, all while choosing the latest fall fashions?

So boot up your laptop, whip out that credit card, log on, and start shopping. Just make sure you put your clothes back on before the UPS man arrives. Or not. It's up to you.

RETAIL VS E-TAIL
WHERE WILL YOU SHOP IN THE NEW MILLENNIUM?

Whether it's makeup or mustard-yellow socks, you can be sure to find it on the Internet. And while e-commerce and Internet shopping are fast becoming all the rage, one question still remains, "What's the fun of shopping without the rude cashiers, 200 elbow-and-purse-swinging fellow customers, and, most important, a nearby food court?"

In the lucrative world of cosmetics, new beauty "e-tailers" are springing up all over. At the same time, existing beauty and cosmetics name brands are scrambling to make a presence online just to compete for the estimated $16 billion that Americans now spend on beauty products. As a retail result, beauty Web sites have truly changed the "face" of shopping for cosmetics.

By the end of 1999, Internet beauty stores were exploding faster than pimples after a sweet tooth marathon, to the tune of thirty-two multi-brand beauty Web sites and counting, including Eve.com, Beauty.com, iBeauty.com, and Beautyjungle.com, all hawking their cosmetic creations in cyberspace.

Which, at first, seems like a makeup match made in hard-drive heaven. Until you "double-click" a little further, that is. There seem to be two kinds of sites:

Welcome to the jungle— Beautyjungle.com, that is. This beauty site's home page welcomes you with soothing purple tones while hitting you with a dizzying array of icons and choices. Cosmetics are organized into different categories, ranging from Elite Street, where products start at $25, to Main Street, where you can pick

up items from such industry icons as Cover Girl for under $6. This kind of shopping may never compete with the testing you can do in a store, but Beautyjungle.com tries to compensate by allowing you to double-click and get a close-up look at shades and colors.

And, once you've filled your funky zebra-striped "shopping bag," why not stick around for some lively reading on the site's "beauwwwty" Web zine. The "Confessions" column answers questions on embarrassing topics like fingernail fungus, while "Celebrity Rip-off" lets you click on different body parts (not *those* body parts—we're talking eyes, cheeks, lips) of today's hyperlinked Hollywood hotties. Try that in your local department store!

Like Beautyjungle.com and many of its other cyber competitors, Beautyscene.com blends convenient e-commerce with easy to understand editorial content. And savvy cybershoppers can make the most of

TOP 5

WAYS "E-TAIL" IS BETTER THAN RETAIL

5 No more blushing with the other losers over at the clearance aisle.

4 You can take all the time you want in the "fitting room."

3 Two words: adults only.

2 No more excuses about your girlfriend's "agoraphobia" when buying women's underwear.

1 Fragrance of Pop-Tarts beats any store's "perfume alley."

instance, the heaviest item for sale on Eve.com is a gallon of bubble bath.) Also, while high-end cosmetic companies refuse to discount, unlike Amazon.com, which has to discount books furiously to fight off crafty competitors, different beauty Web sites must compete by offering user-friendly sites that provide personal advice, beauty tips, and free gifts or samples.

But unless sites like Beautyjungle.com and Beautyscene.com can deliver the product behind the promise, it will take more than aroma therapy, makeup tips, and perfume samples to soothe the manicured masses and compete with such heavyweights as Estée Lauder and Chanel.

In all fairness, it takes time and effort to build a successful brand. Naturally, the quality of that brand is what will determine whether it actually survives or not. Many of these "all-in-one" sites offer niche, boutique brands, and items that are unavailable

the site by signing up for a free membership, which entitles you to free shipping and personal-shopping features like "My Kit," a place to keep track of your favorite products and even be reminded when it's time to stock up.

Certainly, Internet shopping sites like those we've discussed are well funded and dump huge amounts of cash into the market to build brand awareness and personality, drive traffic, and perhaps most importantly, out-do each other.

And, from a business perspective, online beauty certainly makes sense. Unlike bulky books or costly clothes, blush and perfume weigh ounces rather than pounds and as a result are cheaper to ship. (For

or unknown in most other areas. This, of course, makes total sense.

Taking underground industry products and making them accessible to an upscale audience of beauty buyers is a "keystroke" of sheer cyber genius. Pair that with advice from a league of expert e-editors who in most cases have defected from the most reputable media brands in fashion and beauty, and it gets even better.

However, why would the industry superstars that have invested millions of dollars and toiled for countless years protecting and building their picture perfect images all of a sudden hand it over to some Internet ingénue and relinquish total control? This is precisely the reason many fashion e-tailers are having difficulty signing beauty's biggest name producers.

At Eve.com, "the beauty of the Internet" (the Web site's clever slogan), takes on an entirely new meaning. A new "Web mall" devoted to all things cosmetic, Eve.com offers a wide array of beauty products, from women's perfume to bath beads, from men's cologne to pure badger shaving brushes.

But while a few name brands, such as Hard Candy and Anna Sui cosmetics, do hold court among its clickable Web pages, even the most casual user will notice the absence of such department store staples as Estée Lauder and Chanel.

However, while Eve.com and its cosmetic counterparts are waiting for the day when department stores fade into the same historical tar pit as 8-Tracks and leg warmers, their very e-existence opens up great opportunities for startup cosmetic products themselves.

Therein lies the beauty of the Internet: instant access to the global marketplace is now available through a single, convenient point of entry. Therefore a relatively small (not to mention new) cosmetics company yearning to be the next Hard Candy can readily find room, not to mention sales, distribution, and advertising, on a site like Eve.com's wide open Web pages.

They also give up total control to this digital distributor, who may ship their product late or improperly, or even include a competitor's free samples along with those products actually ordered by the customer. And while these may be necessities for a startup company to gain name-recognition and exposure, a big-name company that has spent a career building up their customer relations would never stand for such cyber shenanigans.

As with much of e-commerce, the market is still too young to know for sure whether women will actually start spending time, let alone money, in cyberspace. What is obvious is that not all of the sites currently duking it out will survive. And so, as secure shoppers become increasingly more familiar with the Internet as an all-in-one-stop-shopping haven, stars will rise and fall along with their stocks.

KINKY KEYWORDS

Anyone who's ever used an Internet search engine knows that what's typed in and what pops up are often two *very* different things. For instance, a simple spice search for say, "salsa," is likely to return hits for salsa music, salsa dancing, salsa recipes, salsa dance, salsa clubs, and even a gay and lesbian support group called S.A.L.S.A.

(or, Society for Advancing Lesbian and Straight Affairs). So if a simple condiment can cause such confusion, it's not too far of a stretch to imagine the purple possibilities that might occur when one harried Internet shopper types in the word "underwear."

START YOUR (SEARCH) ENGINES!

So you've heard all about this Internet shopping craze and have finally decided to take the "perpetual purchasing plunge." After all, your days are full enough as it is. With a professional career and enough extracurricular activities to keep you hopping forty-two hours a day, let alone twenty-four, shopping for clothes is the last thing on your list of personal priorities. And, now that you've found out that even if some cyber scammer does manage to get hold of your credit card number and charges it to the hilt, you're only responsible for the first $50, the last barrier has finally been removed.

So, on a rare Sunday evening with no deadlines to meet and no blind dates to blow off, you settle in at your laptop atop the dinette set/"den" to take your first tentative step onto the information superhighway. With your credit card at the ready and a hot cup of coffee steaming next to you like something out of a Pier One Imports commercial, you log on to AOL and wonder where to begin. After checking your e-mail and making sure no one on your "buddy list" is online to muck things up, you twiddle your thumbs for a few minutes and try to focus.

Since you've never done this before, you start with a simple search on Yahoo! But first, what keyword to type in? Truth be told, you're actually doing all of this just to save yourself a trip to the department store's crowded and cramped lingerie department. Although you're certainly no prude, you still feel there's something slightly shady about running your fingers over bras and panties, teddies and camisoles in public. Not to mention that whole "Cathy" comic strip, bloated-in-the-fitting room traumatic experience. You'd just as soon be sitting in the comfort of your own living room clicking on icons and those cute little cyber shopping carts and avoiding the whole scene altogether.

Still, what exactly *are* you looking for? You have enough teddies and nightgowns to last you a lifetime, thanks to the fact that you've slept in the same Garfield Christmas nightshirt since your last serious boyfriend gave it to you three holiday seasons ago.

Meanwhile, every slinky nightgown you've ever been given, or purchased after reading one of *Cosmo's* annual "Treat Yourself" articles, hangs delicately in the back of your closet from its puffy, satin hanger. Bras, likewise, are something you feel

the need to try on for yourself. G-strings, thongs, and satin panties, on the other hand, cram your bureau drawers like so many overdue bills and dead batteries. Since you wear them rarely and indulge in buying them often, your supply and demand ratio is definitely in the overflow mode.

Therefore, you are in the market for your simple, basic, cotton underwear. Something comfortable and not too frilly, i.e. expensive. Something to throw on when you're rushed in the morning and not think about until it's time to do the laundry at the end of the day. Something no one but you and your doctor will ever see you in, but something that wouldn't embarrass you if you got into an accident on the way to work. Nothing too colorful or shocking, just simple, basic, everyday underwear of the feminine persuasion.

And, finally focused, you find the friendly blinking cursor and type the keyword "panties" inside the innocent little box among all of the happy, bright, safe Yahoo! desktop clutter. Waiting a beat while the world's most generic search engine processes your request, you take a sip of coffee and look forward to your seated cybershopping experience.

"Here we go," you smile as the bright blue and black results spread like honey across your monitor. And then, to your horror, you discover that not every Tom, Dick, and "Scary" on the World Wide Web defines the word "panties" in quite the same way.

For in an entire screen filled with so called "hits" for your well-intentioned keyword, you quickly discover that not a single site is actually selling anything as innocent and simple as a plain pair of panties.

Unless, that is, they've been worn, sweated in, and scuzzed up by your favorite porn queen, or so goes the description for a site called "pornpanties.com." Scrolling down as your face widens into a silent scream of hard-drive horror, cyber confusion, and e-commerce embarrassment, you find that *that* site is actually one of the least obscene of the bunch!

TOP 5

SIGNS YOU MAY BE TRAPPED ON AN X-RATED WEB SITE

5 The counter is stuck on 69.

4 The models in the banner ads keep swapping partners.

3 Double-clicking on the icons just makes them get bigger…and bigger… and bigger.

2 Hmm, that's funny, you don't remember the URL changing from amazon.com to amazonchicksontop.com!

1 Two words: Pamela Anderson.

Sighing, squinting, and squirming your way through several screens full of panty-inspired Internet impostors, you try several other, supposedly safer searches using keywords like "underwear," "drawers," "boxers," and "briefs," only to find that the same cyber scammers have long-since clued into the keyword confusion that afflicts so many first-time cyber searchers such as yourself.

In the end, nothing you try turns up anything less than hundreds of raunchy results. Which, of course, makes for quite a stimulating, sinful, and satisfying Sunday evening. Once you've made the decision to quit shopping for underwear, that is.

There are panty stories, panty parties, hidden panty cams, and live panty raids. There are sites devoted to nothing more than clickable thumbnail pictures of panties worn by emaciated models in provocative poses. Then there's the site that's devoted entirely to descriptions of panties bearing the word "cheerleader" in every other line. There's the site where the only panties shown are those worn by clowns, and another where only pregnant women are allowed to "panty pose."

There's Vicky's Panties, where a brash tag line reads, "…as a struggling nurse I need to raise cash any way that I can, and so here's the latest— selling my panties." There's Scent of a Woman Worn Panties, run by "…a sexy female who will send you her very own panties or other items of lingerie fetish."

CYBER CATWALKS

With the inventive Internet now offering top designer fashion shows online, why would anyone in their right mind bother jetting off to Paris, London, or New York? Okay, because they're Paris, London, and New York. But not only can you now enjoy the luxury of viewing the hottest fashions in your very own den, but you get to circumvent that pesky "No Twinkies" runway rule at the same time.

MODEL BEHAVIOR

The crystal clear, full color, hi-resolution image on your glowing computer monitor reveals a pouting model strutting proudly down a gleaming catwalk. And although she is currently located somewhere deep within the bustling city of Manhattan, the gleaming image before you is so lifelike it feels like you can almost reach out and touch her.

In the background, lined up like well-dressed judges with front row seats at some high school quiz-a-thon, celebs and industry elite sit elbow to kneecap on seats that look much more uncomfortable than your cushy desk chair. Pens in hand, notepad or laptop at the ready, they rush eagerly to record the image you see frozen before you, as if for your own private viewing.

Her eyes glazed with flashing bulbs, her cheeks hollow from a tried and true combination of starvation and expensive makeup, her legs long, her chest flat, the supermodel flaunts the newest ensemble from the hottest designer.

The colors are bold, the cut is hip, the attitude fresh. "Fresh" is a word that also describes the show, as it has happened only moments ago (not to mention over a thousand miles away). But, thanks to the power of the Internet, you are looking at it in the comfort of your own home in Poughkeepsie, Fargo, or Tallahassee.

These Internet fashion shows, hi-res runways, and cyber catwalks are, to be sure, a recent phenomenon. One of those "flights of fancy" the old guard fashion establishment said would never, ever, ever work.

"An *online* runway show?" one can almost hear them sneering only a few short years ago. "Clothing via computer? Preposterous. Will there be finger foods, then? Strobe lighting? Fog machines? Rock music? Celebrities? Paparazzi? The smell of flashbulbs and mascara mixing with young, supple flesh? I think not.

"Why, one might just as well get their fashion from a month-old magazine as try and sit at a computer and imagine the real life thrill of attending a catwalk live and in person. Nothing will ever compare."

Yet, despite the lack of champagne, caviar, and strobe lights, "cyber catwalks" are flourishing all over the Internet as cyberseamstresses try desperately to keep up with the jet set in simulcast.

"Who are these start-up companies propagating polyester propaganda on the Internet?" you might ask suspiciously, imagining some gritty grifters setting up a front for cyber porn or some underage-child-worker filled sweatshop, all in the guise of high fashion.

Well, for starters, Victoria's Secret is now an old hard-drive hand at staging live Web casts of their newest, hottest underwear lines. And Firstview.com truly lives up to its name by selling passwords for around six bucks, which allow you to watch fresh fashion runway shows happen via a series of progressive thumbnails zipped to their Web site straight from a fashion photographer's digital camera. Why, you can almost smell the fake fog now.

Indeed, the once secretive world of fashion runways has been introduced to the masses in a way the fashion industry could never have imagined a mere five or six years ago.

Gone are the days of "invitation only" shows and press passes. Passé are the highbrow announcements and clique-y gatherings once considered the end-all and be-all of the fashion industry. Extinct are the Hollywood premiere type openings that once announced a top designer's latest stroke of genius, or self-indulgence. Why, any old schmoe with a modem and AOL can circumvent such "low security" clearance with a few bucks and a color printer. Knock-off entrepreneurs can start sewing long before those rented catwalks in Manhattan are even broken down and even low-techies can garner the bootlegged images from their

more high-tech buds without all that fancy equipment. What can the old-guard do to stop such cyber shenanigans and regain their elitist stature in the fast-paced world of fresh fashion? Not much. The Internet is certainly not going anywhere and it will take a lot more than some "invitations only" notice to stop hemline hackers from bringing the latest designs to their eager e-audiences.

Why not give up? And sign on? You too can view the latest fashions on your very own computer. And, who knows, maybe your next door neighbor will even let you borrow his pork rinds.

"The Internet is so big, so powerful and pointless that for some people it is a complete substitute for life."
—Andrew Brown

DIGITAL
DESIGNER:
www.TODDOLDHAM.COM

admired by the industry's hottest movers and shakers, but as a familiar face on MTV's wildly popular *House of Style*, Oldham successfully introduced himself to a generation full of every day, teenage kids. Kids who would soon be earning, not to mention spending, their very own money.

Maybe it's the simplicity of his uniquely American past that makes him such a rebel on the runway. Born in Texas (not exactly the famed haute couture of snooty Paris), he unwittingly started his clothing career in his teens by making a sundress for his sister out of old pillowcases. From these humble beginnings, Oldham moved to New York in the late '80s and began a gradual climb to the top of the fashion heap by producing fun, lighthearted fashion inspired by the erratic, eclectic funkiness of his city surroundings.

Joining the ranks of Nolan Miller and Elizabeth Taylor, Oldham is not above using his inner child to express his unique vision, recently creating a collector's edition Barbie. And, while you might not want to let your daughter take this one-of-a-kind Barbie out to the daily tea party, for a mere $79.99, she's not exactly out of most collector's leagues. And, after reading the Etoys.com catalog description, you're bound to think it's a downright steal:

Cyberspace might not be the first place you think of when you need a fashion fix, but the hip and hot young fashion designer Todd Oldham is trying his best to change all that. With one of the coolest Web sites anywhere, in or out of the fashion world, Oldham takes you on a cybertrip that's sure to leave you cybersatisfied:

If there is a young, modern, hot, fresh, hip fashion designer who defines the young, modern, hot, fresh, hip fashion of today's eclectic hipsters, it is most certainly Todd Oldham. From Barbie dolls to books to his one-of-a-kind, ready-to-wear Web site, Oldham is, in a word, accessible.

After all, unlike many of his stodgy counterparts in the frigid fashion industry, Oldham welcomes the opportunity to reach out to the average American consumer. Not only are his funky, yet wearable, designs

"In her very first Todd Oldham original ensemble, this Limited Edition Barbie Doll goes totally hip. Her bold, contemporary outfit is the epitome of Todd Oldham's fresh fashion perspective—a point of view that's made him one of today's hottest designers. Todd Oldham has designed for Barbie a full-length leopard-print coat, an aqua satin lining, and a golden satin hip-hugger mini skirt with turquoise and brown embroidery. The outfit's sheer black T-shirt with coordinating decorative stripes makes it uniquely adorable. Besides the 3-crystal barrette in Barbie's long, loose auburn hair, she wears no jewelry, and her dramatic makeup accentuates a beauty mark and healthy tan. The doll includes a Certificate of Authenticity and a doll stand."

Texan. Pillowcase crafter. MTV personality. Celebrity.

Designer. Toy maker. What else could this young man possibly add to his already impressive resume? How about—author! Published in 1997, *Todd Oldham: Without Boundaries* boasts an introduction by famed director John Waters. This lavish photo essay is as much an autobiography as it is a "picture book," in which "…today's premier fashion photographers provide dazzling images of some of the world's most flamboyant people, all of whom wear Oldham's cutting-edge clothes."

And, as if all of that weren't enough, Oldham can add Internet entrepreneur to his repertoire. His vibrant and entertaining Web site, www.toddoldham.com, is just the right thing for anyone in need of a fresh fashion fix. There you'll find funky mood music completely befitting the crowned jester trademark and yellow overtones of this cyber cool shack. Quotes fly out at you from left of center, tossing off such Web site witticisms as "smile with your eyes…" and "…my eclecticism comes from the appreciation of the simultaneity of it all."

Possibly the only fashion site with a reader forum, www.toddoldham.com boasts the aptly titled "talk about it," where fashion devotees can leave messages about everything from their raging vegetarianism to questions about their sexuality. There is a postcard generator, movie reviews, and even a plug for a female rock magazine. But the real attraction here is the clothes.

From glitter tights to a muff portfolio (it's not what you think), Oldham's designs are truly one-of-a-kind. There's the high-style jean jacket, known here as a "snorkle jacket," with a fun, frivolous twist in the form of a hot pink, faux-fur collar. Then there are the cargo-style baggy pants with detachable pocket bag!

But then, devotees of Oldham's quirky style are used to curveballs like these, which are indicative of the young man, a highly creative and colorful designer who makes time to concentrate not on large, lavish runway shows, but instead on more affordable, universally accessible collections.

Not content with conquering the runways, the airways, and the information superhighway, Oldham recently made the inevitable leap to—what else—Hollywood. In 1998, the tireless designer created the outfits for Sarah Michelle Gellar in the 20th Century Fox film *Simply Irresistible*!

In addition, his popular New York and now Tokyo and Miami boutiques house Todd Oldham's imaginative and attractive fashions. Fantastically colorful and eccentric men's and women's clothing is coupled with quirky accessories for the home including dog bowls and welcome mats!

And what's next for Todd Oldham? As if Barbies, babes, books, and bytes weren't enough, the waifish workaholic has recently added handbags, watches, jeans, eyewear, shoes, perfume, and even—throw pillows—to his ravishing repertoire. Not bad for a small-town boy from the Lone Star State.

But then, don't they do *everything* big down in Texas?

COUNTERFEIT CYBER CLOTHING VIA COMPUTER

During the "counterfeit" boom of the mid-1990s, many curbside vendors temporarily flourished selling $10 "Pucci" watches and cut-rate "Channel" handbags. However, today's savvy clothing customers have found a new way to be ripped off, ordering counterfeit clothing online! After all, it's a lot less embarrassing to get ripped off in the privacy of one's own dimly lit den, than to do so live and in person:

OnlineOutlets.com

For your new job, you have come to the decision that you need a new look. More responsibility, more visibility, and more hours translate into the need to be more—fashionable. Right? Certainly your Kmart golf shirts and "wrinkle-free" elastic slacks didn't exactly hold you back from your recent promotion. But there's a niggling little voice in the back of your mind that says you just might have gotten it sooner if your closet, not to mention your argyle socks, had been a little more up to date.

And so, armed with new opportunities, and new issues of *GQ*, not to mention your new Discover card, you take a seat at your slimline laptop and scroll through the hottest wardrobe Web site around, OnlineOutlets.com.

There, sustained by a few slices of pizza and a Diet Coke from the conveniently located dorm fridge beneath your Office Depot desk, (try that in some crowded mall), you forge ahead on your cyber shopping spree. The one that's destined to be your first step toward financial success and freedom, at work anyway.

Unfortunately, that old adage, "It takes money to make money," begins to ring true after only three or four "clicks."

While the gorgeous, sumptuous, and awe-inspiring new styles in the cyber Ralph Lauren outlet may have gone down in price from three digits to two, they're still a long way off from the right two. As in, $2. That song remains the same in the other fashionable outlet stores you visit as well, including Land's End.org, the Gap.com, and Nautica.net.

Depressed and dejected, your cute little cyber shopping cart icon still entirely empty, you realize that it may just not be worth it to spend your new, if meager, raise on clothes that could quickly total one-month's rent by the end of the afternoon.

And then, like a shimmering digital diamond in a sea of online oysters, you see your answer blinking there in between the obligatory Internet poll and the empty shopping cart icon: Bargainbin.com. Flashing lights circle the neon cyber sign and a welcoming slogan printed underneath promises, "Where we sell clothes cheap! NOT cheap clothes."

As you frantically double-click on the garishly colored bulging barrel icon, and on through the virtual mall of bargainbin.com, you visually peruse racks and racks of designer clothing, complete with the appropriate crests, labels, and insignias society deems appropriate, desirable, and, above all, fashionable.

The colors are subdued, the lines flattering, the patterns neither gaudy nor obscene. The textures are rich, sumptuous, and nowhere does the word polyester pop up in any of the hyperlinked fabric labels. (Not even in the fine print.) And, surprisingly, they fall within your admittedly cheap price range.

Adding items to your now bulging cyber cart left and right like a kid in a virtual candy store, you quickly key in your credit card number with only a minor dent. The blinding waterfall of blinking pop-up windows repeating the same mantra: "Absolutely NO returns, refunds, or exchanges under ANY circumstances," are a little disconcerting, but you're so happy with your new "Polo purchases" that you quickly close each one as it opens up.

Exhausted after a long day of scrolling through the online outlets, you barely have the strength to wait around for the long-awaited purchases to arrive at your front door via FedEx in the promised two to four day delivery time. Finally, however, they arrive just in time for you to start your new position. Tired and edgy from nervous days of waiting and anticipating your new responsibilities, you admire your first ever "e-tail" purchases and hang them along your closet wall as if on display, too tired to actually try them on.

"Of course they'll fit," you assure

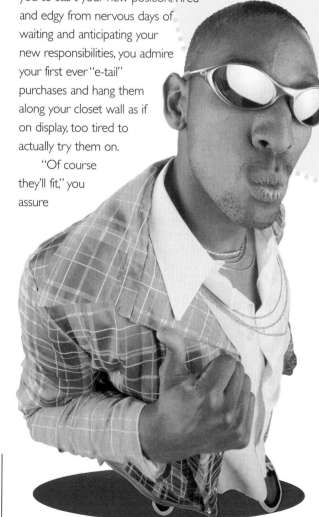

yourself as you stumble into bed that evening. Why would all of those people shop online if it wasn't 100% safe?

Waking up late the next morning, you shower, shave, gulp some coffee, and then proudly slide your legs into your new pleated slacks, only to discover that they have absolutely no pockets and the zipper is made of roughly the same material as a Ziplock freezer baggie!

Surprised, you strip them off and consult the tag to see if you'd somehow picked them from the "non-designer" racks. But nope, right there, you see the recognizable hunter green label and the words, written in a lovely shade of faux gold: "Poko."

"Poko?" you gasp, checking your other five pairs of so-called designer pants and finding sewn pockets, dangling buttons, pinned cuffs, and plastic zippers.

Improvising, you slip into your best pair of old khakis and hope your new shirts will take the emphasis off of them. Unfortunately, your "Nautiza," "Hugo Doss," "Sap," and "Land's Bend" shirts, with their classy blue and gold stripes, checks, lines, and solids, have assorted and various problems of their own. These include, but are not limited to: Sleeves that magically end up halfway down your forearm, missing collars, sleeves that don't quite exist, flawed fabric, and oversized pockets placed in inexplicable positions.

Additionally, most seem to be missing every other button. Several have collars reminiscent of jolly old England at around the time of Charles Dickens's heyday and very few extend below your belly button. And those that do continue on to your knees!

Exasperated, you finally find one "Hilfinger" shirt that actually seems to be in full, working, wearable order. Buttoning up all the buttons, which are magically there, as well as your sleeves, both of which extend equally all the way to your wrists, you tuck it in and proudly step out the door to a thin, fine drizzle.

Not upset in the least, you realize that, for the price of seven failed wardrobes, you actually got a shirt that no one but you will ever know isn't the real thing. All for half the price of a real one. Unfortunately, checking your new look in the rearview mirror, you discover that the rain has magically blended all of the colors into one hideous mosaic roughly the same pleasing shades of a serial killer's nightmare.

Racing back into your bedroom, you peel the shirt off, deposit it in the nearest wastebasket along with the rest of the counterfeit cyberclothing you purchased via computer, and discover that the psychedelic pattern is still finely stained into your skin like some life size tattoo! Now crying freely, despite what the neighbors might think, you grab your best dark shirt, button every single button, and race to work.

After a hectic morning of meetings and assignments, you break for a quick lunch at the mall before spending the rest of your credit limit on real brand name fashions designed by actual people, careful to check each label for reversed or missing letters, invisible ink, and extra fine print!

FREDERICKSOF
OMAHA.COM

Once the over-the-counter version of *Playboy* or *Penthouse* for many middle American boys all across the country, *Frederick's of Hollywood*, along with its wussy Web site, has now evolved into an almost sedate catalog company catering not just to the racy and risqué, but to the rational and realistic as well.

CATALOG
CAPERS

As your first high school reunion draws near, you receive a passionate e-mail asking for your help. The subject line, in all caps no less, reads like something the *real* president might write in response to an international incident: "ALUMNI PREZ SEEKS ASSISTANCE A.S.A.P!" As the president of your former class is too lazy to do all of the work himself, it appears, he has assigned each of his ex-class members five names of absentee alumni to hunt down and inform of the upcoming fraternal festivities.

As you have no idea how to do this, naturally, you take your five names and lay them by the phone for over a week before actually tackling the tardy task. Finally letting your fingers do the walking, you take what little information your former class prez has provided and, within a mere seven hours and 45 minutes, track down four of your five allotted classmates. After several more hours of boring, tedious conversation spent "catching up" on lives you never intended to cross paths with again in the first place, you set down the phone, massage your aching left ear, and resort to doing a "people search" on the Internet for that elusive fifth name.

Typing in "Frederick Frontenac," the former class geek who most likely owns the

mouths and parted legs and cleavage barely contained in bright red bustiers and velvet thighs overflowing silken garter belts. Barely able to contain yourself, you click on the first page and see entirely presentable women in bathing suits, pumps, and sun hats. Checking the Web address again, if only to be sure it isn't actually boringboobs.com instead, you eagerly forge ahead, sure that the good stuff is embedded further on in the deepest reaches of cyberspace to avoid cybercensorship. (Maybe they put the sedate stuff up front just so they won't have to wrap the entire catalog in the Internet version of a plain brown wrapper.)

successful Internet search engine you're using to find him, you return a plethora of hits, none of them pertaining to your intended victim. However, it's kind of hard to compete with your first hit, a whopping 96% compatibility, according to Hotbot's internal calculator. The resulting name, however, hits a 200% in your hotpants hard drive, as it is the mother lode of all mother lodes, the new Frederick's of Hollywood cyber catalog!

Instantly forgetting your reunion (you really didn't want to go anyway) you click on the bulging blue hyperlink and revel in the tense seconds that go by before it finally fills your Web screen, as if savoring the thrill to come like fantasy foreplay. You recall the days of your youth, stealing peeks at all of that pink and tan, black and white flesh before your mother caught wind that her catalog was missing—again.

You remember your first sights of the female anatomy, scantily clad in sheer silk and see-through plastic. Black leather and white lace. Open

You scroll through robes with barely a leg sticking out. Leather jackets straight down to leather-booted calves. Rain slickers and jumpsuits. Teddy bears and umbrellas. A few bras. Not many panties you couldn't find over at Sears.com and absolutely nothing that your girlfriend doesn't currently have scattered around her own living room floor!

Disappointed in your covert cyber catalog carousing, you quietly reflect on your adolescent days spent waiting by the old fashioned snail-

"The difference between pornography and erotica is lighting."
-Gloria Leonard

TOP 5 SIGNS FREDERICK'S OF HOLLYWOOD HAS TONED DOWN ITS ACT

5 The only see-through product in their new catalog is a shower cap.

4 Their new line of "nursing home wear."

3 The most recent catalog's hottest model used to be a *Golden Girl*.

2 Most popular new photo-shoot backdrops are the library and the DMV.

1 You can't decide which is sexier, the centerfold's cane or her walker.

mailbox and wonder if your memory could possibly be *that* bad. Did you imagine all of that half-naked flesh and those provocative poses? But how could you have, when you hadn't even known that such palpable pleasures existed before *Frederick's of Hollywood* came along each month?

Sadly, you realize that, just like the "new" Times Square, *Frederick's of Hollywood* has gone politically correct. The power suits and sensible shoes were just another sign of the times. They may still sell underwear, but you'd have to have x-ray vision to see it underneath all of those clothes they also sell now! Why, you've seen more naked flesh in grocery store flyers lately.

Finally you sigh, keying in the Web address for the *Sharper Image* cyber catalog. There's sure to be some skin over there.